AF478956

Colonial Karma

Colonial Karma

Self, Action, and Nation in the Indian English Novel

Josna E. Rege

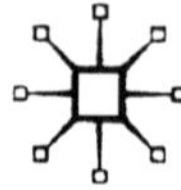

COLONIAL KARMA
© Josna E. Rege, 2004.

First published 2004 by
PALGRAVE MACMILLAN™
175 Fifth Avenue, New York, N.Y. 10010 and
Houndmills, Basingstoke, Hampshire, England RG21 6XS
Companies and representatives throughout the world.

PALGRAVE MACMILLAN is the global academic imprint of the Palgrave Macmillan division of St. Martin's Press, LLC and of Palgrave Macmillan Ltd. Macmillan® is a registered trademark in the United States, United Kingdom and other countries. Palgrave is a registered trademark in the European Union and other countries.

ISBN 1–4039–6400–9 hardback

Library of Congress Cataloging-in-Publication Data

Rege, Josna E.
    Colonial Karma : self, action, and nation in the Indian English novel /
    Josna E. Rege.
        p. cm.
    Includes bibliographical references (p.) and index.
    ISBN 1–4039–6400–9 (alk paper)
        1. Indic fiction (English)—History and criticism. 2. Nationalism and literature—India. 3. Social action in literature. 4. Nationalism in literature. 5. Imperialism in literature. 6. Colonies in literature. 7. Self in literature. I. Title.

PR9492.6.N38R45 2004
823'.009'358—dc22   2004044256

A catalogue record for this book is available from the British Library.

Design by Newgen Imaging Systems (P) Ltd., Chennai, India.

First edition: November, 2004.
10 9 8 7 6 5 4 3 2 1

Printed in the United States of America.

Contents

Acknowledgments

In the journey that has brought me to this point, there are many people to whom thanks and acknowledgments are due, more than I could ever mention here.

Thanks to the University of Massachusetts at Amherst for the Graduate Fellowship in 1993 that supported my doctoral dissertation research in India; to Dartmouth College for the Burke Fund and the Junior Faculty Fellowship that enabled me to make a research trip to India in Summer 1998; and to the Blue Mountain Center for the gift of a month-long writing residency in Summer 2002.

I gratefully acknowledge permission to reprint from *Journal of Gender Studies* and *Studies in the Novel,* where earlier versions and portions of Chapters 3 and 4 were first published, and also permission from the Random House Group to quote from Salman Rushdie's highly quotable *Midnight's Children.*

Farideh Koohi-Kamali, my editor at Palgrave Macmillan, has my gratitude for her confidence in the project, and the editorial and production teams at Palgrave and Newgen have my admiration for their flexibility and their attention to detail. Thanks also to the anonymous reviewer who gave my manuscript a careful early reading.

In India, it was a great thrill and honor to have been able to meet Mulk Raj Anand, and I thank him for his hospitality and gracious help on a day I will never forget. I would also like to acknowledge the help and encouragement of Meenakshi Mukherjee, Rajeswari Sunder Rajan, Vinod Sena, and Gauri Deshpande, who I can hardly believe is with us no more. Much love also to my family in Delhi, Mumbai, Pune, and Ratnagiri who looked after me so well during both my visits. To my Aunt, Kumud Rege, your life of Gandhian social work is a reminder to me that such ideals as selfless service are not just abstract concepts, but are made real through persistent effort.

I would like to thank my Dartmouth colleagues Margaret Williamson, Lynn Higgins, and Agnes Lugo-Ortiz for having read different portions of my work, and especially Doug Haynes, whose help and intellectual generosity has been in a league of its own. I am deeply indebted to my longtime mentors Ketu Katrak and R. Radhakrishnan, as also to Rajeswari Sunder Rajan, Stephen Clingman, and Indira Peterson. To my friends Sangeeta Kamat, Jenny Goodman, Ambreen Hai, and Sabine Broeck, and fellow-members of the South Asian Literary Association: thank you for discussing my work with me and reading portions of it at different stages. Of course, all the help notwithstanding, this book's flaws are my own, and I take full responsibility for them.

To Sartaz Aziz, Marianne Kripps, and Pennie Ticen, our long-distance friendship sustains me. Thanks to Vera Vance for a home away from home. Anita Desai's work was the original inspiration for this project, many years ago. I owe her a special debt of gratitude.

My family, as always, take on my projects as their own. All my love to my father-in-law Ted Melnechuk, for all your editing and proofreading help, and for continuing to work cheerfully with me, in spite of my highly unscientific mind; and to my mother-in-law Anna, for your example of sweet equanimity. To Eve, Dan, and Nikhil Melnechuk, your expert computer and design help, so many times, has meant so much to me—thank you. To my sister Sally and my dear parents, Gladys and Madhukar Rege, who have given me everything, I can only offer my deepest love. And to Andrew and Nikhil, who have always had faith in me, what can I say? You are the best.

PREFACE

Why Karma, Why Now?

Karma, a central concept of Hinduism and Buddhism, was recast under colonialism, partially secularized to denote selfless action in the service of the nation, and eventually, embedded in Indian nationalist discourse and public discourse more generally. In *Colonial Karma* I do not seek to privilege karma as a heuristic through which all Indian novels can or should be read, neither do I intend to reinforce the dominance of a Hindu religious and philosophical concept. Rather, in examining how English-educated Indian writers have variously employed the concept of karma, I seek to subject it to critical scrutiny, to understand how nationalism is culturally constructed and reproduced in colonial and postcolonial cultures, and to consider what happens to nationalism after it has gained state power. More specifically, I seek to understand who is able to speak and act through the deployment of nationalist discourse, and who is silenced and disabled thereby. If colonialism sought to render the colonized quiescent, to deny them their own independent subjectivity and agency, and nationalism sought to mobilize the colonized, to give them confidence in themselves and their ability to act independently, then what kind of subject do we see in the novel, the product of the colonially educated Indian's creative imagination, and what kind of action is possible for this subject? If reinterpreting traditional concepts such as karma solved a problem of action for the nationalist leadership, then what kinds of problems were in turn encoded in that "solution"? In popular parlance, what is the colonial karma of that solution, as it continues to shape Indian thought today?

In this study of Indian novels in English since the novel's emergence in India some century and a half ago, I might have chosen to focus on any one of several concepts. *Atman/Brahman* (self/Self), *dharma* (sacred duty), *jñana* (knowledge), and *bhakti* (devotion) are all "Hindu" metaphysical and religious terms that, like *karma*, underwent changes in meaning and usage during the period of British colonialism, and all of them were variously reinterpreted by Indian nationalists as they constructed new discourses of Indian nationalism in reaction to colonialist definitions. Why, then, privilege the concept of karma, or action? As you will soon see, many of the novels I discuss do not seem to have much plot action in them. Their protagonists may be caught up in a crisis of action only to withdraw from the brink at the very end, restoring the *status quo*; or else the action is largely internalized, mental rather than physical. I examine the obstacles to action and their resolution in selected novels, as well as their characterization of the national subject of action and the nature of his or her engagement in the action. At different times the writers of Indian English novels have perceived different imperatives for action, and I identify these, placing them in historical context. However, at a deeper level I consider the concept of karma—or action—itself, how and why English-educated Indians seeking broader support for their resistance to British colonial subjection developed a new, hybrid idea of action. Indian society is continuing to live out the effects of their actions, their colonial karma, more than half a century after the end of British rule.

I examine the colonial and nationalist genealogy of the powerful and flexible idea of action that has been incorporated into the discourse of Indian nationalism. The Indian English novelists whose work I discuss variously perpetuate and problematize it, reproduce it unquestioningly, and attempt to dismantle it. But just as the *Bhagavad-Gita* has attained the status of official state scripture, karma has become an integral part of the Indian vocabulary of action and therefore must be critically examined as such. What I call colonial karma is a much-traveled concept that has been variously deployed by Indian nationalist discourse since the colonial period. In this study I use the term in a number of different ways. One doesn't have to be a philosopher to understand the commonsense meaning of karma as the law of causality as it applies to the long-term effects of individual or collective human actions. Any happening for which an explanation is not immediately apparent can thereby be ascribed to the karma accumulated by earlier actions. In this broad sense persistent problems of action in the Indian English novel can be seen as its residual colonial karma—more specifically, as stemming from the genre's origins in British colonial rule and from the position of precarious privilege held by the English-educated classes of Indians, in their intended role as agents for the British, rather than independent agents.

I use the concept of colonial karma as an exemplar of the cultural construction of Indian nationalist discourse, in which nationalists selectively drew upon reinterpreted concepts from religious and epic texts to popularize and give orthodox sanction to the new idea of the bourgeois nation-state. Thus karma, drawn from the nationalist reinterpretations of the *Bhagavad-Gita*, came to represent a new, "Indian" model of freedom through action that was both worldly and spiritual. It was open to all yet upheld the caste hierarchy, individualistic yet altruistic and socially conscious, promised freedom, yet required discipline.

Because I am very much aware that millions of people hold the *Bhagavad-Gita* sacred, I want to make it clear that when I discuss the Gita in *Colonial Karma*, I am speaking of the Gita not as a religious text but as a social and political text, in its cultural–nationalist reinterpretations. I must note, moreover, that in the Hindu tradition the Gita is classified as *kavya* (poetry), not as *sruti* (revealed text), and has had a long history of interpretation. In fact, as nationalists sought to draw upon an "authentically Indian" text to give authority to their call to action, the Gita's amenability to a wide range of interpretations while remaining an indisputably orthodox text was one of its attributes that they found the most useful. In most of the novels I discuss, I do not discuss the role of the Gita as such (or, in some cases, even mention the Gita), but rather examine the changing role of the Gita's concept of karma as it was variously reinterpreted under colonialism and has since become embedded in Indian nationalist discourse.

Five Moments in the Life of the Indian English Novel

The reinterpreted notion of the Gita's karma as altruistic action in service to the nation, so central to the discourse of nationalism, both drove and constrained Indian English novelists. Action as karma became so embedded in the dominant nationalist discourse, and the novelists themselves became so identified with the nationalist project, that time and again karma figured centrally in their plots, whether explicitly or implicitly, whether their protagonists accepted it as a responsibility, struggled to reconfigure it, or tried to turn away from it altogether.

Focusing primarily on Indian novels in English at a series of historical "moments" ranging from the 1860s to the 1990s, *Colonial Karma* examines their changing representations of action, as each writer addresses what he or she identifies to be the most pressing problem of action for the time. Although most of the novels I consider in this study were written in English, I wish to draw attention to their multilingual literary–cultural context. The novel genre became well established in a number of Indian languages over the second half of the nineteenth century, but it was not until the 1920s that the Indian English novel emerged as a vehicle for nationalist thought. Accordingly, with the exception of *Rajmohan's Wife*, the novels I discuss in chapter one were all written in Indian languages.

Chapter One calibrates the slow and uneven shift from reformism to cultural nationalism and thence to political nationalism in the late nineteenth century, when the cultural imperative under colonialism was to find a uniquely Indian mode of action. I begin by discussing the first Indian English novel, *Rajmohan's Wife* (1864), written during the period of "nationalist prehistory"[52] when the concept of karma had not yet emerged, and in which the novel's protagonists find themselves unable to exercise agency. With reference to the 1889 Malayalam novel *Indulekha*, I then discuss the significance of the domestic arena "before karma" as one with some scope for agency on the part of the male protagonists and their authors. At the "Moment of Departure" for Indian nationalist thought in the early 1880s,[53] I discuss Bankimchandra Chatterjee's Bengali novel, *Anandamath*, as the first expression of militant nationalism in an Indian novel and the first to advance the notion of karma as self-sacrifice for the motherland. Finally, I consider *Gora* (1907–09), and, briefly, *The Home and the World* (1915), by the great Bengali writer Rabindranath Tagore, who questioned the notion of karma, and increasingly, nationalism itself, as a dangerous expedient.

Chapter Two addresses Indian English novels of the Gandhian era, when the imperative for action on the part of the Indian National Congress was to unify the nation under one inclusive umbrella. The Gandhian era has been characterized as the "Moment of Manoeuvre" for Indian nationalist thought, as the Congress attempted to manage both internal and external voices of dissent, while negotiating with the British for greater autonomy, and eventually, for outright independence.[54] I consider the conceptualization of action in Venkataramani's *Murugan, the Tiller*, a formulaically Gandhian novel, and in novels by the "Big Three" of Indian English writing, Mulk Raj Anand, R.K. Narayan, and Raja Rao, each of which struggles in its own very different way, to present a unified national Subject. As in earlier domestic novels, many nationalist narratives are still plotted as romances, with consummation and union seen as the ideal ends of action. However, the Gandhian concept of karma enjoins celibacy and self-control, and consummation must be deferred until after national independence.

The immediate aftermath of 1947, the nation's long-awaited "Moment of Arrival," was once again a moment of deferral, as independence was attended by the trauma of Partition.[55] By the 1960s and 1970s, a literature of alienation and social disengagement emerged, particularly among younger urban writers. The polarized and gendered nationalist discourse is particularly alienating for those who are not identified with the normative citizen-subject. Chapter Three considers the interiority and alienation in several early novels by Anita Desai in terms of a dominant post-independence nationalism that leaves no space for the individual voice to speak in different terms. Karma remains the dominant model for action, but Desai's female protagonists attempt in vain to make this model serve their personal needs.

Chapter Four shows how Salman Rushdie's 1981 novel *Midnight's Children* discursively reconfigured the relationship between individual and nation, thereby opening up new possibilities for and modes of action in this period of crisis for the once-dominant model of Indian nationalism. In contrast to the earlier post-independence period where an undifferentiated, universalized Self was expected to act altruistically on behalf of the Nation, a unified "I" writing at the Center could now no longer credibly serve as spokesperson for the whole. Rushdie's protagonist Saleem ultimately retreats from his early presumption to speak disinterestedly for the whole, simultaneously undermining his own agency and potentially clearing space for a new politics of engagement.

Chapter Five examines the possibilities and perils of the trope of "return," focusing on two novels each by Shashi Deshpande and Githa Hariharan, featuring women's returns to the father's house, both literally and discursively. In the 1980s and 1990s, in the face of the ongoing crisis of the nation, action as forward movement could no longer take place within the old conceptual frames. Globalization and transnational cultural, economic, and political forces challenged the sovereignty of the nation-state from without; postcolonial, subaltern, and feminist critiques of colonialism, nationalism, and patriarchy questioned its hegemony from within. Both prompted new returns to "tradition," variously defined. At this historical moment, karma is increasingly figured as cyclical action, involving "returns," but with a difference. I see the imperative of action at this time as the perceived need to return, in the effort to recuperate an uncolonized subject. Karma here can be seen as the law that history continues to replay itself until it is fully understood. There is an oscillation between withdrawal and return, a recognition of the limits of discourse, and ultimately, a repudiation of the elite concept of karma as desireless action in recognition of the inevitability, indeed the desirability, of attachment.

My open-ended conclusion considers new directions, at the turn of the twenty-first century, as the Indian English novel has exploded onto the global stage. I discuss Arundhati Roy's celebrated first novel, *The God of Small Things*, with its attentiveness to the "small"—to issues of caste and class—as both a continuation of the trajectory of the Indian English novel I have charted thus far, and, in some respects, as a departure from it. I also touch briefly upon a number of recent Indian English novels in terms of their use of colonial karma. I consider the resurgence of militant Hindu nationalism in the 1990s as the colonial karma of *Anandamath*'s century-old vision. At last, I attempt to move outside the middle-class construct of karma in order to view it from a subaltern perspective, and in so doing, to open up a new critique of the concept, simultaneously pointing to the limits of the English language and the novel form itself.

CHAPTER ONE
SOLVING THE PROBLEM OF ACTION IN THE COLONIAL NOVEL, 1864–1919

As they turned to the novel form in the second half of the nineteenth century, English-educated Indians had an as-yet-inchoate desire for freedom from material, intellectual, and psychological subjection, even as they felt themselves to be indebted to the British colonial presence. Most of them were professionals such as lawyers, doctors, teachers, or journalists, many were employed in the colonial civil service, and a small though influential few were industrialists. Virtually all of them were men. The problem of action preoccupied them: how were they to act under colonialism, on what authority and on whose behalf? Colonial rule drastically limited Indians' advancement in the civil service or the military, denied their civil rights, and censored the press.[1] Colonial education simultaneously inculcated them with their moral, muscular, and military inferiority, their irrationality, superstition, decadence, effeminacy, their lack of ethics, appalling treatment of women, and altogether backward civilization, all the while feeding them an idealized image of enlightened English liberalism through English literary study.[2]

In its native Europe, the novel had historically been the primary vehicle of creative expression for a new middle class who had led their society's modernizing drive. It was also a form that had always focused on the individual in and against the collective. Early Indian practitioners of the genre took up the novel to work out their social aspirations and dilemmas, as individuals, as an emergent middle class, and, increasingly, as Indians. Experimenting with the novel form allowed them to create a world in which they could set their new ideas in motion, put conflicting ideas head to head, work them out, and give them freer play than they could in actuality. But their freedom of action was limited within the confines of the novel as well. Because the novel was largely a realistic genre, writers felt constrained to conform to realism in their representations.[3] However, conforming to the colonial reality meant reforming their own society in its image and reconciling themselves to subjugation. The time came when reconciliation was no longer possible and writers had to seek creative ways of changing the reality rather than conforming to it. Action, therefore, became an increasingly urgent theme, although its scope remained limited. Early novels were often set during a period of transition like the authors' own, an interregnum between one stage of life and another, with the protagonist poised for action yet unsure of how to act, or unable to do so because of sociopolitical limitations.

This chapter introduces the problem of action as it was conceptualized in the literary representations of Indian novelists of this period: how they staged it, and what solutions they enacted. In the 1870s and 1880s there was a decided shift in consciousness in colonial India, particularly among the educated classes, from a spirit of religious and social reform to a cultural nationalism that paved the way for the rise of political nationalism.[4] As this shift took place, it became increasingly urgent to formulate an idea and a strategy of action that could be seen to be uniquely Indian. Part I takes up two early novels, Bankimchandra Chatterjee's *Rajmohan's Wife*, and, briefly, O. Chandu Menon's *Indulekha*, to illustrate the problem of action "before karma"—that is, before Indian cultural nationalism began to draw upon colonialist and indigenous thought to create a new, hybrid concept of action. *Rajmohan's Wife* demonstrates the dilemma of action for English-educated Indians, and *Indulekha* exemplifies their turn to the domestic sphere as a limited arena for action. Part II turns first to Bankimchandra's influential novel, *Anandamath*, to consider how it was able to reconceptualize action in a dramatic new form, and thereby effect a shift to nationalism. Then it examines Rabindranath Tagore's increasingly critical views of action in *Gora* and, briefly, in *Ghare-Baire* (translated as *The Home and the World*), which problematized the "solution" found in the shift from liberal reformism to cultural nationalism, and attempted to find a new synthesis between the two.

Because Bengali writers were early and influential pioneers of the novel form in India, and because the Bengali novel is an important antecedent of the Indian novel in English, I discuss novels by two major Bengali novelists of the late nineteenth century and early twentieth century respectively, Bankimchandra Chatterjee and Rabindranath Tagore. The novel rose early to prominence in several other languages, including Marathi, Tamil, Kannada, and Malayalam, although the time and degree of the shift from reformism to cultural nationalism differed considerably in different regions of the country, as did conceptions of action and the national subject of action.

Between 1857 and 1919, it is in the "vernacular"[5] novels that the construction of a new "Indian" idea of action can best be examined. Of the five novels I discuss in this opening chapter, only one, *Rajmohan's Wife*, was written in English, although all the others were translated into English soon after their first publication. I situate the Indian English novel in a multilingual frame, because its early development cannot be understood in isolation from the emergence and development of the novel in the Indian languages. By the turn of the century the novel had already become the preeminent literary genre in a number of Indian languages, and the English language had gained considerable ground among the reading public, especially in the periodical press. However, as I shall discuss further in Chapter Two, it was not until the 1930s that the novel in English became a significant site for the cultural construction of nationalism, or indeed a major presence on the literary-cultural scene.[6]

Part I: The Problem of Action "Before Karma"

The First Indian English Novel: Rajmohan's Wife *(1864)*
Bankimchandra Chatterjee (Chattopadhyay, in Bengali) must figure importantly at the outset of this study. Besides being the author of the first Indian English novel, *Rajmohan's Wife*,[7] he was the first Indian to adopt the novel form successfully into an

Indian language,[8] and the first nationalist interpreter of the *Bhagavad-Gita*.[9] His eighth novel, *Anandamath*, was the first Indian political novel, the first to challenge foreign rule with militant action, and the first to use the figure of the Mother Goddess as a symbol of the Motherland, thereby elevating patriotism to a religion.[10] In *Anandamath*, Bankimchandra was to craft a newly "Indian" call to action. However, *Rajmohan's Wife*, written nearly twenty years before *Anandamath*, conspicuously lacked a paradigm for action under colonialism.

After an early grounding in Sanskrit scholarship from his father and in popular Vaishnava devotionalism from his mother, as well as an English-medium secondary education, Bankimchandra Chatterjee sat for the entrance examinations of the newly established Calcutta University in 1857, the year of the abortive Revolt (or Sepoy Mutiny, as the British called it). The historical simultaneity of the army's uprising and Bankim's sitting for the examination ironically underscores the instrumental nature of the British attempt to mold a new class of Indians as their agents of colonial rule, at a time when the first major challenge to that rule had already been issued. It also suggests the internal conflicts that a "proud and sensitive" young Indian was likely to have felt in submitting himself to a "punishing syllabus" of English colonial education.[11] Bankimchandra took his B.A. from Calcutta University in its first graduating class of 1858 and, shortly thereafter, a law degree from Calcutta's Presidency College.[12] That same year, he took up the post of Deputy Magistrate in the British colonial administration, where he was to stay for 31 years without a promotion, except for an interlude in 1881–82 when he was appointed to an Indian position specially created to appease Bengali employees of the colonial administration. However, the appointment was terminated unceremoniously a few days after the publication of a particularly inflammatory instalment of his Bengali novel, *Anandamath*, then being serialized in his own journal, *Bangadarshan*, and Bankimchandra was back in his old job again, where he remained until his retirement.[13] Tapan Raychaudhuri writes that it was the source of the "fundamental contradiction" of Bankimchandra's life "that his livelihood depended on service to and collaboration with alien rulers whose contempt for Indians was a fact of daily experience" (115).

During his long tenure in the middle ranks of the colonial bureaucracy, Bankimchandra had a parallel and distinguished literary career as one of the leading intellectuals in Bengal, a prolific philosophical and political essayist, humorist, and founder-editor of the literary–cultural journal, *Bangadarshan*. He devoted himself to the cause of promoting and enriching the Bengali language and literature, crafting a modernized Bengali capable of great subtlety of nuance and range of expression. He pioneered the novel genre in Bengal, writing, before his death in 1894, twelve vastly popular Bengali novels in a number of different modes, from the romantic and fantastic to the historical and political. After his debut novel, he abandoned creative writing in English, restricting his literary production in that language to the occasional essay and public exchange of opinions. Nevertheless, he had received his education in English and once "confessed that both in writing and speaking he was more at ease in English than in Bengali."[14]

In view of his double life, it is no surprise that "conflict was central to Bankimchandra's personality."[15] This conflict gave his work what Sudipta Kaviraj has called its characteristic "unhappy consciousness" as he alternated between "tragic fiction and comic commentary…both rationalism and its critiques…both enlightenment and religion," and in the process, "managed to retain the complexities of these contradictions through his characteristic mode of irony."[16] The dramatic shift in the character of his late work augured the more general shift toward cultural nationalism in the country as a whole. His early work showed sympathies toward social reform, although never without ambivalence. Both tendencies are clearly present, even in his very first novel.

Bankimchandra's first work of fiction exemplifies the struggle of Indian writers under colonialism to formulate a coherent subject and agent of action. It is a slight, uneven effort that begins with an ambitious scope but peters out at the end. It would seem that colonial rule and conflicting colonial and feudal social, moral, and legal codes preclude both action and the constitution of an autonomous subject. Neither of the novel's protagonists is able to act effectively in his or her own interest, and the narrator appears to be ambivalent toward his hero, so much so that he eventually seems to lose interest in the project, bringing it to a hasty and unsatisfying close. *Rajmohan's Wife* was originally serialized in the journal *Indian Field*, but disappeared for seventy years, before it was rediscovered and published as a book.[17] The exigencies of Bankimchandra's colonial employment, the language and narrative conventions of his English education in an Indian colonial setting, and the tension between the norms of feudal social orthodoxy and emergent middle-class sensibility combine in this work to narrow the range of his creative options to an unacceptable degree. It is significant that it was the first and the last novel that Bankimchandra wrote in English. Of course it was in Bengali that he was to become known as the preeminent practitioner of the novel genre in Bengal, and indeed, in India as a whole. Many scholars simply dismiss *Rajmohan's Wife* as a failure and a false start, or attribute Bankimchandra's switch to Bengali to his patriotism, but I see its failure to define and direct a subject of action as the problem that Bankim continued to struggle with until he found his solution in *Anandamath* (1882) and the works that followed it in the last decade of his life.[18]

An overview of the novel's plot will suffice to show how unsatisfactorily it is able to realize a subject of action. The eponymous heroine (significantly unable to be named in the title) is Matangini, a spirited young woman married to the lazy scoundrel Rajmohan. The novel begins with an indiscretion on Matangini's part, in which, when she is returning from the village well in direct contravention of her husband's orders to stay at home, the wind fatefully blows her sari and reveals her face to two men. The older, Mathur, is a local feudal landlord, lustful and corrupt, and the younger is his cousin Madhav, a man of refined sensibilities—English-educated, Calcutta-returned, and already quietly, desperately in love with Matangini, although he is married to her sister. Each of these three characters attempts to act, but is ultimately unable to do so.

Matangini runs to Madhav one dark and stormy night to warn him of her rascally husband's involvement in Mathur's plot to send robbers to raid Madhav's house and deliver Madhav's uncle's will to his wealthy cousin, thereby disinheriting him. Matangini's action successfully foils the robbers, but in the process she commits yet another indiscretion: she goes shamelessly before her brother-in-law and finds herself confessing her love to him.[19] However, both of them have the self-control to forswear their love and Matangini returns to her husband, who discovers her treachery and vows to kill her. She manages to escape, taking refuge with Tara, Mathur's senior wife, and leaving a despondent Madhav brooding on the impossibility of his situation.

In addition to his forbidden love for Matangini, Madhav is facing legal action instigated by his cousin in which his deceased uncle's widow[20] is suing him for his property, which Madhav has inherited with the provision that he care for her during her lifetime.[21] Because the English-educated Madhav will not take a second wife or keep a woman as a concubine, he persists in his self-denial, knowing that his sister-in-law is suffering a husband who is far inferior to her. Kidnapped by the robbers, he is taken to the dungeons of the scheming Mathur, who, hampered by none of Madhav's scruples about monogamy, has also kidnapped Matangini in order to seduce her. He threatens to starve her into submission, but she is fully prepared to starve to death rather than acquiesce to him. Fortunately, Tara ventures into the dungeons, where she frees Madhav and, together, they find and free Matangini.

Here Bankimchandra abruptly loses interest in the possibilities of his novel. In short order, one of the robbers is captured, Rajmohan is sent to prison, and Mathur hangs himself before he is caught. With her husband in prison, Matangini must return to her father's house, and live out her days in celibacy as a near-widow. The best that the author can do for his heroine is to make her life thereafter mercifully short, and all he can give Madhav is the satisfaction of increasing his regular allowance to his father-in-law. The only way Matangini could have found happiness is if she could have realized her passion for Madhav, but to Bankimchandra, this was impossible for a married woman. Similarly, Madhav's only happiness lay in fulfilling his passion for Matangini, but as a modern, English-educated man he would never have dreamed of betraying his marriage vows or violating hers; on the other hand, Mathur's feudal values allowed him to womanize with impunity. Ultimately, with the exception of the shadowy figure of the robber chief, who evades capture (and who, it is hinted, was once a person of high social rank), the British magistrate is the only real agent in the story, the final arbiter of the action.

There are two chief modes of action on the part of the characters in *Rajmohan's Wife*: direct, aboveboard action and indirect, surreptitious action, of which the latter is by far the most pervasive. Most of the action in the novel is forced underground, as it were, by social and political constraints on the actors. Hardly anyone, except the robber chief, acts on his or her own, but rather, through others acting on their behalf. In spite of Bankim's need to restore British colonial order at the end of the novel, there is more than a hint of narratorial admiration for, perhaps even envy of, "bad" characters like Mathur, Madhav's grandfather Bangshibadan, and the robber chief—those who are uneducated, feudal, beyond the reach of the law, or otherwise unedified by British rule. By contrast, the English-educated Madhav, though valorized for his generosity and self-restraint, is portrayed as somewhat bloodless.

An almost-Gothic romance, *Rajmohan's Wife* is jam-packed with abductions, robbers, dungeons, impossible love, punishment, and death, but at the center of the novel lies a curious malaise: Madhav, the English-educated hero, has nowhere to go. Without either capital or government patronage, he is obliged to return after completing his higher education in Calcutta to the management of his family's land, where social reality remains unyieldingly feudal and his liberal ideas are decidedly out of place. Throughout the novel, this refined, decent young man remains unable to act, either in his own interests or in others', while all around him, corrupt feudal landlords, robber chiefs, lawyers, and even hapless widows seem to be able to work the system to their own advantage. A strange, dreamy chapter consisting almost entirely of one three-page paragraph depicts Madhav alone in his well-appointed room on a dark night, reflecting on his predicament. The reader finds him "reclining on a mahogany couch covered with satin," with "some two or three English books scattered" over it, and one in his hands that he can hardly read, tormented as he is by his anxieties, uncertainties, and suppressed emotions. As he stares out into the night with unfocused eyes and "listless gaze," Madhav's mind ranges over the circumstances of the lawsuit against him, "the unprincipled agency employed by cunning and clever antagonists, whom he had neither the will nor the power to fight with their own weapons." Tears spring to his eyes as he suffers the torments of his forbidden love, "the deep and tender feeling which he had stifled in his breast at such cost," but no solutions offer themselves to him. In this distracted state he is easy prey for the two large, rough men who overpower him and carry him off to Mathur's dungeons. They turn out to be the robbers, "vigorous and well-armed." Indeed, in the paragraph describing the abduction, Bankimchandra uses the word "vigorous" to describe his assailants no less than three times in six lines, while the words "powerless," "submitted," and "uselessness" are used to describe Madhav, whom they carry off "without much difficulty" (94–97). When the sardar (the robber chief) visits him in the dungeon, he mocks Madhav sarcastically, as Englishmen regularly mocked English-educated Bengalis: "The Baboo seems particularly submissive tonight."[22] The narrator is clearly suggesting that however else Madhav's English education may ennoble him, it certainly does not make him more of a man.

It is the logic of the colonial situation that dictates the dull ending, one that was clearly unsatisfying to the author himself: the long arm of British justice apprehending and sentencing the brutish Rajmohan and the robber chief's henchman to the Andaman Islands. But while the corrupt feudal landlord Mathur hangs himself rather than allowing himself to be shamed and humiliated by the British, and the robber chief disappears, evading colonial law as well,[23] the blameless hero Madhav cannot find happiness. His English education, Victorian middle-class morality, and high-Hindu principles of self-restraint keep him away from his love, even when her husband is well out of the way. After describing Mathur's suicide, Bankimchandra wraps up the rest of the story with apparent indifference (or perhaps stoicism): "As to Madhav, Champak and the rest, some are dead, and the others will die." In the end, it is only the British who can dispense a measure of justice, and our hero's only consolation must be that he and Matangini have acted honorably. As for our heroine, however courageous she may be, and however churlish her husband, she must remain, to the end, merely Rajmohan's wife.

For Madhav, the English-educated hero of his English-medium novel, there was no realistic solution to the problem of action within the discursive framework of colonialism. Like him, his creator would have to exercise self-restraint, and find other sites for his imaginative expression. After *Rajmohan's Wife*, Bankimchandra turned to his mother tongue, Bengali, as the medium for his creative work and the outlet for the humiliations of his day job. But he continued to struggle with the problem of action, both in his life as a Bengali intellectual in the British colonial employ and in his fiction, where critics note his continual shuttling between violent acts of transgression and repudiation of those acts.[24]

An "English Novel" in Malayalam: Indulekha *(1889)*

With little scope for action in the colonial framework, and political agency arrogated to the colonial rulers, the English-educated intelligentsia set out to cultivate themselves as a modern middle class who could rule India along with—not yet in place of—the British, and to shape a new Indian subject who would be capable of such action. In this context, the modernization of middle-class gender norms became central to their modernizing project. One of the earliest expressions of cultural nationalism was the molding of an ideal Indian woman, who combined what her (male) creators saw as the best of high-caste Hindu and Victorian ideals of womanhood.[25] Besides their role in preparing the ground for future political action on the part of the English-educated middle classes, I suggest that the large number of exceptional female protagonists in nineteenth-century Indian novels represented an effort to enact in the domestic realm the still-unrealized (or unrealizable) desires of their male counterparts (and creators) in the realm of the political.[26]

From Rammohan Roy, who campaigned against sati (widow immolation), to D.K. Karve, who championed women's education, it was men who initiated social reforms for women in nineteenth-century colonial India.[27] Of course, their motives were not entirely altruistic. "In all societies it was men who always laid down the ways in which women should behave," wrote Bankimchandra Chatterjee in the early 1870s, noting that "self-interested men are mindful of the improvement of women only to the extent that it furthers their self-interest; not for any other reason."[28] This was the case with novels as well. The representation of women in Indian novels during the transitional period between social reformism and the rise of nationalism was almost entirely the prerogative of men. Even when women were the ostensible subjects, and even, on occasion, the narrators of the novels, they were figures created by men. Male writers asserted their agency through the very creation of such characters. In so doing, they also created a model of a new middle-class Indian family and a new Indian woman. A few women were writing in English in the late nineteenth century, chiefly autobiographies and autobiographical fiction, but even the voices of their female protagonists were muffled by larger agendas of colonialism, nationalism, and religious conversion or revival.[29]

It was in the vernacular languages that English-educated men had to write the new literary form of the novel if they intended to reach educated, upper-caste women as well as a broader spectrum of the literate classes.[30] Take *Indulekha* (1889),[31] for example, written by O. Chandu Menon, who was employed by the colonial administration in the Madras Presidency.[32] It was the first novel in Malayalam, and immensely popular in its time. Its cautious nationalism and liberal social reformism demonstrate the regional unevenness in the development and character of Indian nationalism. (As we shall see presently, the militantly nationalistic *Anandamath* had appeared in Bengal six years earlier.) Paradoxically, because *Indulekha* was intended to promote English education for women, it was written in the mother tongue; however, it was also intended for English translation from the start.[33] Thus, like many Indian English novels, it had a dual address, both to the British colonial administration and to its fellow Malabari Nairs—and within the Nair community, both to the women who were its ostensible addressees and to their male guardians who would in fact be making the decision to educate them. Its subtitle, *Matiriyilulla Oru Katha* (a story in the manner of the English novel), frankly proclaimed its imitative intentions.[34] *Indulekha* was a strenuous advocate of English education as creating just the sort of Indian the British wanted. At the same time, it disavowed just as strenuously any perceived threat to British power represented by that sort of Indian. However, the burning political questions of the day burst out of the confines of the love story almost against the author's will, as it seems, even though he attempts to bracket them off in a chapter of their own.

Indulekha is a model of that as-yet-nonexistent figure, the Nair woman who has been educated in both English and Sanskrit and is as beautiful and good as she is witty and intelligent. After describing her radiant beauty according to the highest standards of Sanskrit literature, the author/narrator describes her education, which has included a thorough grounding in English, Sanskrit drama, and music (both Indian and European). He makes sure to praise the liberal-mindedness of the uncle who arranged for this education and to point out that Indulekha has not been "spoiled" by it, noting "her punctual observance of caste ritual, her dress and her conversation, the reverence she paid to her mother, her grandmother, grandfather and uncle, her religious faith" (10–11). Far from being a corrupting influence, her English education has actually taught her greater self-restraint. Although she has been given a great deal of freedom, her chastity is at no point in question. She remains obedient to her grandfather, never going against his wishes directly, even though she is in fact dead set against an arranged marriage to the lecherous old Nambudiripad and has vowed to marry Madhavan with or without permission.

Madhavan, the handsome young hero, is a paragon. He has never attained less than a first-class First in any examination he has taken, he is manly as well as modest, and he has cultivated his body as well as his mind. In his ingratiating introductory letter to his English translator, Chandu Menon specifically notes that Madhavan "excelled in sports and English games, such as cricket and lawn tennis." To top it off, he has been offered a coveted "assistant's place in the Secretariat" in Madras.

In *Indulekha* we encounter an ideal of marriage that will become a recurring trope of the national narrative and a metaphor for the different unions that the new middle class were attempting to bring about: the marriage of "modernity" and "tradition," English education and Indian thought, social reform and religious revitalization. Marriage is seen as an act of cultural synthesis that promises a future flowering of creative forces. The representation of a harmonious marriage in the new literary genre helped to domesticate the cultural hybrid of Indian nationalism and to allow it to take root in the private sphere by redefining the middle-class family. Conversely, a troubled marriage allowed for the staging and resolution of nationalism's internal conflicts within that contained arena.[35] The novel presents marriage as the highest ideal, as a union not only between two well-matched and complementary people, but also between the highest Indian and English ideals. Romantic love itself, the fuel that drives the story, is seen as a harmonious balance of Indian and English elements. Linked to the heroine's effort to overcome the obstacles to a love marriage in the private sphere is the effort of the hero Madhavan to achieve a balance in the public sphere, between loyalty to the newly formed Indian National Congress and loyalty to the British rulers.

The acts of resistance in *Indulekha* are those of liberal young Indians to the entrenched power of feudalism and religious orthodoxy, encouraged by English education and empowered by colonial employment. The challenge to both Indulekha and Madhavan is to gain greater individual freedom, more room to move within a restricted social framework.

Indulekha must gain her ends by staying at home and holding her ground, maneuvering in the limited space she has. Her education does not necessarily enlarge her arena for action, but it does give her a stronger sense of self and help her to hold fast to her goals, and she must use all her subtlety and wit to attain them indirectly. Indulekha's circumscribed scope for action and her need for cautious mediation can be compared fruitfully to the predicament of the English-educated Indian man, between colonial loyalism and nationalist action, between orthodoxy and reformism, between culture and politics. It is paradoxically her exercise of *self*-control that gains her greater control over her restricted circumstances. Her strategy is one of apparent nonresistance: she consents to the match with the old Nambudiripad at first but, despite her seeming compliance, she is determined to resist it to the end. Getting her way is a delicate business that involves being willing and qualified to "play the game," in the sense of knowing the prevailing rules of conduct and behaving in accordance with them, but also in the sense of mastering all possible moves so as to be able to outmaneuver one's opponents. There are, of course, two sets of rules in play in the novel, the Indian and the British, and part of being able to win is to know which sets of rules apply at any given time. Sometimes, especially for a woman, they are both in force.

Looking back from *Indulekha*'s fairy-tale ending—a companionate love marriage and a secure job in the colonial administration—to examine what kind of action has taken place in the novel, one finds that there has in fact been very little. Madhavan gains his ends both times by leaving home, and in the process broadening his arena for action. But just as Indulekha remains chaste even though she is given freedom, so Madhavan returns and remains loyal, thus vindicating his English employer's wisdom in having given him a long leash. While a larger national field of action is being mapped, Madhavan, like Indulekha, is playing a waiting game, to win.

With works like *Indulekha*, the Indian novel came to the limits of English liberalism. No matter how much characters like Madhav in *Rajmohan's Wife* and Madhavan in *Indulekha* cultivated themselves, the best they could hope for was a middle-level civil service position and the paternalistic benevolence of a British superior. In *Rajmohan's Wife*, Madhav's English education was no consolation for the yawning gulf between his liberal ideals and his semifeudal, semicolonial reality. In such settings, writers found themselves in the uncomfortable position of setting up Indian orthodoxy as their primary antagonist and British colonial rule as their ally. The domestic plot did provide some scope for agency on the part of the male protagonists and their authors during this early period. But while the new heroines served as a means by which nationalism was naturalized and Indianized, the novel could not remain in the domestic sphere forever.

While the English-educated classes continued to chafe under its colonial leash, the novel's refined heroes and domestic plots offered no emotionally satisfying avenues for action. How were they to step into the public arena? Madhav of *Rajmohan's Wife* and Madhavan of *Indulekha* shared a name of the Lord Krishna, the deified ally of the Pandavas in the epic *Mahabharata* and Arjuna's charioteer in the *Bhagavad-Gita*; but, accomplished as they were, both men paled by comparison to that manly, omnipotent leader, worshipped all over India as an *avatara* (incarnation) of the God Vishnu.[36] In the 1880s cultural nationalism began to turn away from the English book[37] and the English language and to re-create its heroes in a newly "Indian" image, in order to provide inspiring models for effective anticolonial nationalist action.

Part II: Karma in Action

Bankimchandra Chatterjee's Anandamath *(1881–82)*

This militant historical novel is set in the Bengal famine of the 1770s, a century before it was published, ostensibly based on the so-called *sannyasi* (world-renouncing ascetic) rebellion.[38] When the novel first appeared on the Bengali literary scene, serialized in its author's own literary journal *Bangadarshan*, no militant secret society such as the one depicted in it was anywhere in sight.[39] There was no national political organization either, neither would there be for three years to come, when the moderate, loyalist Indian National Congress was to be formed. As for militant action against colonial rule, it was to be nearly a decade after Bankimchandra's own death before anything approaching the passionate nationalism of the guerrilla renouncers would materialize in Bengal. When it did, however, it would consciously pattern itself on Bankimchandra's imagined community. Thus the Motherland was imagined and projected in a literary text well before it was embodied in an actual political movement. It was a text that reached back selectively to (re)construct a nationalist past and a text that would cast a long shadow into the future, one that is still making itself felt, indeed even experiencing a resurgence, well over a century later. It heralded the "New Hinduism" that its author was to develop over the next decade. It addressed itself lovingly, seditiously to Bengalis in their mother tongue, while its English-educated author worked by day as a bureaucrat in the British colonial administration. The novel's name was *Anandamath* (translated as The Abbey of Bliss).[40] It is its author's most influential novel and has been translated into many other Indian languages, although it is considered to be flawed artistically, its fame resting on largely "extra-literary" qualities.[41] The haunting strains of its anthem, "Bande Mataram" (Hail to the Mother), still echo today throughout India—and beyond, on the website of the Bharatiya Janata Party—as the novel's colonial karma continues to unfold.

Anandamath is a secret forest stronghold inhabited by a secular monastic order of men of all castes, many of them householders, under the leadership of the sage Satyananda. The *santans* (or "Children," in this translation), have dedicated themselves wholly to freeing the Mother Country from the foreign yoke, taking strict vows of celibacy until their mission is accomplished. Besides Satyananda, the main characters are Bhavananda, Jivananda and his wife Shanti, and the landlord Mahendra and his wife Kalyani.

Although the armed struggle to free the Mother Country from foreign control constitutes the primary action of the novel, of equal though less visible importance is the internal struggle for self-control. Other questions gradually assume even greater weight than the problem of driving out the foreign enemy: just who the enemy is and what constitutes right action in the long term. *Anandamath* functioned as an inspiration to militant action, a source of spiritual sustenance, and an imaginative haven from the humiliations and psychic violence of colonial domination. My particular interest here is to inquire in what sense this landmark novel represented a point of departure for Indian cultural nationalism, and specifically, how it sought to resolve the problem of action.

The title alone evokes a number of important points about the novel's religious and philosophical underpinnings. *Ananda*, or bliss (one of three states used to approximate a description of the transcendent Self), also denotes the monastic order of Shankaracharya, the eighth-century commentator on the *Bhagavad-Gita*, who sought to purify, regenerate, and unify Vedic Brahmanism in the face of internal decline and external challenges, the title suggests that the central concern of the novel is not merely the political freedom for which the Children are fighting, but a higher, spiritual freedom.[42] It imparts a religious intensity to the Childrens' fervor to liberate their Motherland and introduces a paradoxical pairing of worldly action and world-renunciation.

After affiliating itself with Shankaracharya's preference for knowledge over action, *Anandamath* begins with a epigraph from the Gita that invokes neither.[43] In *Gita* 12:6–9, Krishna promises liberation to those who worship him "with single-minded devotion," surrendering all their actions to him. In the prologue a man's voice penetrates the forest stillness, asking insistently for his desire to be fulfilled. Not even his very life will be enough to realize that desire, another voice replies: nothing but devotion. Thus Bankimchandra inaugurates the shift to cultural nationalism by introducing the popular element of *bhakti*, or religious devotion, marking a clear departure both from Shankaracharya's austere monism and from the abstract unitarianism of Bengal's reformist Brahmo Samajists.[44] This mood of intense desire and longing is the predominant emotion in *bhakti* poetry, although as yet the desire is free-floating, its object as yet unknown.

Forced out of his village by the famine, the landlord Mahendra is captured by a British convoy of sepoys. In a daring rescue, Bhavananda gets himself captured too, and his band of Children ambush the convoy, killing the British Captain, and causing the sepoys to flee in terror. Mahendra follows Bhavananda into the night, wondering what manner of men these robbers are. Now comes the most powerful scene in the novel, a scene whose beauty is intensified by its contrast with the violence in the preceding one, the parched land, the famished villagers, and the callousness of the British in the opening chapters. As they step into a moonlit meadow, Bhavananda undergoes a sudden transformation, as he is uplifted into a joyous, lyrical mood. "He . . . [sings] softly to himself:

> Mother, I bow to thee [*Bande Mataram*]!
> Mother, I bow to thee [*Bande Mataram*]!
> Rich with thy hurrying streams,

> Bright with thy orchard gleams,
> Cool with thy winds of delight,
> Dark fields waving, Mother of might,
> Mother free.[45]

Astonished at such lyricism from a robber, Mahendra inquires as to the identity of this Mother. "We own no other mother," replies Bhavananda, fervently. "The mother and the land of birth are higher than heaven. We think the land of birth to be no other than our mother herself. We have no mother, father, no brother, no wife, no child, no hearth or home…only…the mother" (32). He tells Mahendra of the Children's devotion to the Mother, their sacred vow to drive the foreigners out of the Motherland, and the asceticism they practice to cultivate courage and perseverance. At Anandamath, Satyananda takes him before three images of the Mother in turn: "as she *was*," in the prosperous form of Jagaddhatri, the protectress of the world; "as she has *now* become," in the fierce form of the goddess Kali, "garlanded only with skulls, covered with the blackest gloom, despoiled of all wealth, and without a cloth to wear" (40); and "as she *would* be," in the radiant form of Rajrajeswari, goddess of power, trampling her foes underfoot. In each case Bankimchandra's iconography adopts the existing forms of Durga-worship in Bengal.

It is worth taking another look at the scene of the ambush to better understand the relationship between violent action, sexuality, and nationalist passions. Dressed in the saffron robes of a Hindu holy man, one of the Children allows himself to be captured. When a sepoy treats him roughly, he responds with seeming servility, but "his eyes flash[ed]." Suddenly, a shot rings out, and the Hawaldar (lieutenant) falls, "shot through the head." The captured man strikes a sepoy with his pistol, cracking his skull. Two hundred armed men encircle the sepoys. Somebody tears the captain's sword from his belt and cuts off his head: "When the saheb fell down headless from his horse, the order to fire could no more be given." Standing upon the cart, sword in hand, crying "Hari, Hari" and "Kill the sepoys, kill the sepoys!" is Bhavananda, the same man who is soon to sing so sweetly to the Mother in the moonlight (27–28). The silent man who fired the first shot turns out to be Jivananda, and the two embrace.

Note the captive's feigned humility, seeming quiescence, controlled anger, and biding of time, followed by climactic violence—swift, decisive, cold-blooded—and an overwhelming show of force. And when the job is done, just as swiftly follows the affectionate embrace, an unwinding of tension, and the heightened, near-spiritual state in the moonlit forest, accompanied by lyrical outpourings of joyful emotion. The spasmodic intensity of anticolonial violence in *Anandamath* has a Fanonian purgative force and an elevated aftermath.[46] The cycle repeats: suppressed passion, self-control, intense bursts of terrifying violence, quasi-religious expressions of emotion. Revolutionary action is one parallel: the other obvious analogy is sexual. When Shanti reminds her husband Jivananda to uphold his vow by controlling his sexual desires, they join in singing "Bande Mataram" in a trembling excess of sublimated desire. Singing or intoning together stands in for sexual intercourse, as in their last encounter (as they believe) before they are to die fighting for the Mother. At the top of a hill, above the British army encampment, Shanti says to Jivananda, "Leave alone the talk of death just now…and cry 'Hail Mother'" (180). This, too, is how the novel leaves them, walking out of sight hand in hand, singing "Bande Mataram," after Shanti has decided that they will take a lifelong vow of celibacy and retreat to the Himalayas together.

The militant asceticism of the sannyasis, their stirring anthem, their devotion to the Mother Goddess and their invocation of her *shakti* (female power) was a potent concoction designed to transform the most hard-hearted in a pulse-quickening conversion that would fill them with a spirit of passionate self-sacrifice. They would resolve to renounce everything, to fight British might with might until their Mother was restored from her current state of degradation to her future radiance and power (41). According to Meenakshi Mukherjee, in *Anandamath* Bankimchandra linked, "perhaps for the first time in Indian history, the concept of the mother goddess with its connotation of shakti ... with the idea of the motherland as a political unit." The novel "fused among the Hindus a revived religious fervour with a newfound patriotic zeal"[47] by yoking a rechanneled popular religiosity with an as-yet-unfamiliar national feeling and locating a desired future in an anachronistic imagined past, since it was not materially feasible in the historical present. This masterful move exemplified what Partha Chatterjee has called "the moment of departure" for Indian nationalist discourse, a move that modeled a specifically Hindu nationalist appropriation of action.

In *Nationalist Thought and the Colonial World*, Chatterjee considers how Bankimchandra broke the impasse he had reached in pondering the problem of how to encourage Hindu action in resistance to British domination. The problem, as the English-educated Bankimchandra saw it, was a cultural one: Hindus lacked a desire for liberty, and a sense of solidarity with other Hindus because of the diversity and divisions in Hindu society. He concluded that for Hindus, the goal of knowledge was salvation, whereas "Europeans are devotees of power. That is the key to their advancement. We are negligent of power: that is the key to our downfall" (57). He saw Bengalis' lack of power as arising from "lack of enterprise, solidarity, courage, and perseverance," all attributes that could be cultivated. In *Anandamath*, Bhavananda contrasts the British soldiers' courage and adherence to duty with that of their Muslim counterparts: "an Englishman would die sooner than fly;—the Mussulman will fly with the first breath of fire and look about for *sherbet* [a chilled drink]." Asked by Mahendra if the Children have the qualities of the British, he responds, "No, but ... they come by practice."[48] Bankimchandra also saw physical strength as something else that Hindus needed to acquire, and it is in his work that the origins of the Hindu nationalist obsession with physical culture can be located. Partha Chatterjee points out that since Bankim's whole mode of reasoning was entirely consonant with Orientalist discourse on India, he still needed to find a way for Hindus to gain a positive sense of nationalist identity, which is always defined in terms of an essential difference from other nations. How were Bengalis-Hindus to prepare themselves for power by cultivating the qualities of the colonizer without entirely capitulating to the colonizers and losing themselves in the process? It is here, he argues, that the assertion of spiritual superiority became essential, allowing Hindus to define themselves in positive terms, and not solely in terms of lack.

Examining the ending of *Anandamath*, however, nationalism's very moment of departure appears to become a moment of deferral. In the final chapter,[49] Satyananda is in deep meditation after having won the battle against the British forces. But Providence has decreed that the Children's final goal of freedom for Bengal remain on hold for some time to come. A mysterious "physician" or "great man" appears and tells him that the fighting must stop: Muslim rule has come to an end and his mission has been fulfilled. Satyananda insists that "the power of the Hindus has not yet been established," since the British still hold power.[50] He calls on the Mother with tears flowing down his cheeks, lamenting that she will again "fall into the hands of infidels," wishing that he had died on the battlefield (198). Telling him not to grieve, the physician explains the cease-and-desist order from on high.

Satyananda is told that in true Hinduism, knowledge is superior to action, but that "this knowledge is of two kinds, subjective and objective." Although "subjective knowledge is the essence of the True Faith ... till you have objective knowledge, the subjective knowledge can never grow." Because the English are "great in objective sciences" that have long since "disappeared from our country," swallowed up by superstition and polytheism, a period of English rule is the only hope for a revival of "the True Faith which *Mlecchas* [foreigners[51]] call Hinduism" (198–199). Apparently the Children's rebellion was intended to force the British, formerly mere traders, "to take charge of the administration." The "great man" asks Satyananda to give up fighting, and to come away with him to gain knowledge. Satyananda cries furiously, "I will soak the earth with the blood of enemies and fertilize it,"[52] but the voice of reason prevails at last: "Where is the enemy now?" it asks; and the answer is, "There is none." Not only are the British a friendly power, but no one has the power to defeat them. Satyananda is eventually obliged to come to terms with the necessity of curtailing action against the British by the rationale that although spiritual knowledge is still the higher Truth, it is first necessary to gain material knowledge. Satyananda proposes to sacrifice his life before the Mother's image, but the great man advises him instead to accompany him to a temple of the Mother in the Himalayas.

> So saying, the great man took Satyananda by the hand. What a lovely sight that was! ... It was as if, knowledge took the hand of Devotion, Faith of Action; sacrifice, of active duty, Kalyani of S[h]anti! This Satyananda was S[h]anti and the great man Kalyani! Satyananda was Active Duty and the great man Sacrifice. Sacrifice took away Active Duty.[53]

Thus, the novel that inspired the Swadeshi Movement of 1905–08—indeed, the whole Indian independence movement—concludes with the suspension of action by an act of self-sacrifice. But according to Tanika Sarkar, such an ending is characteristic of Bankimchandra's later novels, in which he "formulates and fills out a violent Hindu agenda and immediately proceeds to deconstruct it. He powerfully projects religious militancy as a resolution to the problem of colonization," yet has "an equally powerful certainty about its untenable future."[54]

Where does this leave Indian nationalism at its moment of departure? Who does Bankimchandra see as capable of acting, and under what circumstances? Jivananda and Shanti walked off hand-in-hand at the novel's penultimate ending, their sexual passions controlled. Let us examine the implications of Bankimchandra's new model of action for others—women, lower castes, and Muslims.

The shift from social reformism to cultural nationalism was accompanied by a shift away from the earlier concern with "women's uplift." This shift is evident in *Anandamath*, and Bankimchandra signals it at the outset in his Author's Preface to the First Edition: "The wife of the Bengalee is very often his chief support: sometimes also she is not."[55] Nationalism required a sterner, harder ethos in which men had to seek modern forms of power and women could participate only by shoring up male power. The focus moved perceptibly away from women to a fetishized masculinity—physical culture, the cult of the leader, the glorification of blood—in a partially secularized worship of power. One can detect in Bankim's cryptic statement about "the wife of the Bengalee" an impatience with the social reformers' focus on the wife as companion. As often as not, he seems to suggest, she is a clinging vine who stands in the way of her husband's performance of his duty.

Besides the figure of the Mother herself, the two important women in the novel are very nearly polar opposites: Kalyani, Mahendra's dutiful wife, who is willing to take poison and die rather than stand in the way of her husband's joining the Children, and Shanti, Jivananda's strong-willed young wife, who disguises herself as a man in order to join the Children along with her husband. After the victory of the Children over Warren Hastings's forces, both couples meet in Mahendra's village and Kalyani steps back into domestic seclusion again. However, Jivananda and Shanti are never again to take up normal married life.

I suggest that Bankimchandra endows Shanti's desireless action, the *nishkama karma* of the *Bhagavad-Gita*, with the highest value in the novel. She joins the Children to fight alongside her husband, renouncing all sexual desire. Although she is a fighter by nature, Shanti decides on behalf of herself and her husband that they will become lifelong celibates, denying themselves both the conjugal pleasures of married life and the joy of serving the Mother through militant action. Her freely chosen act of renunciation is the domestic parallel of Satyananda's reluctant withdrawal. As the two plots come together in the closing paragraph of the novel, and the great man takes Satyananda away, Bankimchandra equates Satyananda with Shanti and action and the "great man" with Kalyani and renunciation. For the time being, suggests Bankim, it is necessary for the Shantis of India, male or female, to yield to the self-effacing Kalyanis. Despite patriots' burning desire to free their Motherland, the times call for self-control, not militant action.

While Jasodhara Bagchi is right that Shanti's heroism opens up a new space for women's action, it would appear to do so only temporarily.[56] It is only in times of crisis that an exceptional woman like Shanti may emerge from the home and fight alongside men, as a man may temporarily renounce caste and his duties as a householder. But in so doing, as Sangeeta Ray points out, such a woman must "become" a man and renounce home and hearth forever.[57] Although Bankimchandra does indeed delink wifehood from domesticity in Shanti's exceptional case, he simultaneously reaffirms the gendered social norms. Bankim does not redefine women's karma as selfless service to the Motherland: their highest duty is still to their husbands, and their karma still consists primarily of ritual actions, duties enjoined by their place in the social order. From the outset, the discourse of nationalism constructs the normative patriot as male, and sets the terms and the boundaries of participation in nationalist action. Those who breach those boundaries or attempt to set their own terms must pay a high price for their transgression.

The normative patriot is upper-caste as well as male. Although the order of the Children is theoretically open to all, regardless of caste or religion, as long as they are willing to abide by the terms of initiation, Bankimchandra does not introduce a single leader who is not high caste. We are told that Mahendra is a Kshatriya and Nabinananda and Jivananda are Brahmins. Not a tear is shed for the thousands of Children who follow Jivananda unquestioningly into the jaws of death under British cannonfire. We shall see the same discrepancies in Indian nationalism more generally: the declaration that all citizens are equal, regardless of caste or creed, and yet a leadership that is overwhelmingly male, upper-caste, and Hindu.

Apart from the question of who is able to fight and on what terms, the question of who is being fought is also an ambiguous and troubling one. Although the Children's goal is to drive all foreign rulers from their soil, most of their battles with the British are in fact proxy battles fought against British troops sent to Bengal to protect their trade interests and only ostensibly to help prop up the fading Muslim ruler. When the Muslims have been defeated and direct British rule becomes imminent, the Children are ordered to cease hostilities. The ambiguity is compounded by the number of different editions and widely varying translations of the novel, some altered by Bankim himself for obvious pragmatic reasons during his civil service career, and others changed at various times to suit the reigning political climate. (For instance, the abridged English translation by Basanta Koomar Roy, the only English translation currently in print, first published on the eve of the Quit India Movement, entirely omits the final chapter in which the physician tells Satyananda to suspend the action against the British.[58]) Bankimchandra's own intentions are complicated by the fact that he himself progressively "softened the adjectives applied to the British as enemies" in the five editions in his lifetime, changing *Ingrej* to the ambiguous *yavana* or *bidharmi* (which could refer to anyone of a different religion).[59] Some critics have downplayed Bankim's explicitly Hindu vision and his unquestionable hostility to Muslims.[60] Others have suggested that he deliberately wrote a historical novel with Muslims as the alien enemy to avoid personal repercussions. But even if this was the case, the action valorized in the novel was achieved at the heavy cost of excluding Indian Muslims from the national vision.

Anandamath's portrayal of a militant nationalist struggle was sharply at odds with the moderate, gradualist politics of the Indian National Congress, which was to be founded in 1885, three years after the novel's publication. And yet Bankimchandra's notion of *anusilan* (culture)[61]—learning from the British in areas where Indians were weak, and, as in Bankimchandra's interpretation of the Gita, cultivating a balance among the different qualities of worldly action, knowledge, and renunciation, or self-control—was entirely congruent with a gradualist model of preparation for self-rule.[62] Nevertheless, although *Anandamath* justifies the abrupt cessation of armed struggle in the jarring final chapter, its argument for the providential nature of British rule cannot match the religious intensity and the emotional appeal of its patriotism.

Anandamath sought to invent a Bengali past of militant action against foreign rule with which to inspire courageous action in the present. But Bankimchandra also saw that the conditions for such action were not yet ripe. Indeed, it was to be twenty years before life would imitate art in the form of the terrorist movement in

Bengal. A revolutionary *anusilan samiti* was founded in 1902 by Aurobindo Ghose and others directly inspired by Bankimchandra Chatterjee's works. This group and others like it sought to implement his idea of *anusilan* in order to prepare themselves physically and spiritually for the struggle to free the Motherland. They used Bankimchandra's emotionally charged language, with the Mother as their source of *shakti*, the Gita's karma yoga as their call to action as selfless instruments in a righteous war, and "Bande Mataram" as their mantra. By 1907–08, some of these groups began to organize terrorist actions such as assassinations of British officials, one of which landed all the organizers in jail, including Aurobindo.[63] However, their base was restricted to a minuscule section of the educated urban elite. Even though such activity was carried on sporadically throughout the independence movement, it remained limited to upper-caste youth.[64] New nationalist journals both in Indian languages and in English, such as *Yugantar, Bande Mataram*, and *The Karmayogin* in Calcutta, and *Kesari* and *The Mahratta* in Poona, were founded during this time and enjoyed wide circulations. "Bande Mataram" became the anthem of the nationalist movement, and was sung at the opening of the annual Indian National Congress sessions, despite the objections of Muslim Congress members to its clear references to the nation as the Goddess Durga. But many of the divisive elements of Bankimchandra's nationalist vision were to play themselves out in the ensuing years, both outside the Congress, where Muslims and the lower castes were forming their own separate organizations, and within it, where conflicts between exponents of militant and moderate action would lead to a paralyzing split.

Tagore's Dual and Dueling Protagonists, 1905–19
The Partition of Bengal and the decade-long split in Congress dominated the cultural politics of this period. Indian nationalism felt the possibility of mass mobilization for the first time, but also faced paralysis as leaders clashed over means and ends. In 1905, in an explicit and effective divide-and-rule move along both religious and class lines, the British Viceroy Lord Curzon partitioned the state of Bengal into East and West Bengal.[65] The resultant *Swadeshi* Movement that raged for three years in Bengal marked the first time that anticolonial sentiment acquired a militant political character. Taking a vow of *Swadeshi* ("of one's own country" or self-reliance) involved buying Indian and boycotting British goods, particularly cloth, and the movement mobilized educated, urban Bengalis, most of them Hindus, in larger numbers than ever before. It developed rapidly into a broader struggle for *Swaraj*, or self-rule, with newly formed regional organizations and a proliferation of periodicals calling for *Swaraj* from 1906 on.[66] The *Swadeshi* Movement spread beyond the boundaries of Bengal and began linking up with counterparts around the country, leading to the beginnings of a truly national movement and a struggle between the men and methods that were to lead it. However, the Congress remained a body that met annually to make resolutions but not to organize action. Militant activists challenged the "mendicant" Congress (as its critics called it) to open up its ranks and engage in more concerted action. Moderates criticized "Extremists" for their tacit endorsement of terrorist acts and their resistance to social reform. This led to a major split at its Surat Session in 1907 between the "Moderates" and the "Extremists," or

"Nationalists," that was not to be reversed for nearly a decade. During this period, the primary problems of action for a self-rule movement with national aspirations involved overcoming internal divisions and broadening its base of support. Rabindranath Tagore tackled both these problems head-on in his novels of the time, considering how best to reconcile split selves and how the national Self was being defined and constituted. *Vis-à-vis* action, he became increasingly ambivalent, as we shall see.

Rabindranath Tagore (in Bengali, Thakur) was a scion of the wealthy and illustrious Tagore family, and the grandson of Debendranath Tagore, an early member and leader of the reformist Brahmo Samaj. He was the undisputed literary/cultural giant of his time, and it was the young Tagore to whom Bankimchandra Chatterjee passed the torch as his literary successor in Bengal and who revived and took over the editorship of Bankim's journal *Bangadarshan* for a time after his death.[67] Rabindranath was a poet, songwriter, educator, painter, Nobel Laureate, Bengali *eminence grise*, and universal humanist. Besides poetry, he also wrote plays, short stories, novels, and essays. Educated at home in Sanskrit, English, and Bengali literature, he absorbed European liberal ideas, modern science, and reformist heterodoxy from his Brahmo Samaj family. Although he was fluent in English, Tagore, like Bankimchandra, wrote almost exclusively in Bengali (with the exception of some of his essays and lectures); however, he transcreated some of his work into English, most famously his long poem *Gitanjali*, which won him the 1913 Nobel Prize for Literature.[68] He was awarded a knighthood, which he returned in protest in 1919 after the Amritsar Massacre. Although Tagore's freedom songs inspired millions, and today, two of them, "*Janaganamana*" and "*Amar Sonar Bangla*" (Our Golden Bengal), are the national anthems of India and neighboring Bangladesh respectively, it is ironic that from 1907 on, he increasingly distanced himself from the prevailing tendencies of nationalist politics. Two of his novels, *Gora* ("fair-skinned"; also slang term for the British, 1907–09) and *Ghare-Baire* (*The Home and the World*, 1915), engage most eloquently with the problems as he saw them, "vividly expressing the tensions and ambiguities of the age."[69] With these novels, both written in the aftermath of the *Swadeshi* Movement, Rabindranath Tagore mounted a powerful critique of the trajectory of the nationalist movement in Bengal.

While Bengal was the first headquarters of British rule and English education, it was also a center of the all-India nationalist movement. Bengalis continued to value their Bengali language and literary heritage highly, even as they pioneered British-influenced religious and social reform, and to this day Bengal produces some of India's finest writers in English. The point here is that for many Bengali intellectuals, including Tagore, the conflict was not between English and Bengali. Rather, the dilemma was how to identify the vital elements of both of the cultural and linguistic traditions and combine them in a unique synthesis that would enrich both India and the world. They did not wish to cut themselves off from the intellectual currents of the world or from those of the Indian traditions, and they were determined to shape their national–international vision actively, rather than merely reactively, in spite of the fact of their country's colonization. Although it was inevitable that the inequities and indignities of colonialism would color their vision to some degree, many early cultural nationalists refrained from framing their conflicts in the polarized terms of Orientalist discourse. Since members of the high-caste educated elite were trained to value highly abstract, text-based religion, many Bengali intellectuals tended to belittle popular religious beliefs and practices, but Tagore was also deeply influenced by the songs of popular Bengali groups such as the Bauls, the traveling mystics of Bengal. The discourse of nationalism in Tagore's *Gora* is therefore many-sided, and like Tagore himself, resists polarization, even when driven to the wall.[70] In his work, Tagore variously sought to reconcile both his own apprehensions about nationalism, and the tensions within educated Indian society between liberal reformists and socially conservative militants. National self-determination was the goal, but there was a great deal of disagreement as to who the national self was, and what constituted right action in pursuit of that goal.

Gora *(1907–09)*

Gora is a rich, complex novel, peopled with fully developed characters.[71] It shows Tagore at his most sympathetic toward the constructive potential of nationalism, even as it presents a clear-eyed critique of its pitfalls. In seeking solutions to his problem of action, Tagore reached back thirty years to set *Gora* in Bengal of the late 1870s (the very time when Bankim would have been starting to write *Anandamath*), illuminating the precise historical moment when the religious and social reform movement was shifting into a movement of religious and cultural revival, in preparation for its next phase of mass political mobilization.

Set in the respectable, upper middle-class *bhadralok* (educated "gentlefolk") society of Calcutta, *Gora's* action is played out primarily through internal conflicts between and within the Westernized, reformist Brahmo Samaj and orthodox Hindu society. The fiery, charismatic protagonist Gora is an English-educated young man, once a reformist Brahmo Samaj supporter, but now an aggressively—and defensively—orthodox Hindu revivalist leader, defiantly practicing the idol worship, observances of caste purity, and religious rituals that were anathema to Brahmo society. His best friend Binoy is a tolerant, mild-mannered youth who seems to agree with Gora on everything. *Gora* opens with both young men in an extended transitional state, having completed their education and as yet having neither married nor taken up a paid position.[72] As members of the English-educated elite, they would have been expected to seek a job in the colonial administration; indeed, Gora's elder brother Mahim has just such a job, in which he must continually kowtow to his British superiors and do what is expedient rather than what is right. By contrast, Gora and Binoy have the time to organize and attend meetings and to contribute fiery articles to the newspapers. They also have the freedom to travel when and where the spirit takes them and to defy colonial authority. Then, in his passionate quest to define Bharatvarsha (India), Gora reaches out beyond the English-educated *bhadralok* to the Bengali peasantry, and Binoy reaches in beyond English-educated men to the equally unfamiliar territory of Bengali women. Neither high-caste Hindu orthodoxy nor elite reformism can accommodate both subalterns and women; neither has a national vision inclusive enough to contain them all. As Gora and Binoy become estranged from society and each other, the novel's central conflict becomes the split between the two male protagonists and how it is to be healed.

Tagore differed from many of the nationalist interpreters of the *Bhagavad-Gita* in that he questioned both the colonialist idea of action and the nationalist notion of karma, which he sees as disturbingly similar to each other. He did not privilege action, even while he recognized the need for it under colonialism, and he distrusted nationalist claims to selfless action. After two years of intense participation in the *Swadeshi* Movement, he began to withdraw from nationalist politics. He was frightened by the rabble-rousing polemics, in which he saw power-hungry leaders inflaming passions and inciting people to destructive action at the expense of reasoned thought or judgement. In *Gora*, the problem of action facing Gora and Binoy in their extended moment of transition is not merely *what to do* but, as importantly, *how to be*. Tagore's ideal remains synthesis, in this case a synthesis between action and contemplation. But in a period of increasing polarization, when people are forced to choose which side they are on, can a true synthesis be achieved or is a parting of the ways inevitable? As the rift between Binoy and Gora widens—a rift that can be seen both as the Brahmo split in the late 1870s between the reformists and the revivalists at the moment of transition from cultural to political nationalism and as the Congress split in 1907 between "Moderates" and "Extremists"—how will Tagore resolve their seemingly irreconcilable differences?

Gora is the very epitome of a Hindu nationalist ideal of action. Tall, fair, and vigorous, he is a powerhouse of passionately focused energy and religious–patriotic zeal. Like the fighting *sannyasis* in Bankimchandra's *Anandamath*, and the young Swami Vivekananda (who is one of the people thought to have been Tagore's model for his character[73]), he has decided not to marry but to remain celibate, dedicating himself wholly to a nationalist ideal of karma, selfless action in the cause of a united, revitalized Bharatvarsha. He is devoted—again, like the *sannyasis* of *Anandamath*—to the masculinist ethos of action and physical culture characteristic of Hindu nationalism, and even runs physical culture classes open to young men of all castes.[74] Binoy, by contrast, is a gentle soul and a seeker, as yet uncommitted to a particular path in life. The novel opens with Binoy listening from his window to the strains of a mystical devotional song sung by a Bengali Baul, an itinerant street singer. Binoy often agrees with Gora for the sake of peace, but he is less drawn to ideas than he is to people, and he himself is the least dogmatic of people. At the same time, he admires Gora for his energy and direction, and is content to be his follower and friend, until he meets Poresh Babu's reformist Brahmo Samaj family and, in particular, his daughter Lolita, who taunts him for being a mere satellite of Gora and not standing up for his own ideals.

Gora's hypermasculinity is marked by the defensive nationalism with which Indians defied the colonial stereotypes of Indians as passive and effeminate, and of their British colonizers as dynamic and virile. In contrast, Tagore portrays the sensitive Binoy as rather too passive at times, even though for much of the novel Binoy appears to be the central and the more sympathetic character. While Gora is too driven to have the time or patience for introspection, Binoy, the more contemplative of the two, has self-knowledge but sometimes lacks the drive to translate his ideals into action. Clearly Tagore's ideal would be a synthesis of the two. Differences between them are often resolved by Binoy's backing down—again, for the sake of peace, rather than by genuine negotiation or mutual compromise. In a novel structured by a series of dilemmas, the first and central dilemma posed by Tagore is what path the two friends will take into their adult life, whether it will be a united one, or whether their differences will ultimately be irreconcilable.

Given the large number of fully developed characters in *Gora*, several of them near-protagonists, it is worth asking why Tagore named the novel after the character seemingly least like himself, the character who for most of the novel espouses Hindu nationalist views that were repugnant to him. As Meenakshi Mukherjee has noted, centerstage at the novel's opening is the gentle Binoy, to whom at least as many chapters are devoted as to Gora himself. Is Gora the protagonist, or are Binoy and Gora dual protagonists, their differences, debates, estrangement, and eventual reunion representing the author's own shifting ambivalence toward nationalist action?[75] As the novel progresses, several chapters are also devoted to Sucharita and Lolita, the two young women with whom the two friends fall in love and who are responsible for restoring gender balance to Gora and Binoy's exclusively male vision of India. Several more chapters deal with a series of paired characters, every one of whom is an essential aspect of a multifaceted vision of India's pluralism and diversity. Nevertheless, if there can be said to be a central focus, it is the two young men's understanding of what it means to belong to India, an understanding that begins as shallow and entirely abstract, and that deepens over the course of the novel. Ultimately it is Tagore's concern with the complex meaning and means of this "belonging to India" that places the ardently religious activist Gora at the center of the novel, rather than the agnostic, essentially private individual Binoy. This placement reflects a recognition on Tagore's part of the urgency of his historical time, in which, whether the philosopher-poet himself liked it or not (for he was temperamentally much more akin to Binoy than to Gora), the burning question of the day was how to realize the idea of India in principled political action.

Tagore was to become increasingly disillusioned with the strategy and tactics used by the nationalist movement to mobilize its forces, distrustful of short cuts to building a mass movement that sought to win support not by providing real economic resources for the poor or by reasoned argument, but by demagoguery and the manipulation of popular and religious symbols. He particularly disliked the nationalist recourse to Hindu religious images, such as identifying the nation with a Hindu mother-goddess (as Bankimchandra had in *Anandamath*), and tactics that inflamed hatred, whether for the British or for fellow Indians, such as Indian Muslims. Social inclusivity, religious tolerance, genuine cultural synthesis, and economic self-help were the central articles of Tagore's faith. As time went on, he saw the nationalist movement gaining ground at the expense of these ideals, and he foresaw that, in the long term, India—and the world—would be compelled to reap the results of the hatred, violence, and deep social divisions it had sown. But in 1907–09, when he wrote *Gora*, Tagore still sought a positive construction of the nationalist ideals. As Vivekananda did, Gora sets out on foot into the countryside to search for the spirit of Bharatvarsha by attempting to get in touch with ordinary people. He recognizes the insularity of Calcutta *bhadralok* society, and feels a burning need to reach out and serve the larger, still-undefined entity that is his homeland. For all his faults, Gora's nationalist vision is broad and generous, seeking both to restore faith in India's ancient traditions and to realize a vision that includes the whole of society. However, major blind spots in his vision are the inequities of gender and caste discrimination in Indian society. These are the contradictions that he must face and resolve before his vision can hope to be complete.

In addition to recognizing the internal hierarchies of power that divide Indian society, Gora must acknowledge the exclusionary nature of Hindu caste society, deterministically based as it is on birth. He comes to see that Hindu nationalism functions to exclude "insiders" such as women and the lower castes and outcastes of Hindu society, as well as "outsiders" such as the British. Beyond barriers to belonging based upon nature, it also erects barriers based on culture by its excommunication of those who do not observe its rigid codes and rituals of purity. Tagore asks how such a society is ever to achieve national unity and whether the whole nationalist project is bankrupt if it is capable of attaining only a negative, reactionary unity.

Because Tagore is at pains to de-link national belonging from biology, all *Gora's* protagonists—Sucharita, Binoy, and Gora himself—are orphans, and neither of their nurturing parent-figures—Poresh Babu and Anandamoyi—are their biological parents. Furthermore, in portraying his protagonists changing their identities and identifications dramatically over the course of the novel, Tagore shows identity to be a developmental process rather than a given. Poresh Babu and Anandamoyi give their love unconditionally, never favoring their biological over their adoptive children. In fact, it is ultimately revealed that Anandamoyi, although the essence of motherliness, has no biological children at all. But it is also seen that this discovery makes absolutely no difference to the fact of her love. Tagore shows us a range of people who are motherly to a greater or lesser degree, but only one who serves as a model for all mothers, and for Mother India herself, matrix for the nation-in-the-making.[76]

At first it is the open-minded Binoy whose life is enlarged by contact with the free women of Poresh Babu's reformist Brahmo Samaj household—Sucharita, his calm, wise adoptive daughter, and his own daughters, one of them, Lolita, bold and principled. Binoy is soon drawn to Lolita, whose temperament is complementary to his own. Gora is initially contemptuous of these unorthodox Brahmo women who do not observe seclusion, but begins to visit their household after Binoy makes him recognize the importance of women to a complete vision of India. Gora finds himself falling in love with Sucharita in spite of himself, and begins visiting her daily, trying to make her see India and the nationalist task with the same urgency that he does, and to understand her powerful role in carrying out that task. When Sucharita's orthodox aunt points out to him that it is improper for him to be spending so much time with the girl, he resolves to cut off from her altogether and renew his vows of celibacy in service of the nation. But he finds himself changed by his contact with her, and when he finally discovers that he is not a Hindu and will never be accepted as one, his first act is to go to Sucharita and to seek her father's blessing for their marriage. For his part, Binoy marries Lolita, standing by her in the face of universal censure from both the Hindu and the Brahmo communities. His steadiness balances her impulsiveness.

Sucharita and Lolita are very different: Lolita needs to be active out in the world, while Sucharita is naturally retiring. Tagore makes it clear that Lolita is no less a woman than Sucharita, just as the gentle Binoy is no less a man than the aggressive Gora, and that all sorts of people have a role to play in society. Gora and Binoy eventually realize that it is not only the symbol of Woman that is necessary to complete their masculinist nationalist vision, but also the participation of real women themselves, helping actively to shape the new India. Although Tagore is remarkable in his portrayal of a full spectrum of women, he does remain a Bengali man of his time in his glorification of motherhood and of women's quiet capacities for service, silent suffering, and self-sacrifice. In spite of his inclusion of the rebellious Lolita, the quiet, decorous, obedient Sucharita is clearly his ideal consort for the fiery protagonist Gora. And in spite of his insistence that the vision of India needs women to complete it, his female characters serve primarily as complements to his male protagonists. Still, Tagore portrays the callow youths, who begin by spouting ideological abstractions, learning from Sucharita's wisdom and Lolita's courage. He also contrasts Anandamoyi's open-minded tolerance with her orthodox husband's rigid and entirely self-centered obsession with ritual purity.

In setting *Gora* back in the 1870s, on the eve of the Hindu revival and at the time of a historical split in the Brahmo Samaj (between those who dissociated themselves from Hinduism entirely and those who still considered themselves Hindus), Tagore explores the roots and possible resolutions of the polarized conflicts of his own time. Sucharita is the only character who has the potential to mediate successfully between the rigidly orthodox Hindu society and the self-righteously liberal Brahmo society. An orphan from a Hindu family, she is being raised in Poresh Babu's Brahmo household, but when her orthodox aunt comes to stay, she begins to cook for her and to observe caste purity for her sake. At the same time, she has begun talking to Gora and, under his influence, comes to feel that socially conscious Hindus should not cut themselves off from the great mass of Hindus who worship images and engage in ritual. The moment comes when she courageously declares herself a Hindu, which is anathema to the Anglophile, Christian-leaning Brahmo society to which her adoptive family belongs. However, knowing that Sucharita is from a Hindu background, the wise Poresh Babu has raised her not to be ashamed of her cultural heritage. It is significant that Tagore uses the *Bhagavad-Gita* to set Sucharita apart from Brahmo purism and link her to her Hindu heritage:

> At that time in Bengal, those who were English-educated people did not generally study or discuss the *Bhagavad-Gita*, but Poresh Babu used to read the Gita occasionally with Sucharita...Haran Babu [her Brahmo suitor] did not approve of this. He was in favor of banishing all such texts from Brahmo households...wishing to keep *Ramayan-Mahabharat-Bhagavad-Gita* separate as the property of Hindus. (94)

As nationalists used the Gita to popularize the movement and to mediate between reformism and orthodoxy, so Tagore uses the figure of Sucharita to address the social isolation of the Bengali reformist elite and to mediate between Brahmo liberalism and Hindu orthodoxy. She attempts to chart an independent, quietly constructive course between her two suitors, Haran Babu, the tight-lipped leader of the Brahmo purists, and Gora, the fiery leader of the Hindu revival. However, neither side is prepared to compromise, and a breach between the two becomes inevitable.

In *Gora*, Tagore seems to endorse women's full emergence into the world. Without them, he asserts, the idea of India will remain just an idea. At the same time, his favored women are natural mothers, modest, empathetic, self-effacing. It is interesting to compare Tagore's differential portrayal·of Binoy's and Lolita's independently taken decisions not to participate in the play being rehearsed for the English magistrate, with Sucharita's decision to stay behind and take part in it. The play, a drawing-room performance of English songs, poetry, and a dramatic recitation accompanied by a costumed dumb-charade, to be staged at the home of Mr. Brownlow, can be taken to represent the English-educated Indian's problem of action under colonial rule. Binoy and Lolita, Sucharita and Haran Babu have all been rehearsing for it, until they learn that Gora has been jailed for siding with Muslim peasants against a Brahmin landlord, and has chosen to remain in jail on principle, in solidarity with the defenceless peasants. He is tried by the same magistrate in whose home they are preparing to stage the dumb-charade, and is sentenced to a month's hard labor. Both Binoy and Lolita leave the Englishman's house and take the night steamer back to Calcutta, withdrawing from the play in silent protest against Gora's sentencing. Binoy's act simply follows from his quiet, unceremonious decision to go away; there is no discussion, no authorial censure, no suggestion that perhaps he ought to stay and see the play through, or at least to explain himself to his hosts. It is enough that Binoy loves Gora, has always been uneasy about the play, and feels that he simply cannot go on with the charade while his friend languishes in prison. For Lolita, however, the same decision is immeasurably more fraught with consequences. Her slipping away in the night without permission, and on the same steamer as Binoy, inevitably exposes her to gossip and her reputation to ruin. Characteristically, Lolita does not stop to consider the ramifications of her actions, either on herself or on her family. By contrast, Sucharita, tormented by the situation, and deeply but silently in love with Gora, stays behind and follows through with her commitment to act in the play simply because Poresh Babu asked her to do so, even though she had never wanted to be involved in it at all. Here Jane Austen's *Mansfield Park* comes inevitably to mind, with Sucharita having drawn back from the play with the same natural modesty—and authorial approval—as Austen's heroine Fanny Price. The important difference is that despite her disinclination to parade herself on a stage, Sucharita is prepared to take part in the play out of duty to her adoptive father, rather than withdrawing from it as Binoy and Lolita do. Without offering any hard-and-fast answers, Tagore thereby raises the difficult question of when withdrawal from social engagement constitutes right action and when it is a self-indulgent escape from doing one's duty. Of course, in withdrawing from the Brownlows's drawing-room stage, the young people are stepping out into the much larger public arena of action.

The figure of Sucharita (or Little Mother, as she is called) is more than just a mediator between the divided male protagonists, even if she is not quite a fully developed character in her own right. Rather than an idealized Sucharita merely triangulating the Gora–Haran Babu opposition or the Binoy–Gora dyad, the pairs of Binoy–Lolita and Gora–Sucharita form a complementary square, encircled within the love and guidance of the parent figures of Poresh Babu and Anandamoyi. In the end, it is Anandamoyi who promises to heal the rift between Binoy and Gora, seeking their reunion above all else. When Gora is finally forced to accept the fact that he is adopted and of Irish parentage (the reader has suspected the truth all along but, like Gora himself, has been unwilling to look it in the eye), he realizes that despite his desire to embrace orthodox Hinduism, orthodoxy has always rejected him and will always continue to do so. Binoy had already been forced to recognize this truth when Hindu society shunned him for his decision to marry Lolita, despite his refusal to marry her according to Brahmo rites and his insistence on a (modified) Hindu ceremony.[77] Gora is now freed to follow his heart, rather than to feel compelled to conform to a society that will never accept him. Going straight to Sucharita, Gora takes her with him to the feet of Poresh Babu, and begs the old gentleman to become his guru.

On many occasions throughout the novel, Poresh Babu's withdrawal into contemplation, especially under pressure, is contrasted with the action of younger men such as Gora and the ambitious Brahmo leader Haran Babu, Gora's rival for Sucharita. Poresh Babu frequently counsels his children that it is better not to act at all than to act hastily, in passion; at the same time, when no one else, Brahmo or Hindu, will attend Binoy and Lolita's wedding, it is only Poresh Babu and Anandamoyi who have the courage to stand against the whole of society and support them—even Gora had refused to attend his best friend's wedding. In the end, it is their courage, tolerance, and wisdom that is vindicated, when Gora realizes that now, as an outcaste of Hindu society, he belongs to India all the more. Tagore clearly upholds quiet action born of mature reflection over knee-jerk action-for-action's-sake, bravado born of insecurity and wounded pride.

In the paragraph-long Epilogue, Gora returns home to his adoptive mother, Anandamoyi, and claims her as his own and as the India of his dreams:

> "Ma, you are my only mother. The mother I have looked for everywhere—all the time she was sitting in my house. You have no caste, you do not discriminate against people, you do not hate—you are the image of benediction. You are my Bharatvarsha..." (477)

Gora then asks, "Ma, will you call Lachmiya and tell her to get me now a glass of water?" In accepting water from his mother's servant Lachmiya, something he has consistently refused to do throughout the novel, Gora is finally rejecting the orthodox rituals of caste purity, since Lachmiya is a low-caste woman and a Christian convert. It is Anandamoyi who has the final words of the novel: "Gora, let me send for Binoy." These words suggest the coming-together of the two friends,[78] but their reconciliation is not accomplished within the frame of the novel—it remains unfinished business, as does the resolution of the sharpening conflict between the Brahmo reformers and the socially conservative Hindu nationalists in society at large. The novel's resolution of the protagonists' personal dilemmas, then, leaves us a social and political vision that Tagore is already painfully aware is not likely to be realized on larger national scale, and that, in fact, leaves them as involuntary outcastes from the very Hindu society they have been seeking to unite and transform.

The religious, social, political, and ideological differences that have driven a wedge between the two friends have not vanished, but instead have been taken up into Mother India's inclusive, all-embracing love. They share a mother who does not discriminate among any of her children. Neither blood nor caste status confer a greater claim to this mother's love. Tagore resolves the conflict between orthodox Hinduism and non-conformism as Binoy did when he married, and as Gora does when he finally realizes his freedom: he has not rejected Hinduism, although he feels free to redefine it, but it has rejected him. This resolution leaves caste society intact—as Meenakshi Mukherjee has noted, the device of his Irish parentage frees Gora from the constraints of caste society by default, without compelling him (or the author) to reject it actively.[79] Nevertheless, Gora's realization of the biological determinism of caste society forces him to recognize the discrepancies between his idealized vision of India and the harsh social realities, and in the end Tagore puts forth his ideal of a tolerant, loving Motherland from which none of her children is cast out. Tagore's vision remains aristocratic and abstractly intellectual, since Lachmiya remains a mere principle, not a flesh-and-blood character, never seen or heard in her own right. Nevertheless, written nearly thirty years before Mulk Raj Anand's *Untouchable, Gora* was far ahead of its time in rejecting the upper-caste rituals of caste purity, even as it still attempted to embrace the spirit of Hindu India. In view of the seemingly irreconcilable differences between educated Indians on the problem of anticolonial action when *Gora* was first serialized, the novel's conclusion was remarkably optimistic, if not about Hindu nationalism, then at least about the prospects for a new cultural synthesis that could include a broad spectrum of differences. But by the time Tagore wrote *Ghare-Baire*, he was far less sanguine about the possibilities for reconciliation between its divided protagonists.

The Home and the World *(1915)*

Ghare-Baire—in English translation, *The Home and the World*—was serialized in 1915 and set in 1908, toward the tail-end of the *Swadeshi* Movement. By the time he wrote it, Tagore had become completely disillusioned with the direction the movement had taken. Not only is his critique of nationalism more sharply drawn in this novel than in *Gora, The Home and the World* is also narrower, less generous, and deeply pessimistic, and its characters often little more than ciphers. Sandeep, the nationalist character, is cynically portrayed as an unscrupulous, self-serving villain, while Nikhil, the Tagore-like feudal landlord, is portrayed as well meaning, but entirely ineffectual.[80] Even though Nikhil thoroughly disapproves of his old college friend's hypocritical behavior and unprincipled political tactics, he allows Sandeep to remain in his home, wearing his foreign clothes, smoking his foreign cigarettes, and seducing his wife. Both English-educated men, each in his own way, lure the naïve Bimala, Nikhil's wife and the figure of Bengal, out of domestic seclusion only to betray her trust and abandon her to her fate.

By 1916–17, when Tagore delivered his lectures on nationalism in Japan and the United States, his position was fully formed: that the idolatrous "cult" of modern nationalism "with all its paraphernalia of power and prosperity, its flags and pious hymns, its blasphemous prayers in the churches, and the literary mock thunders of its patriotic bragging" was an entirely pernicious "machine of power," a dangerous capitulation to divisive, dehumanizing tendencies rather than a positive force for human development.[81] He saw nationalist action that merely reacted in kind to European colonial aggression as reproducing the same will-to-power, rather than offering an alternative vision. In *The Home and the World*, Tagore poured his abhorrence for any such behavior on the part of Indian nationalists into lengthy debates between the moderate, rational Nikhil and the militant demagogue Sandeep—debates in which the author's own disillusionment tends to reduce the characters to puppets, and make Nikhil a mouthpiece for his own views. Nikhil disapproves of Sandeep's forcible coercion of Muslims who refused to support *Swadeshi*: "If the idea of a United India is a true one… Muslims are a necessary part of it." Sandeep's responds, "Quite so…but we must know their place and keep them there."[82] Tagore saw such coercive tactics on the part of the Hindu leadership as only deepening the rift between Hindus and Muslims and thus reinforcing Britain's own divide-and-rule policy.

As liberal Bengali reformists opposed to all ritual and idol-worship, both Nikhil and Tagore himself found the idea of the worship of the country as a god repugnant in the extreme, and Sandeep and Nikhil argue about the ethics of using the mantra of "Bande Mataram" for political purposes. However, Bimala, speaking for the uneducated populace, insists, "I have my desire to be fascinated, and fascination must be supplied to me in bodily shape by my country. She must have some invisible symbol casting its spell on my mind." Nikhil's distaste for any exploitation of peoples' baser instincts makes him, in his wife's estimation, "too good to be useful" (37–38), and he, too, castigates himself for his failure to act. In his own life, Tagore faced a continual struggle between the desire to live a quiet, principled life and the historic necessity for mass action. When the battle lines were drawn and individuals were faced with the prospect of fighting dirty if they hoped to win, Tagore's personal inclination, like that of his fictional Nikhil, was to withdraw from the fray altogether, and repair to his feudal estate. As Martha Nussbaum notes in her brief discussion of the novel, "Tagore would never act. Action was too contaminating."[83]

Tagore's growing disillusionment with the nationalist movement was accompanied by a less optimistic view of the prospects for the reform of Hindu society. By the time he wrote *The Home and the World*, the consequences of Bimala's indiscretions were not merely troublesome, like Lolita's, but tragic. In *The Home and the World*, the reformist domestic novel and the militant political novel come together with disastrous results. Nikhil's uxorious pride in his wife's accomplishments in learning English and modern ways, leading to him bringing her prematurely out of seclusion to meet Sandeep, turns out to be not just a forgivable weakness, but a fatal flaw.[84] The sheltered Bimala does not have the strength of character to withstand the seductions of the world. She falls prey to Sandeep's considerable charms, losing all modesty and self-control when he sets her on a pedestal as Mother Goddess and nationalist muse. The innocent, idealistic student Amulya is caught up in the movement, seeking Bimala's blessing as Mother India, and carrying a gun and the Gita to justify its use. Now that it is being used to sanctify killing, Tagore no longer takes the benign view of the Gita that he did in *Gora*. Bimala is horrified by the nationalist passions that render a human life worthless, but she is too much in Sandeep's thrall herself to halt the chain of events that has begun to unfold.

There is no redemption in this novel for the fallen woman. She must be punished, and Bimala's vanity and betrayal brings about the death of the innocent Amulya, and perhaps the death of her husband as well, since the novel leaves his life—and thus Bimala's fate—hanging in the balance. When a husband died before his wife, orthodox society blamed and punished the inauspicious widow, and interestingly, Tagore the enlightened reformer affirms that social judgment by making Bimala the indirect cause of her husband's fatal or near-fatal injury. Allegorically, Bengal herself is exposed to the corruption of the West and to the seductions of modernity in being forced too soon out of her age-old seclusion.[85] Here Tagore would seem to be reproducing what he himself has censured, making real women into symbols of the country. In the end, the sensual Sandeep gets off scot-free, while the naïve woman faces the tragic consequences of acts for which she was not mature enough to take responsibility. The author's fear of women's uncontained sexuality speaks clearly through Bimala's voice: "When, like the river, we women keep to our banks, we give nourishment with all that we have; when we overflow them we destroy with all that we have" (51). Despite Nikhil's attempts to exonerate his wife's actions and take the blame upon himself, Bimala's emergence from seclusion and its disastrous consequences remain the focus of the novel. Any hopes the reader might have nurtured that this bright, newly educated woman was maturing into an independent subject, the mistress of her own fate, are unequivocally crushed.

While the ending of *The Home and the World* is clearly much darker than that of *Gora*, the ambiguity of both allows some space for hope, in the former, for the reunion of Nikhil and a contrite Bimala, and in the latter for the reunion of Gora with Binoy and with Sucharita. However, Tagore is clear that these reunions can take place only outside the folds of Hindu nationalism and Hindu orthodoxy, respectively. In 1916, the Congress was to be reunited after its nine-year split, but Tagore was as critical of the Moderates' isolation from the Indian people as he was of the Extremists' manipulation of them. The Extremists had been marginalized in the Congress, but had by no means been discredited in the nation at large. Tagore's critique of nationalism included tactics that were soon to be adopted by the Congress mainstream, such as the adoption of Hindu religious texts and symbols that would alienate Muslims, the burning of foreign cloth, and the deification of the nation as a mother goddess, but "his was increasingly a voice crying in the wilderness."[86] Although Gandhi's masterful mediation had managed to reunite the Congress, and the Indian nationalist movement stood on the threshold of mass action, Tagore saw the dark shadow of colonial karma stretching ahead, and continued to envision in its place a genuine cultural synthesis.

C HAPTER T WO

S HAPING A N ATIONAL S UBJECT
OF A CTION , 1920–47

The national Sahitya Akademi's *A History of Indian English Literature* characterizes 1920–47 as the "Gandhian age," and indeed, as a defining figure of the period, M.K. Gandhi was tremendously influential, in literature as in society at large.[1] This chapter examines the efforts of prominent Indian English novels of the Gandhian Age to create a coherent national subject of action, during a time when the Indian National Congress, under Gandhi's leadership, was attempting to establish its own hegemony over a host of pressures from below.

"Reunification without Reconciliation"

The decade-long Congress split between the so-called Extremists and Moderates ended, at least nominally, in 1915, but it was a "reunification without reconciliation,"[2] in that no breakthrough had been made between the two polarized factions. Gandhi had arrived on the scene, already famous for the nonviolent civil disobedience campaigns he had organized in South Africa, and after the 1919 Amritsar Massacre, a new era in Congress politics began with the Non-Cooperation Movement, under his leadership. Politically, 1920–47 was a turbulent period during which the independence movement acquired a mass character for the first time, thanks to the Congress' nonviolent civil disobedience campaigns and its focus on peasant and youth mobilization. During the Non-Cooperation Movement of 1919–22 and throughout the 1930s, Congress was to organize hundreds of thousands of Indians in acts of nonviolent resistance. A brilliant political strategist and master of compromise, Gandhi developed a winning strategy that has been described as Struggle-Truce-Struggle (S-T-S), a model of highly disciplined mass resistance as a tactic to pressure the British into negotiations and concessions, combining the pressure politics of Tilak and some of the "Extremists" with the politics-by-negotiation of the Moderate Congress.[3]

Although the Gandhian Non-Cooperation Movement had swelled its ranks in the early 1920s, the Congress was still composed largely of upper-caste, upper- and middle-class professionals and industrialists. By the mid-1920s, it had not achieved hegemony over the movement, and was feeling compelled to be more inclusive. There were still numerous different tendencies within the organization, some of which were to become increasingly intractable in the 1930s. Two of the biggest challenges to a unified Congress came from the political left within the organization itself and from low-caste organizations outside it. Non-Brahmin movements were developing in the West and South, outcastes or "untouchables" were organizing, and various peasant groups were emerging. None of these groups would give unquestioning allegiance to a national organization led by the overwhelmingly high-caste Congress.[4] Although some Muslims were working with the Congress, others were organizing separately, and their allegiance to a unified national movement was by no means assured. As Gail Omvedt writes of political challenges to the Congress during the 1930s: "Beneath the folds of the Congress and the hegemonic claim over almost all other political movements, a large number of forces and identities simmered but remained unconnected and ineffective."[5]

While the Congress did expand its base considerably to become the organization capable of leading the nation to independence, it never succeeded in becoming fully representative of India as a whole. A distinct brand of Congress nationalism asserted its dominance during the 1930s, but even under the Congress umbrella there was a broad continuum of tendencies, from socialists and communists to conservative "nochangers." As the nationalist imperative gathered force, so did the pressure to suppress and defer internal conflict by reconciling, synthesizing, and effecting compromises among all the dissident voices under the broad umbrella of the Congress.

Because English had always been the medium of intra-national communication for the Congress, it is no surprise that the novel in English asserted itself during this time, when the Congress was attempting to establish a unified national identity. Meenakshi Mukherjee suggests that fiction in English played a specific role at this particular historical moment: "It may not be a coincidence that the novel in English emerged in India in the 1930s, the decade prior to independence, when there was an urgency to foreground the idea of a composite nation."[6] She points out that writing in English facilitated the construction of a pan-Indian national identity across internal differences—an imperative crucial to the nationalist project—by "eras[ing] the differences within the border and accentuating the difference with what lies outside,"[7] during a time when the Congress was struggling to uphold its claim to be the sole spokesperson for the Indian subject and soon-to-be-citizen.

During the earlier periods of religious reform and cultural nationalism, writers often conducted their imagined action on a domestic stage, with female leads, but with political power almost in sight at the level of the state, the novelistic action moved into a public arena, with the leading roles increasingly occupied by men. Over time, we will find novelists placing less emphasis on split protagonists and instead attempting to define a unitary or collective subject, in the face of a number of external forces pressing upon that subject. However, we shall see that they are unable to present their protagonists in an untroubled relationship either to the nation or to the forces that challenged its unity.

In this context, it is not surprising how many novels written during the height of the independence movement are focused not on the struggle between Indians and the British, but rather, on conflicts within Indian nationalism. It is incorrect to assume that literary texts of this period would be focused on driving out the colonizer, and that it is only in the aftermath of political independence that disillusionment and internal soul-searching would set in. In fact, whether or not the texts are explicitly nationalist, they are more often than not engaged in internal struggle and self-criticism from the outset. Disjunct individual and national selves jostle with each other for dominance, colonial rule more often being manifest in the Indian protagonists' struggle with colonial ideas and institutions, and in conflicting constructions of self and nation, than in the physical presence of the colonizers.

In the 1930s, R.K. Narayan, Mulk Raj Anand, and Raja Rao published their first novels, and went on to become prolific and influential writers who were canonized by the Indian literary establishment as the "Big Three" of Indian English literature. It is a measure of the reach and flexibility of the Congress that Anand, a socialist and secular humanist, Narayan, a social conservative and political agnostic, and Rao, a Gandhian with a Brahminical vision, could all be claimed by the dominant nationalism and contained under its broad umbrella. It is also a testament to the integrity of these writers that, during a period when the political pressures must have been intense, none of them descended to the level of producing mere propaganda. Mukherjee asserts that despite their tremendous differences in ideology, background, and narrative style, they "shared an unspoken faith in a distillable Indian reality which could then be rendered through particularized situations."[8] However, as we shall see, their works during this period suffer from the strain of containing conflicting social forces within a unified national vision. Interestingly, of the dozen novels in all which they wrote and published before independence, only two have important British characters or a substantial British presence, and only two have the independence movement as their central theme.

Of the novels by the "Big Three," I focus on Anand's *Untouchable*, Narayan's *Swami and Friends*, and Rao's *Kanthapura*, first novels all, after considering K.S. Venkataramani's *Murugan, the Tiller*, a somewhat earlier novel that allows us to examine an idealized Gandhian subject and model of action.

The Indian English Novel in the "Gandhian Age"

K.S. Venkataramani: Murugan, the Tiller *(1927)*

Murugan, the Tiller was one of the first Indian English novels with a Gandhian hero.[9] K.R. Srinivasa Iyengar recalls the novel at the time of its first publication in 1927 as one that spoke personally to every Indian professional who had to struggle for success in British colonial India.[10] Despite its moral and emotional force in its time, the novel is formulaically Gandhian. With Ramu as the spiritual hero and Kedari as the materialistic go-getter, the dualities that structure *Murugan* have none of the nuanced complexities of a novel like *Gora*. This reading focuses on its formula, and on the characteristically Gandhian notion of karma it offers as a solution to its problem of action.

Murugan, the Tiller incorporates a spectrum of internal and external forces into a dominant Gandhian paradigm of Congress nationalism. The novel simultaneously stages the reconciliation of internal forces through the now-familiar trope of twinned protagonists, and effects the pacification of hostile external forces through its selfless hero. With respect to the internal conflicts of the protagonists, we see in the estrangement and ultimate reconciliation of the two friends Kedari and Ramu the synthesis of the active/material/masculine and the passive/spiritual/feminine, with the distinctively Gandhian difference in emphasis that privileges the feminine, redefining as strengths traits labeled in colonialist discourse as weak or effeminate.[11] The central conflict of the novel becomes the struggle between the two young protagonists over which qualities of leadership will prevail—"Indian" contemplative wisdom or "Western" energy and ambition. With respect to threats from below, we see a process of accommodation, neutralization, and unification under benevolent, altruistic upper-caste guidance. In Tagore's *Gora*, the primary conflict was within urban-educated, upper-caste society, with the problem of the lower castes and rural poor recognized but located outside the frame of the novel. Tagore recognized the narrow class/caste base of the emergent nationalist movement, but was unable to do more than point to the problem.[12] In *Murugan*, however, the title itself announces the desired shift in focus to the tiller of the soil.

English education plays a prominent role in *Murugan*, as in so many other novels of the colonial period. It begins with the young Brahmin Ramachandran (Ramu) telling Murugan, his old family servant and landless laborer, that he has failed his B.A. exams. Ramu's English education has contributed to the drain of the family wealth and to the dwindling of his family's ancestral lands. Murugan, the natural patriot, who prefers his native Tamil to English, wants nothing more than to have his young master back from the city to oversee the farming. But Ramu's friend Kedari exhorts him to return to Madras and retake his exams, writing, "the meek will never inherit the earth. You must show a little more 'go.'" Although the gentle Ramu is hurt by his friend's "mere call for action on the morrow of his failure" (25), he does return to Madras for another try.

Kedari is a doer by temperament, while Ramu is a thinker; Kedari is flashy, Ramu slow-moving. While the former seems destined for a successful, highly lucrative career, the latter is hard put to pass his exams, and indeed, fails them a second time. Ramu and his city bride Janaki return to the village for a time, but leave it again when Ramu's go-getting mother-in-law procures him a civil service job. Leasing the family land to the faithful Murugan, Ramu vows to return after having paid off his debt. Despite his newly gained independence, Murugan is heartbroken at his young master's leaving the land yet again. While Ramu struggles as the lowly camp clerk of an autocratic British District Collector, Murugan and his nephew Thoppai make the land yield abundantly back in the village. Ramu is eventually forced to sell the ancestral land, except for the lucrative coconut garden, which he gives to Murugan. In the meantime, Kedari, whose ambitions have seduced him into corrupt practices, loses everything.

Just when it begins to look as if Ramu has abandoned the land for colonial servitude, Kedari is sunk, and Murugan is set to inherit the earth, the tables turn. Ramu's honesty and diligence earn him a promotion from the District Collector, and an assignment to rid the area of a notorious robber gang. Ramu gets himself captured and brought to their hideout, where he also finds Murugan and the once-rebellious Thoppai. Apparently Thoppai had persuaded Murugan to start a toddy (palm wine) shop with the surplus capital from his farming, but they had been wrongfully jailed for some "agrarian trouble" in a nearby village. They have been living with the robbers since Thoppai and the robber chieftain master-minded an escape, and Murugan's benign influence has been working to pacify the chieftain. Prostrating himself before Ramu, Murugan begs Ramu to save the robbers and to give them land so that they can "work day and night...and...grow fruits and flowers and most delicious things for you." Ramu duly arranges amnesty for all and establishes an agrarian commune in the hills, where they will work honestly to attain self-sufficiency. They hail him as their guru. The British, well pleased, name Ramu to the position of District Collector, but Ramu renounces politics and joins the commune himself.[13] Even Kedari now renounces the things of the world and joins them, vindicating Ramu's life of selfless service over the life of ambitious action.

By the end of the novel, a new Indian order has been established. The British have withdrawn, leaving the administration in the hands of Indians, who have themselves withdrawn from the materialism of the British system into a life romantically reminiscent of the Brahmin sages of antiquity, whose guidance was sought by kings yet who chose to live away from the hurly-burly of the city and the court. Although Murugan has proved himself capable of hard, honest work and of generating considerable wealth, he has not shown himself to have the judgment or moral authority to maintain and direct that wealth. Thus, the novel ends with the social hierarchy restored in the form of a consensually authorized benevolent dictatorship, in which the leader is entirely selfless, and the masses toil not for personal gain, but for the common good, the love of their leader, and the work itself.

In the many long dialogues, Ramu or Murugan serve as mouthpieces for Gandhian ideas. In a typical conversation, Murugan counsels his rebellious nephew, using the doctrine of karma to preach deferral of revolutionary action and acceptance of their low place in society: "Let us win our place not by revolt but by patient work; Thoppai, wait for better times. Surely, it will come when your *karma* is ripe for it." Thoppai (who has arrears in wages and an empty stomach), responds, "I don't care for the ripening of my *karma* in the long, long births to come." Murugan: "Remember, once our days were even harder. Now they are better. Times are improving. Work and wait. You will have your day" (90–91). In another such dialogue, as Ramu and the reformed Kedari discuss philosophy, Kedari declares: "...you preach, great Ramu, a life of utter inaction." Ramu replies, advancing nonaction as the highest ideal and selfless action in the world as self-sacrifice: "You are right, Kedari, that is the ideal no doubt...action is misery for you and your fellow. For where action is, there conflict will be...But still you must act in this transitional world till man reaches a higher plane of life" (284–285).

Murugan is an imaginative expression of Indian nationalism at the Gandhian "moment of manoeuvre in the 'passive revolution of capital' in India," in which contradictions within nationalism were reconciled through the ambiguities of Gandhian thought. As Partha Chatterjee notes, "There was a fundamental incompatibility between the utopianism which shaped the moral conception of Gandhian politics and the realities of power within a bourgeois political order."[14] It was the task of the nationalist discourse to bridge that gap, "to reconcile a national political movement with the institutional processes established and run by a colonial state." In spite of its rhetoric of self-determination, nationalism in fact required the peasantry "to become willing participants in a struggle wholly conceived and directed *by others*" (124). Thus in Venkataramani's utopian state-within-a-state, Ramu's power is represented as renunciation, Murugan's labor as loving service to his feudal master; both are contained in the Gandhian conception of action. The discrepancies between morality and power are all smoothed over in the glorious vision of Meenakshipuram, somehow already achieved.

Venkataramani removes all political obstacles from the realization of Meenakshipuram, which leaps from idea to reality, from future to perfect tense in an instant. He projects an almost seamless transfer of power from the British to English-educated, upper-caste Indians. Meenakshipuram is described as a "new colony" (306), in the administration of which the (colonial) government has given Ramu "the fullest powers to employ men of his own choice" (298). The novel manages to avoid having to address actual political struggle, whether for national independence or against British colonial rule. Meenakshipuram is such a complete world unto itself, that the reader may forget that it is a world created within and under the dispensation of a colonial state. One contemporary reviewer commented on Ramu's "extraordinary power due to sheer benevolence," as both the hard-nosed British Collector and the troublesome Thoppai become malleable in his gentle hands.[15] Partha Chatterjee cites Gandhi as having instructed Congress members not to make any effort to get elected.[16] He believed that if they were to accede to power, it should not be through their own efforts, but merely a by-product of their desireless action. Like Gandhi, Ramu too shuns political office, rejecting his appointment to the coveted position of Collector. However, he warns Kedari not to tell the women, because while he himself is immune to the trappings of power, "we never know women's mind in these great turns of luck. They will clutch at pomp and power" (331).

As Ramu patronizes the women by withholding information from them, so he patronizes the low-caste members of Meenakshipuram as having a limited capacity to wield power wisely. Even the faithful Murugan cannot be entrusted with power. Although Murugan tills the ancestral soil on his behalf and makes it fruitful in Ramu's absence, it remains fruitful only as long as Murugan remembers his place as the servant, not as the master. When Thoppai makes him overreach himself due to lack of self-control, they both fall hard and wind up in jail. It is Murugan whose innate goodness pacifies the dacoit chief so that the chief is quite ready to renounce his anti-social ways and turn to farming, It is Murugan who ultimately redeems Ramu, and Murugan who is glorified in the title as the ostensible subject of the novel. However, he is glorified only as long as he remains the faithful servant, content with subsistence and subservience in an idealized new version of the old feudal order. He is the "good" *padayachi* (member of a low caste in southern India), and the uppity, unconverted Thoppai is the "bad" *padayachi*, influenced by dangerous ideas and elements in the city. In the end, Thoppai's imminent marriage to Murugan's daughter wishfully projects his domestication and reclamation into the new-old order.

Given the recent popular movements in India against big dam projects, it is interesting that Meenakshipuram is founded on a dam that has submerged a valley under an artificial lake. Ramu's latent feminine power is shown to have been harnessed and made productive by his stern, ambitious, masculine mother-in-law driving him from the village to work for the Collector and thereby for "the people"; likewise, Venkataramani depicts the dam as a "marital girdle" on the Arni River and the realization of the project as her "bridal" day: "She, the girlish Arni river, seemed to enjoy and welcome the marital girdle round her youthful, slender waist." Venkataramani drives home the analogy in no uncertain terms:

> Brick and mortar are to a river, strange and alien though they be to the babbling, freedom-loving water, what love and marriage are to human life. Bondage is bliss when the binding threads are threads of love. (301)

Not only does Venkataramani envisage no opposition to the project, either from displaced people in the valley or from the British rulers who are footing the bill, but he also represents the union of the strange bedfellows of Gandhian decentralized agriculture and rural self-help and Nehruvian capital-intensive, large-scale industrialization in gendered terms as a blissful bondage, a discipline not imposed but joyfully accepted. Ranajit Guha quotes Gandhi in 1929 as having articulated the desired reconciliation of a spectrum of political forces within the Congress in terms of a social *consummation*. Through the imagery of patriarchal marriage, Venkataramani inserts an imagined future into a colonial present as if the consummation has already taken place. Ideally, according to Gandhi, "...the Congress would be admitted by all to be the only national organization to which the members of the other organizations, while retaining their own, would deem it a pride to belong. For this consummation, Congressmen should show striking results in constructive effort and broadest toleration towards those holding opposite views..." However, according to Guha, this desired consummation "never materialized," but was deferred into the postcolonial future. "On the contrary, the Congress claim to speak for all was contested more and more vigorously on both...the communal and class axes...of Indian politics."[17]

Peasant unrest is defused early in the novel, with Ramu voluntarily giving his land to Murugan, but the excellent Murugan refuses to consider the land his own, despite the fact that he and his people have always been the ones who have actually worked the soil. Murugan thinks of himself as merely a steward of his master's land until his nephew begins to influence him, and it is only so long as he remains a steward that he has the narrator's approval. In this sense, the novel is a cautionary tale, warning against the dangers of going too far in actually fulfilling the revolutionary potential in the slogan of "Land to the Tiller."[18] In the utopian vision of Meenakshipuram, each family is given three acres of land to farm and all are ostensibly equal. Nevertheless, Murugan remains "the God-anointed Tiller...born to the plough," and continues to "st[and] respectfully, like a tiller of old of Alavanti, with folded hands, whenever he s[ees] his Swami." And in the new "casteless" order, the Brahmin children still marry within their own community, as do the lower castes. Thoppai marries Murugan's daughter, but not before prostrating himself before Ramu and craving his leave. Ramu magnanimously bestows his blessing on the couple. Although K.S. Venkataramani was considered a champion of the oppressed in his novels and a staunch, Gandhian opponent of untouchability, both *Murugan, the Tiller* and his later novel *Kandan, the Patriot* feature as their heroes ascetic Brahmins who renounce worldly wealth to serve the people selflessly, and portray the subaltern classes and castes as children who need the wisdom and guiding hand of their betters. Nationalism itself regularly repeats a similar sleight-of-hand—promising a starring role to the masses, but keeping an elite leadership firmly in control.

Partha Chatterjee has characterized the Gandhian moment of maneuver as "a national framework of politics in which the peasants are mobilized but do not participate, of a nation of which they are a part, but a national state from which they are for ever distanced."[19] Thoppai and his like must be accommodated within the new order, and their ambition and sense of injustice must be appeased. Thoppai is given the position of "commander-in-chief" of the workforce employed in building the dam. He goes about boasting that the whole project is his conception, and Ramu finds it convenient not to disabuse him of this notion:

> Ramu nodded assent discreetly to Thoppai's proclaiming words...already feeling...that Meenakshis and Thoppais had their place, though not the very first, in the...scheme of things. *Even courage and action* [my emphasis] tended life in their own way. (328–329)

Like the white man who in his normative centrality does not recognize the privilege of his color, Ramu disavows his power and position in the new colony. As Ranajit Guha has characterized Brahmin liberalism, Ramu is the "mentor and warden" of the utopian society but declines to hold any other political power.[20] By contrast, in the person of Kedari it also shows another kind of leader, corrupted by "Western" ideas and values. When Kedari suggests that the colony be named after Ramu, Ramu declines emphatically, denying his own agency and ascribing it to Murugan: "No, no, Kedari, never. I am but an instrument, like that spade in Murugan's hands" (317). So did subjects of action in the nationalist Gitas disavow their own agency, characterizing themselves as mere instruments of a divine will. So too was the high-caste Congress leadership able to present its role in the struggle as entirely altruistic, working for the good of "the people" with no personal stake in the outcome of the action. There is even a place in Meenakshipuram for the lone Muslim in the novel, "the Muhammedan Boy, Abdulla, who had made their escape from...jail possible, by sacrificing himself...[Ramu] felt that the colony would not be complete without Abdulla" (300). It is telling that this nationalist fantasy represents the peasants and national minorities as reformed criminals and their leaders as upper-caste renouncers who have assumed power only with great reluctance.

In the penultimate chapter, "The Vision Splendid," Ramu and Kedari discuss the future of Meenakshipuram in a rapidly changing world. Ramu advances the ideal, while Kedari, as devil's advocate, challenges its realization in practice. In the end, Ramu makes some concessions to capitalism and social inequality:

> Man must buy and sell and stand at the marketplace a slave to himself and to others for a long, long time to come. But...Civilisation is now only a matter of the body and a little of the mind. Make it a matter of the spirit and the soul...I don't want all the trees in the forest to be equal. Each has its own...individual beauty. But let none live on another...[T]here is room for all in this wide, free and rich world.

As Gandhi himself did when the nationalist realization of state power was in sight, Ramu concedes the need for civil society "to enforce the common good against greedy and aggressive individuals," but suggests that state power will eventually wither away: "[Government] must act its mission and recall itself by the very act. Before it dissolves as a superfluity through individual perfection...." (314–315).

In spite of his repeated failure of the English exams, *Murugan* restores to Ramu what he has lost and more. In his new status as patriarch and founder of Meenakshipuram, he names it not after himself as Kedari suggests, but after his aggressive mother-in-law, who lit a fire under him and thrust him out of the village. And by the end, being in a position to turn down the Collectorship, Ramu has been able to have his cake and eat it, turning failure into success, ambition into renunciation, and power into altruistic guardianship. For though he has declined to name the project after himself, he, like the Mahatma himself, is still recognized by all as the "father of the nation."

In this idealized *Ramarajya* (reign of Rama), the mythic future often evoked by Gandhi, Ramu even gets two Sitas—his wife Janaki, formerly dissatisfied and critical of him, now properly submissive and respectful, and the village Sita he was to have married, now widowed and settled with them in Meenakshipuram.[21] To both their satisfaction, Sita's son Ramu, will marry their daughter, whom Ramu has symmetrically named Sita. The novel's highest consummation, however, is imagined not in terms of heterosexual marriage, but is reserved for the reconciliation of the two male friends after their period of separation. "Ramu and Kedari at last realized the final bliss and peace of union and love. They are twin souls—the dual expression of a longing inherent in all life."[22] Kedari and Ramu, the "Western" and "Indian" principles of action, are entirely reconciled, forming a complementary whole in which the former's ambition and dynamism serves and defers to the latter's quiet wisdom and moral leadership.

The final scene leaves the reader with a dreamlike tableau depicting the true subject and center of the novel:

> In peaceful evenings, on the water-laved and velvet-turfed shores of the lake, Sita, Kokilam and Janaki sat around Ramu in a ring of love, and stirred his rich and philosophic mind to rare depths of cosmic peace and joy. The air was radiant with the light and grace of the Eternal Feminine. Ramu then spoke in a voice that seemed to come from beyond the hills and the falls of water. (336)

Ramu's renunciation of power has elevated him to a godlike status that by denying itself has become naturalized and omnipresent, like the Word. The feminine principle is declared ascendant, with immature worldly action properly disciplined and subordinated to contemplation. While appropriating the feminine, however, Venkataramani upholds a patriarchal ideal, disguised in disembodied transcendence. In the novel's Gandhian solution to the problem of action, selfless service—spurred on by a little ambition—prevails over power, achieving its ends without conflict. Despite the prominence of the tiller in the title, its nominal hero turns out to be only a bit player. The subject of action is the upper-caste man, served by the hardworking peasant who knows his place.

The 1930s and the "Big Three": Mulk Raj Anand, R.K. Narayan, Raja Rao

Mulk Raj Anand: Untouchable *(1935)*

With the moderate Congress struggling in the 1930s to contain challenges from the Left and from below, *Untouchable* is conversely marked by its struggle to chart a politically radical social position while remaining within the dominant nationalist framework. Its socialist–humanist author, recently returned from study in England, attempts to construct his outcaste hero as an autonomous subject, but pressures of the dominant nationalism simultaneously work to construct him in the nationalist image of Gandhi's Harijan (child or person of God). The conflicting demands of Anand's worldview and a "Gandhian socialism" combine to frame the primary conflict as an internal struggle within the protagonist. The contradictory ends of the Congress' secular Left and Hindu Center further render a resolution impossible within the frame of the novel, forcing its deferral to an ambiguous postcolonial future.

As his first and most famous novel's title proclaims, Mulk Raj Anand's hero is an untouchable, an outcaste of the four-tier Hindu caste system.[23] The plot is a deliberately simple one, and the novel is slim, pared down until it achieves a kind of symbolic luminosity. It covers a day in the life of the eighteen-year-old Bakha, who lives in a hovel in an outcastes' colony with his father, brother, and teenage sister. Both he and his father are sweepers, charged with cleaning out public latrines every morning. Over the course of the day Bakha, a strong, healthy, naturally optimistic youth, suffers a series of humiliations at the hands of caste Hindus. But he is resilient, and the day also offers small compensations. The climax—or nadir—of his day is the incident of the "touching," which occurs accidentally as he brushes by a Brahmin man who causes a big scene, draws a crowd, and showers abuse upon him. This experience turns out to be an epiphany for Bakha, suddenly bringing home to him the existential realization of himself as an untouchable. (Of course he has known this before, but has never before stood self-consciously apart from the knowledge of his difference, never before understood what it means in terms of his individual identity and his relationship to society.) Running away in misery, Bakha happens upon an eccentric Christian missionary, who intrigues him, but only momentarily, with the idea that his God sacrificed himself "for the Brahmin and the Bhangi."[24] Then he comes upon a mass of humanity of every conceivable race, caste, and creed on the way to a meeting where Mahatma Gandhi is to speak. Bakha climbs a small tree to be out of the crush and the rest of the novel consists of Gandhi's speech, the critiques of a couple of educated Indians in its aftermath, and Bakha's mixed reactions.

Although he is delighted when Gandhi speaks out against the abomination of untouchability, Bakha is bemused and alienated when the Mahatma begins to glorify the work of a sweeper, even going so far as to say that he himself would like to be reborn as a sweeper in his next life. Moved as he is by Gandhi's compassion, Bakha does not think much of being condemned to cleaning latrines lifetime after lifetime, and is drawn instead to a poet in the crowd who eulogizes the flush toilet, a technology that he declares will sweep away the sweeper caste more surely than all the well-meaning campaigns against untouchability. Even though Gandhi did clean his own latrines and insisted that everyone who stayed at his Sabarmati ashram do the same, his position on caste upheld the fourfold order as the Gita did, declaring like Swami Vivekananda that all occupations were equally valuable to society, and that a person could achieve the highest fulfillment by desirelessly performing his or her socially ordained role in life. *Untouchable* offers Bakha three "solutions" to his condition: conversion (which he rejects), Congress, and the flush toilet. At the end of the day, Bakha goes home with his mind buzzing to tell his father everything he has heard—"what Gandhi said about us... and all that that poet said" (157).

In the 1920s *Murugan, the Tiller* was an example of the new literary attention to common folk, particularly the peasants, largely as a result of Gandhi's mass outreach to the villages. In the 1930s this attention began to be extended to untouchables and factory workers, as a result of the self-organizing of lower castes from the 1920s, the leadership of Dr. B.R. Ambedkar and Periyar E.V. Ramaswami Naicker, Congress' work in the villages, Gandhi's campaign against untouchability, the rise of socialism and communism both inside and outside the Congress, and the Progressive Writers' Movement. Even organizations of the Hindu Right like the Rashtriya Swayamsevak Sangh (RSS) were campaigning for reforms such as temple entry for untouchables and *sahabhojan* (eating together) across caste lines in temples, seeking, like Gandhi, to strengthen and reform Hinduism and to stem the tide of lower-caste and outcaste conversions to Christianity and Islam. As we have seen, in spite of the nominal subjecthood conferred on "the Tiller," Venkataramani's focus was squarely on the upper-caste protagonists. *Untouchable*, by contrast, was one of a wave of new novels that genuinely attempted to cast an outcaste as the protagonist. Nevertheless, the narrative perspective in many of these novels remained that of high-caste humanism, seeking to inspire pity, compassion, and reform on the part of caste Hindus.[25] Anand certainly identifies with the figure of Bakha, and in his creation of Bakha as an isolated individual, he may also be projecting his own modernist individualism and feelings of social alienation.

In renaming untouchables as Harijans, Gandhi sought to give them a sense of self-worth, to give Indians a respect for all work, no matter how menial, and also to strengthen Hinduism and the independence movement by eradicating the blatant injustice of untouchability. However, untouchables were acting on their own behalf as well. Periyar's Self-Respect Movement, founded in 1925, and Dr. Ambedkar's 1927 Mahad Satyagraha, in which untouchable Mahars burned the *Manusmriti* and attempted to draw water from a well reserved for caste Hindus, are just two examples from the 1920s, but there had been ongoing movements against caste discrimination and high-caste privilege since the 1870s.[26]

In its drive to become the representative of all the Indian people, the Congress exerted pressure on groups with other agendas to subsume themselves under the overarching Congress umbrella. As it gathered strength, it demanded full allegiance on its own terms. If other groups and social movements insisted on advancing their own agendas, the Congress accused them of succumbing to British divide-and-rule politics. However, *Untouchable* does not represent Bakha as antinational; rather, it represents the nationalist struggle from Bakha's perspective, as largely irrelevant and somewhat bewildering. Gandhi's stand against untouchability is similarly represented from Bakha's perspective, such that there is no mention of either Gandhi or the nationalist movement until the very end of the novel, when he stumbles upon the Congress rally by accident, and absorbs Gandhi's message only very selectively, rejecting a great deal, even of the little that makes sense to him. The novel does not give Gandhi the last word, or the penultimate word, either—that is reserved for a poet, and even he is presented with tongue playfully in cheek as the author mocks his own romantic dilettantism. The last word is reserved for Bakha himself, and although it is inconclusive, it does reserve to untouchables themselves the right and the ability to make their own judgments. Anand's day in the life of an untouchable challenged not just untouchability but the caste system as a whole, at a time when neither nationalists nor communists would do so. Although some elements in Congress opposed caste inequities, many others were staunch Hindus whose support for the anti-untouchability campaign was largely opportunistic. Even the communists, having determined that British imperialism was the "principal contradiction," considered anything that did not contribute to the anticolonial struggle to be irrelevant or antinational.[27]

Much of the current criticism of *Untouchable* revolves around the novel's denouement, during and after Gandhi's speech. Both Teresa Hubel and Gauri Viswanathan point to the conspicuous absence of Dr. B.R. Ambedkar in a novel about untouchables written in 1930–32, when Gandhi and Ambedkar were locked in conflict about who could legitimately represent untouchables, and particularly in a novel that purports to represent Gandhi from the perspective of an untouchable.[28] They both elaborate on the conflict between Gandhi and Ambedkar on the issue of separate electorates for untouchables, Gandhi's "territoriality" on "his" issue of untouchability, and his insistence on being the sole spokesperson in negotiations with the British. Both charge that Anand reproduces Gandhi's relegation of untouchables to passivity in his failure to give Bakha any direct agency, Viswanathan noting that Anand quotes Gandhi nearly verbatim several times.

Hubel acknowledges that Anand presents a critique of Gandhi's ideas from an untouchable's perspective and offers an alternative solution to the problem of untouchability in the form of the flush toilet and all that it represents. However, she also argues that the narrative perspective is limited in positing the nationalist elite as the leaders and spokespeople of the untouchables, and that Anand projects the possibility of Bakha's organized resistance into the distant future. Hubel further asserts that Anand's very commitment to social realism, with its element of "that's the way it is," limits his ability to give narrative agency to Bakha. She contends that Anand's brand of modernist social realism, like its Victorian antecedents, is blind to the limitations of its own middle-class perspective, which it takes unproblematically to be "the Truth," and which cannot help but project Bakha as a passive object of pity, dependent, grateful, servile. In the same vein, she argues that Bakha's epiphany is problematic because it reinscribes him in the mental prison of his untouchability. While I concur broadly with both these critiques, I am more interested in offering a context for the ambivalence of Anand's representation of Gandhi and the corresponding ambivalence of Bakha's response.

It is true that the novel continually reinscribes Bakha's servility. Again and again Anand depicts the strong, spirited Bakha lapsing into the "passive contentment" of gratefulness, when a caste Hindu condescends to show him a small kindness. Again and again he depicts him reacting angrily to an insult, but being pulled up short by his long-ingrained subservience, and then subsiding into sullen resignation. Anand describes Bakha's free will as having been ideologically imprisoned through generations of his hereditary occupation as a sweeper. He is perpetually racked by the tension of suppressing his natural urge to fight back, and this tension gives him a characteristically clumsy, lumbering look that belies his body's natural grace.[29] I see Anand's depiction of Bakha's epiphany in positive terms, as a significant moment of breakthrough.

Rather than merely reinforcing his subservience, the episode of the "touching" gives Bakha a new self-awareness, akin to the encounter in *Black Skin, White Masks* that forced the young Frantz Fanon to become aware of his blackness.[30] As such, it is an essential—and existential—starting point for the raising of his consciousness and for any action he may take on his own behalf in the future. Earlier in the day, when Bakha met two Hindu boys on their way to school and offered to pay them to teach him English, the omniscient narrator reflected on his gradual realization, as a boy, that as a sweeper he could not go to school: "He was a sweeper, he knew, but he could not consciously accept that fact. He had begun to work at the latrines at the age of six and resigned himself to the hereditary life of the craft, but he dreamed of becoming a sahib" (39). After the incident of the "touching," Bakha is jolted into a new self-consciousness, and thereafter, every experience of abuse is a new and painful humiliation for him, driving home that consciousness and piercing his soul with it. After the touching, although he bears the abuse silently as he is used to doing, and begins to call out, "*Posh*, keep away, *posh*, sweeper coming," he thinks:

> "[W]hy was I so humble? I could have struck him!... Why are we always abused? They always abuse us. Because we are sweepers. Because we touch dung. They hate dung. I hate it too... They don't mind touching us, the Muhammadans and the sahibs. It is only the Hindus, and the outcastes who are not sweepers. For them I am a sweeper, sweeper—untouchable! Untouchable! Untouchable! Sweeper—untouchable! ... That's the word! Untouchable! I am an Untouchable!"
>
> Like a ray of light shooting through the darkness, the recognition of his position, the significance of his lot dawned upon him... "I am an Untouchable!" he said to himself... He repeated the words in his mind, for... he felt afraid it might be immersed in the darkness again. (51–52)

From this moment on, Bakha becomes so self-conscious that he feels like an actor in a play. His hereditary profession has become suddenly defamiliarized. He looks upon Hindus and sees them as alien, Other. But he himself feels a tremendous alienation as well; he longs to be drawn into something larger, all-encompassing. He tells his comrades, the other low-caste and untouchable youths, and they sympathize with him, but their sympathy merely "accentuate[s] Bakha's self-pity and churn[s] up all the suppressed, frustrated emotions of the day." Any act of kindness or fellow-feeling, however small, melts him when he is in such a mood, and this is what renders him vulnerable to the clumsy Hindustani of the missionary.

The experiences of Bakha's day have heightened his sense of alienation from the larger society, and this alienation persists even through the rapturous crowd experience, when everyone else seems to be exalted and united in a shared group feeling. He had felt a similar group feeling at the Hindu temple before he was ejected from it. But here no one seems to notice him in their eager anticipation of the Mahatma's arrival.

> It seemed as if, in trampling on the blades of green grass, they were deliberately, brutally trampling on a part of themselves which they had begun to abhor, and from which they wanted to escape to Gandhi.
>
> Beyond the bowers... was a tumult, and the thronging of the thousands who had come to worship. The eager babble of the crowd, the excited gestures, the flow of emotion, portended one thought and one thought alone in the surging crowd—Gandhi. There

was a terror in this devotion, half expressed, half suppressed, of the panting swarms that pressed round. Bakha stopped short as he reached the pavilion end of the cricket ground. He leant by a tree. He wanted to be detached...there was an insuperable barrier between him and the crowd, the barrier of caste. He was part of a consciousness which he could share and yet not understand. He had been lifted from the gutter...to partake of a life which was his, and yet not his. He was in the midst of a humanity which included him in its folds and yet debarred him from entering into...contact with it. (137–138)

Will Gandhi be able to break down the barrier that separates him from the crowd? Bakha suspends his disbelief, waiting for the Mahatma. Gauri Viswanathan has pointed to the above passage describing Bakha's state of mind as he both shares and cannot share the crowd's anticipation as "partaking of the language of transcendental mysticism." She also sees it as duplicating the assimilation of the Dalit by Gandhian nationalism and as bringing Bakha back firmly into the Hindu camp.[31] However, in my view, both Bakha and the determinedly secular Anand are as ambivalent about the near-religious emotions called up by this nationalist devotion as they are about Hinduism.[32]

Getting drawn up into the shared devotion of the crowd is something Bakha desires, yet fears. "He felt he had lost something of himself and was uneasy on account of it, yet thrilled about it, happy."[33] What Bakha stands to lose is his sense of caste difference, so recently and painfully acquired. He is disarmed, indeed deeply touched, by Gandhi's speech, and by being the object of the great man's sympathy and the subject of his address. Yet he retains his critical faculties throughout. When Gandhi says that he has been on a fast for the untouchables, Bakha wonders what the point of that is, and whether Gandhi will be giving the food to anyone else. When Gandhi exhorts untouchables to purify themselves, Bakha feels that he is unfairly blaming the victims. And finally, when Gandhi says that untouchables should feel pride in their work, Bakha rejects the clear implication that Gandhi expects him to continue carrying out his karma, his socially prescribed duty of cleaning latrines, all his life. What he does gain from the Mahatma, however, is a sense of validation and self-worth. In the end, Bakha retains a distinct sense of identity as an untouchable, but one that is now stronger and more positive. He returns home eagerly to tell his father about what he has heard, where earlier he had been unable to go back to his hut, feeling in his misery and alienation that he had nothing in common with his family. He has not been reclaimed for Hinduism, neither has he suddenly become a nationalist, but the rally has made him feel the first inklings of a possible kinship with other Indians.[34]

The ambivalence of Bakha's responses to Gandhi reflects Anand's own, as well as the pressures on Indian writing in English in the 1930s to valorize the nationalist movement. Although he does show Bakha thinking for himself and making critical judgments and choices, Anand does not ultimately show his young protagonist acting on his own behalf, instead presenting him and the other untouchables in the book as creatures who have been dehumanized by centuries of oppression.[35] He also shows Bakha admiring Gandhi and suspending his disbelief about the liberatory potential of the nationalist movement for his sake. At the same time he remains skeptical, even while hoping for a better future through the offices of the Mahatma and/or the machine. And in fact these alternatives may have been the only ones open to him at the time. As Gail Omvedt declares in her historical survey of the contours of Dalit thought: "the 1930s failed to consolidate a radical alternative to the Congress."[36] By 1942, even Ambedkar had had to accept a British government position as law minister in Nehru's "brahman bourgeois" Congress Ministry.

Anand's own position is a Left-wing Congress one closely akin to Jawaharlal Nehru's own brand of liberal-democratic socialism at the time. In *The Twice-Born Fiction*, Meenakshi Mukherjee identifies Anand's basic worldview: "He is a rational humanist in the western tradition, believing in the power of science to improve material conditions, in progress and the equality of all men." Further, there is "no nostalgia or sentimentality in his attitude toward Indian traditions."[37] Anand believes strongly in a human-centered universe and in the sanctity of the individual, freely acknowledging his intellectual preferences in his 1946 *Apology for Heroism*: "I am conscious that much of my insistence on the role of man in the universe derives from European Hellenism."[38] He is dead-set against religion and caste hierarchies, and tends to draw sharply polarized pictures of Modernity vs. Tradition after the fashion of the social-democratic Old Left of the 1930s to the 1950s. His critical attitudes toward caste Hinduism partly reflect his parentage. His gentle, pious mother came from a Sikh family, and his gruff Army clerk father, who mocked her piety, was associated with the reformist Arya Samaj. Additionally, his family, "though Hindu, still retained its loyalty to the Aga Khan Ismaili sect."[39] Anand combines a violent aversion to Brahmanism— his Brahmin priests are invariably lustful, hypocritical, and constipated—and indeed all religious belief, with a genuine concern for the downtrodden, and a modernist-socialist humanism which, however, is perpetually at war with his individualism.

An element of guilt enters into the novel's portrayal of Bakha's life, for Anand himself was the model for the high-caste child in *Untouchable* whom Bakha carried home after he was injured in the hockey match and the child on his way to school whom Bakha watched wistfully as he wished he too could learn to read and write.[40] However, Anand is also driven by a strong identification with Bakha, not only as a representative of an oppressed caste, but as a rebellious individual in a stratified, colonized society. Throughout the novel, Bakha's numerous critiques of Indian—and especially Hindu—social customs are Anand's own. So also is Bakha's fascination with English dress and all things "phoren." In an essay on the writing of *Untouchable*, Anand recalls his embarrassment, after traveling from England (where he had completed his Master's degree and his Ph.D. in philosophy) to Gandhi's Sabarmati Ashram in India, when, sweating in a ridiculously inappropriate English collared suit, he came before the loinclothed Gandhi.[41] Under Gandhi's influence he reverted to Indian dress during the period he lived in the ashram. During that time he maintained the required celibacy and vegetarian diet with impatience, and mocked Gandhi's puritanical attitudes to sex and his expensive food faddishness. Gandhi's perspective certainly shaped the editing of *Untouchable*, as Anand records that Gandhi read and commented on the novel at his request. It was Gandhi who made Anand edit out large sections of Bakha's interior monologues as the thoughts of a Bloomsbury intellectual, not those of an uneducated *bhangi*. Nevertheless it is the intensity of Anand's personal identification with his protagonist that makes Bakha come to life.

Mulk Raj Anand's agenda and that of Gandhi's overlap in *Untouchable*, both conflicting and collaborating. While Gandhi seeks to reform Hinduism without abolishing caste, Anand's primary target is the caste system itself. It is Gandhi's stand against untouchability, not his campaign against British rule, that interests Bakha. Nevertheless, Bakha's developing consciousness and identity are shaped in reaction to his treatment by representatives of the various institutions of power in society around him—members of Hindu caste society and the British military, Christian missionaries, educated Indians of different political persuasions, and his fellow untouchables. As the novel closes, it is clear that his personal and social alienation will be overcome only to the extent that he is able to identify himself with one or more of these social groupings. The two choices left facing him at the open end of the novel are Gandhi and the flush toilet, and although Gandhi's compassion and mass following have been inspiring, it is the flush toilet—or industrialization—that offers him the better prospect of liberation from a lifetime of cleaning latrines. The ending reflects Mulk Raj Anand's mistrust of Gandhi's mysticism and his love affair with Nehru's vision of Indian industrialization. Ultimately, Bakha is portrayed as an isolated and exceptional individual whose fellow untouchables' political consciousness is even lower than his own, and both he and Anand remain ambivalent as to what nationalist politics will be able offer him or his people.

Like many Indian novels of its time, *Untouchable* is driven by a desire to identify with the poor of India, to rouse them to action, and to effect a social transformation in the process. Yet the nationalist discourse itself seems to dictate a strangely indirect, incomplete, circular ambit, in which action is desired and undertaken, but eventually obstructed, renounced, or deferred. Gandhi's exhortations to the Gita's *nishkama karma* or, as his disciple Vinoba Bhave put it, "inaction in action," appear to be enacted structurally or metaphorically in novel after novel, even in the works of writers like Anand. In the 1930s, the Indian National Congress was attempting to incorporate and speak for the broadest possible spectrum of social forces that were often mutually antagonistic and persisted in wanting to speak for themselves. Yet as the Congress-led imperative for independence intensified, it silenced dissenting voices or pressured them to silence themselves. Many Indian English novels of this period thus struggle with contradictory forces, whose resolution they project into the future. The pressure for unity despite strong internal dissent is reflected in individual protagonists who discipline themselves to identify with a larger collectivity despite persistent doubts and contrary desires. Bakha resembles many of his creator's later protagonists in that he is an individual, an unrepresentative representative of a larger downtrodden group, who eventually chooses to identify himself with them, but returns only reluctantly after escaping. The pressure to engage and the desire to escape thus set up an internal shuttling movement often traced by Anand's picaresque hero who is acted upon far more than he acts, thereby ironically replicating the very passivity he so abhors in "Traditional" India.[42]

R.K. Narayan: Swami and Friends *(1935)*
Like Mulk Raj Anand, R.K. Narayan (Narayanaswami) was a prolific writer who between 1935 and his death in 2001 produced, almost without a break, novels, short stories, autobiography, film scripts, and retellings of Indian mythology. Like Anand,

he wrote exclusively in English and both their first novels were published in the same year, introduced by prominent British novelists,[43] but here the similarities between them would appear to end. Anand is a socialist who takes a dim view of religion, while Narayan supported the *status quo* and was content to locate his characters in a pervasively Hindu social milieu. Anand is a champion of the downtrodden and the marginalized, while Narayan charted the bounded universe of the middle and lower-middle classes. Anand, whose worldview is cosmopolitan and whose characters are wanderers, evokes rural life in Punjabi villages and urban life in the large Indian metropolis; Narayan, focusing almost exclusively on small-town life in South India, maintained a determinedly provincial worldview firmly rooted in one place. However, despite very differently motivated efforts to distance themselves from the dominant politics of Congress nationalism, both their first novels are compelled to recognize some of the very elements they seek to refuse. I examine the character and the actions of Swami (Swaminathan), Narayan's schoolboy protagonist, in response to the social forces around him as Congress nationalism seeks to shape a pan-Indian national identity.

In *Swami and Friends*, a socially conservative nationalism is located within Swami, while a liberal reformism is projected onto the character of Rajam, the worldly and highly Anglicized new boy in town. Swami is powerfully infatuated by Rajam throughout the novel, to the extent that other children start calling him Rajam's "tail," but he must ultimately distance himself from Rajam. However, he can do so only passively, and in the end, his farewell to Rajam is the most poignant scene of the book, as painful as if he were being severed from a precious part of himself. Swami and his schoolfriends Mani and Rajam can be seen to make up a composite Indian protagonist. If Swami is the moderate nationalist and social conservative and Rajam the modern, Anglicized liberal reformist, Mani, Swami's loyal old friend and sidekick, is portrayed as the belligerent but not very bright Hindu nationalist who may threaten violence but is ultimately all bluster. The primary pairing for most of the novel is between Swami and Rajam, but toward the end a rift develops between them, which remains unresolved by the end of the novel.

It must be noted at the outset that while it may be based on the city of Mysore,[44] Narayan's fictional Malgudi, the sleepy little South Indian town that is the setting of *Swami and Friends*, and subsequently of all his novels, is an imagined community. As such, it is built out of desires and shaped by a worldview. In Narayan's *oeuvre*, Malgudi attains the status of a character who passively but steadfastly resists change; no matter what social and political changes threaten it, a Hindu ethos always reasserts itself comfortingly at the end. The language that constructs Malgudi and its citizens is the language of an Indian nationalism whose makeup and contours had become quite well established by the early 1930s. However, the novel does not explicitly reject British rule, although Narayan finished writing *Swami* in 1931, two years after the Indian National Congress had declared *Purna Swaraj* (full independence) as its goal, and during the period of Gandhi's Salt *Satyagraha*.

In his now-classic *Indian Writing in English*,[45] K.R. Srinivasa Iyengar eulogized *Swami and Friends* as the story of everyone's Indian boyhood:

> As one reads it, one becomes nostalgic almost, for one has been oneself one of these boys—
> Swami the average, even the obscure...Mani "the mighty good-for-nothing"; ...and

Rajam with his dash, romance, and propensity for leadership. One has also studied under the "fire-eyed" Vedanayakam and the fanatical Ebenazar. One has…quarreled with one's friends, fought pitched battles, and made sensible treaties. One has taken part in hartals and strikes…One has played games—even Cricket the "King of Games"—or at least has cheered one's comrades. The whole of one's boyhood is recalled here…the story of Swami and his friends would be true anywhere. It is as though everyday actuality has taken Narayan's pen and written out this universal epic of all our boyhood yesterdays that are now no more. (364–365)

Who is this "one" who is the Indian Everyman? What does it mean to universalize Narayan's protagonist? To Ved Mehta, writing in *The New Yorker* in 1962, the same year that *Indo-Anglian Literature* first appeared, Narayan's books,

> …though they were written in English, a language foreign to most of his countrymen and also to most of his characters, had the ring of true India in them. He had succeeded where his peers had failed, and this without relying on Anglicized Indians or British caricatures to people his novels…For me, the magic of his unpretentious, almost unliterary novels was his astonishing marriage of opposite sides of the compass.[46]

Both Srinivasa Iyengar and Mehta considered Narayan's work authentically Indian, with his characters and settings so realistic that they seemed to be writing themselves through the medium of his pen, as if he were only a passive instrument. Iyengar spoke of his work in terms of "everyday actuality" shining forth as "universal epic," Mehta in terms of its "unpretentious…almost unliterary" quality. Yet Mehta also suggested that Narayan's unpretentiousness was a kind of magic, a literary sleight-of-hand that seemed to unite "East" and "West" effortlessly. Let us consider Narayan's "magic" at work in *Swami and Friends* and attempt to identify the subject position (or positions) that are so seamlessly married to create its authenticity-effect.

Swami's is an upper-caste Hindu worldview, content to accept the socioeconomic *status quo*. His world is circumscribed, and he likes it that way; he is afraid of the world beyond. His country is a small part of South India, and the larger "India" has no real meaning for him. When he is studying the map of Europe, he wonders whether he could get a bird's-eye view of India from the top of the town hall, the tallest building in Malgudi. Yet "he had never been there nor did he ever wish to go there"(56). Even Madras is something vague and distant, and Bombay is another world, where political action happens. Rajam, more enterprising, more socially and economically mobile than Swami, also has a more secular view, the kind that will take him far in a new Congress-led administration. His English is good, and he is less geographically rooted. Ironically, his family is presented as antipolitical, because his father works for the colonial government. But in an independent India, or the quasi-autonomous provincial ministries (that were established for a time before the World War II), Rajam will be invaluable. After Swami has transferred to the Board School (which, as an Indian school, confers less prestige than the loyalist English mission school), Narayan contrasts Swami's and Rajam's views on religious community and caste in the only direct mention of Muslims in the novel, when Swami speaks defensively of a classmate at the Board School who is "a very fine Mohamedan" who "calls Mohammed of Gazni and Aurangazeb *(sic)* rascals."[47] In a tone that is hard to pin down, but that the narrator would seem to be mocking as 1930s Congress political correctness, Rajam replies provocatively: "We Brahmins deserve that and more." He adds that it is the Board School that has given Swami this communalist mentality, and that his own father will not have orthodox rituals in their house.

Swami is a coward. Most of his actions consist of running away. Nevertheless, the novel opens with Swami uncharacteristically in direct confrontation with authority in the person of Ebenazar, his scripture teacher at the Albert Mission School. His first act of resistance is a reaction. Ebenazar has been abusing Hindus as idolaters, and charging the God Krishna with immoral acts such as "gadding about with dancing girls" and stealing butter. When Swami retaliates boldly, asking why Jesus drank wine and ate flesh if he was a god, Ebenazar almost twists his ear off. Swami complains to his father, who writes to the headmaster for an explanation, but Swami is so terrified that when the headmaster summons him, his friend Mani has to drag him there.

Swami's second act of resistance comes about when he and Mani attend a nationalist rally to protest the imprisonment of a "Bombay political worker." In the only explicitly political scene in the novel, Narayan's mildly derisive description of the speaker and Swami's ignorant, emotional responses undercut both speaker and patriots. The speaker is "an earnest-looking man clad in khaddar" (homespun cotton) and his voice is a "high, piercing" shriek. His demagoguery whips the boys into heights of emotion and the burning of British cloth begins. Someone suggests that Swami's cap is foreign and in the heat of the moment he flings it in the fire, "with a feeling that he [was] saving the country." The crowd ignores the headmaster's pleas to return to school, and goes on a rampage. As an "unobserved atom in the crowd" Swami is caught up in the destruction, smashing numerous school windows with giddy abandon until the police move in with their *lathis*, when he runs away in terror. Later, at school, the boys involved are beaten in turn. After the third blow of the cane Swami, with a sudden access of desperate courage, runs out of the school, refusing ever to return. Luckily for him, his father, who turns out to be a nationalist sympathizer, does not press him, and instead enrolls him in the Board School.

The third act of resistance is over cricket. The Malgudi Cricket Club (MCC) is gearing up for a big match on Sunday, and they are counting on Swami's bowling—Tate, they call him, after the great British bowler.[48] But cricket practice conflicts with after-school drill. Swami tries but fails to get excused from drill and is hauled before the headmaster once again. Again a caning is imminent, but this time Swami reacts very swiftly: "A flood of emotion swept him off his feet, a mixture of fear, resentment, and rage. He hardly knew what he was doing. His arm shot out, plucked the cane from the Head Master's hand, and flung it out of the window" (144). Then he runs for it. But note the last sentence: it is hardly he who has acted, so involuntary the movement seems. Once again, Swami finds himself acting in spite of himself. Since there are no more schools in Malgudi, Swami has now burned his bridges, and he will have to run away. Striking out for the Grand Trunk Road, Swami gets lost in the Mempi forest, and suffers the forest ordeal of myth and epic. Night falls, and terrified in the dark, he screams for help, weeps and prays, hears noises, sees ghosts, imagines demons, monsters, and wild beasts, and eventually collapses and falls asleep, dreaming wildly of fantastic cricket victories.

There is one more set of conflicts to be mentioned: not with the British colonizers or the school authorities, but with the lower classes/castes of Malgudi. Although Swami is subject to multiple layers of authority, he is also a perpetrator of power himself, at home, at school, and in the community at large. During his school vacation, longing for a hoop, Swami confides in the coachman, who cheats Swami out of two installments of money. Rajam and Mani hatch a plan to kidnap the coachman's "dirty black rascal" of a son and drag the terrified Swami along to the hovels where the family lives, but the boy outwits them and the residents drive them away with stones. The boys take out their feelings of humiliation by bullying a powerless village cart-driver. Later, when Swami goes to the English Club with his father, dressed in his best dhoti, he is terrified to find that same coachman's son working there, dressed in the khaki uniform of a ball boy and menacing him with a penknife. But the reassertion of an organic Hindu community is an important aspect of the novel's resolution. Although it was the forest officer, a British government servant, who had arranged for Swami to be brought home, it was Ranga the cart-man who had been responsible for rescuing him from the forest. Puzzled to find the boy sleeping in the road, he "gave up the attempt to solve the problem himself, feeling that he had better leave such matters to learned people like the sircar officer… He would just take the boy gently to the officer" (163). This is the last we hear of the cart-driver, except in a conversation between Swami and Mani after Swami is safely home in Malgudi. Swami is mortified that he has forgotten to thank the forest officer, and has no recollection of being picked up by the cart-driver. But Mani advises: "If he happens to come to your place during Deepavali or Pongal festival, don't behave like a niggard. He deserves a bag of gold. If he had not cared to pick you up, you might have been eaten by a tiger." This is a reference to the fable of the tiger and the Brahmin on Swami's final Tamil examination earlier in the novel. In that exam, Swami had failed to give the right answer for the story's moral: the Brahmin was eaten because of his greed. Swami had earlier begrudged the coachman 1-1/2 annas, but now the humble cart-driver has rescued the young Brahmin boy with no thought of reward. Mani, representing indigenous authority now restored to itself since Rajam's departure, warns Swami to be properly grateful to the cart-driver. The idea of the mutual interdependence of the Hindu community is restored, and the threat of the upstart lower castes is neutralized.

In *The Twice-Born Fiction*, Meenakshi Mukherjee identified the basic structure of the typical R.K. Narayan plot as the "clear mythic design (order—dislocation of order—restoration of order)."[49] In *Swami*, Rajam and Swami must part so that order can be restored. After the night in the forest, the returned prodigal must be received safely back into the bosom of his family, who, he realizes, love him deeply after all. His mother spoils him again, his grandmother has made special vows to the Lord of the Seven Hills, his father makes everything all right with the headmaster of the Board School, and even the servants are loving. But everything is not forgiven and forgotten between him and Rajam, for Swami missed the cricket match while he was away in the forest, and the MCC has suffered an ignominious defeat. Rajam doesn't care to speak to Swami when he returns, and Swami, afraid and ashamed, keeps putting off going to visit him and explain himself. Swami has always taken the path of least resistance in his relationship with Rajam by acquiescing or signaling his submission in every decision or disagreement. In the all-important match, Swami does not give Rajam what he wants, once again taking action by running away, "letting the side down" when he has assured Rajam that he will be there for the game. Their friendship does not survive the incident.

When Mani tells him one day that Rajam's father has been transferred and the family will be leaving the next morning, Swami is filled with "a great sense of desolation," as if the whole world is suddenly blank. He must go to the station and see Rajam off. Searching through his things, he decides to give Rajam a book, "the only book he respected," a volume of Andersen's *Fairy Tales* that his father had bought in metropolitan Madras. Swami inscribes it "to my dearest friend Rajam." He never could read the book very well, anyway, because of all the "unknown unpronounceable English words in it." At the station, Rajam, "dressed like a 'European boy,'" is unapproachable. "His very dress and tidiness ma[ke] Swaminathan feel inferior and small. He [shrinks] back and trie[s] to make himself inconspicuous" (176). Mani is the one who pushes through the crowd with him at the eleventh hour. Swami's eyes meet Rajam's, and he cries out, "'Oh Rajam, Rajam, you are going away. When will you come back?' Rajam [kept] looking at him without a word and then (as it [seemed] to Swami), [opened] his mouth to say something" as the train begins to move (178). There is just time for Mani, running alongside the moving train, to pass the English book to him. When the train is out of sight, Swami says to Mani, "'I am glad he has taken the book. Mani, he waved to me. He was about to say something when the train started. Mani, he did wave to me and to me alone. Don't deny it.'" As Swami bursts into tears, Mani tries to reassure him that Rajam will write to him. But although Mani claims that he gave the address to Rajam, when pressed, he cannot say what it is (179).

The reconciliation has been one-sided, after all, and although Swami is restored to his family and Malgudi is restored to itself, there is a place of irretrievable loss where Rajam has been. Swami will just have to get over his infatuation with modernity and Englishness. As a cricketer, he had briefly been hailed as Tate, the English hero, but he had ultimately let Rajam down and failed to play the game. However, there is a strong sense that he had never had a passion for it anyway. The MCC had been wholly Rajam's idea, and when Rajam had first proposed it, Swami had thought "in his heart of hearts" that cricket was a boring game, although he would never have uttered such a travesty out loud. Now that Rajam has gone, he consoles himself that he had always intended to play in the match, but had been prevented by circumstances from doing so.

Discussing Narayan's tendency to take refuge in myth and "tradition," Fawzia Afzal-Khan writes that "myth often reigns supreme" at the end of his novels, creating "the possibility of a whole existence for the fiction as well as the characters." She argues, however, that this fictional wholeness requires that "present reality is diluted or made palatable by the comforting presence of the indigenous past."[50] In *Swami*, Narayan attempts to restore fictional wholeness while still maintaining his realism and characteristic comic mode. He succeeds in maintaining Malgudi's "purity," perhaps, but at the expense of a hole in Swami. Is this anxious anticipation of the British departure, or resistance to an urban, "Westernized," pan-Indian identity? The narrative clearly distances itself from the political views and actions at the rally, but it does not similarly undermine Swami's resistance to Ebenazar's Missionary School arrogance. Nationalist resistance, therefore, is reduced to a socially conservative "defense of tradition" rather than an active movement for political independence or social justice.

In Malgudi, Indian tradition is depicted as deep-rooted and fundamentally intact; however disruptive or dominant an outside force may appear to be, it does no more than ruffle the surface of life. This is in keeping with Narayan's representation of Indian (Hindu) society as flexible and self-perpetuating. Traditional forces may appear to fall in line with the alien authority, but they remain internally untouched. Thus Narayan shows Granny, his repository of tradition, being unimpressed by Rajam; she assures Swami that yes, she does believe every word of his story about Rajam shooting a tiger, but she merely says it to soothe him. Similarly, Ebenazar at the Albert Mission School attempts to discredit the *Bhagavad-Gita*, but Narayan does not portray this as a threat, since "this generous piece of writing lends itself to any interpretation," and the students pay no attention to the teacher anyway. But although the desire that Swami and friends have for Rajam and all that he stands for must similarly be rendered a mere infatuation that they will soon get over, the novel ends with a clear sense that the desire runs deep, and will not simply go away with Rajam. In the face of the realism of the ending, Narayan's restoration of Malgudi's innocence seems a little disingenuous.

The recovery of Swami by the forces of tradition and the departure of Rajam from Malgudi represent a reassertion of social and political conservatism through a myth of cultural wholeness. To the extent that they also represent resistance, it would seem that the site of resistance is also the site of social conservatism and the failure of action. *Swami and Friends* represents its world as indigenous, distancing itself from an Anglicized way of life on the one hand and from nationalist politics and reformism on the other. Malgudi's timeless, essentialized quality draws attention to its mythic status, ostensibly unaffected by colonialism. But ironically, it is with Swami's loss of Rajam and his voluntary but unreciprocated gift of his precious English book that this novel leaves us, and it is in English that the novel represents itself as so essentially "Indian." Many early R.K. Narayan novels follow a similar formula, in which the Indian protagonist faces a choice between a British and an Indian—more specifically, a Hindu—set of norms and finds himself making the latter choice with little real struggle—and herein lies their considerable charm. With humor and gentle irony, Narayan presents a provincial India whose way of life is so deep-rooted that colonial rule can never achieve any real hegemony. Nevertheless, his representation of Indian society reproduces many of the colonialist stereotypes of the "Indian mind," and glosses over a colonial influence that has in fact been far greater than his novels admit.

The Bachelor of Arts *(1937),* The English Teacher *(1946), and*
The Dark Room *(1938)*[51]
The Bachelor of Arts and *The English Teacher* chart a reverse movement to that of *Indulekha* only two generations earlier, demonstrating how much nationalism has changed the social climate, but also the degree to which the English language has taken hold. Whereas Chandu Menon wrote *Indulekha* in Malayalam to convince

Nair women (and their guardians) of the benefits of studying English, these two Narayan novels, while written in English and clearly the product of an English education, paradoxically make a case for their superfluity in the Indian social setting. In these Narayan novels, nationalism often becomes indistinguishable from the rejection of English education and the re-embrace of an indigenous tradition. By contrast, in *Indulekha*, English education was advocated for the express purpose of weakening the grip of orthodoxy and enacting social reform. While *Indulekha* promoted the superiority of love marriage, *The Bachelor of Arts* is designed to demonstrate the superficial hold of alien notions of romantic love. *Indulekha* ridiculed orthodox social practices as comically antiquated, even perverse, while the Narayan novels normalize them and instead mock Anglicized Indian social conventions as imitative affectations. To Chandu Menon, English education conferred upon its youthful recipients maturity and wisdom beyond their years, whereas in Narayan, the adoption of English norms is presented as evidence of an extended adolescence that must inevitably be outgrown. Chandran, the Bachelor of Arts, settles happily down to an arranged marriage after his brief period of youthful rebellion. Krishna, the English teacher, throws over his sterile, meaningless college lectureship to work in a Tamil language preschool. By thus seeming to subscribe to Tamil linguistic nationalism, Narayan's English-language works appear to be making a curious case for their own inauthenticity here, thereby giving Narayan a reputation for "authentic Indianness" both in and out of India.[52]

Plot action in *The Dark Room* follows the familiar pattern of Narayan novels in its formula of "order—dislocation of order—restoration of order," but, as in *Swami and Friends* and unlike in most of Narayan's work, the restoration of order does not bring reassurance. What is also different about this novel is its female protagonist, unusual in Narayan, and its tone, in which his characteristic tolerant, gently ironic humor is absent. The protagonist is the middle-class Brahmin woman Savitri, named after the devoted wife of Indian mythology. Married with two children, she is entirely powerless and Narayan does not romanticize her or her situation. Her husband Ramani continually abuses her both verbally and psychologically, and her only defense is to withdraw periodically in silence into the "dark room," a storeroom next to the kitchen. Eventually, when Ramani begins to have an affair, she can bear it no longer, and leaves home to drown herself in the river. Quite against her will, she is rescued by a low-caste locksmith. Since Savitri insists that she must work and become self-sufficient, he and his wife take her to a temple, where the priest grudgingly agrees to allow her to clean the premises in return for shelter and a few crumbs of food. However, Savitri finds herself too weak to renounce family life, although she struggles to cultivate nonattachment. Homesick and worried about her children, she soon returns in defeat to a completely unchanged status. "A part of me is dead," she reflects, dully. A few days later, as she sees the locksmith who saved her life going by her house, she has a momentary impulse to invite him in and offer him thanks with food, water, and a reward, but then checks it, not because she is not grateful, but because she does not have the authority. After all, she thinks, "Why should I call him here? What have I?" The novel ends desolately with Savitri sitting alone by the window "haunted by his shining hungry face…long after his cry had faded out in the distance" (209).

Like *Swami and Friends*, order in *The Dark Room* is restored with a sense of high-caste indebtedness to a person of low caste who has offered his service voluntarily, and a sense that if the social order is to be maintained, the high-caste person must give something back. But while in *Swami* there is a positive reassertion of Hindu community, *The Dark Room* ends with an oppressive feeling of arbitrary patriarchal power. Savitri owes her life to the generosity of the low-caste couple, but she does not have the authority to respond in kind. There is the uncomfortable implication that she is no better off than they are, yet must remain complicit in upholding an order that oppresses both of them. Savitri has no agency, even in her own home. Although she is a high-caste woman from a middle-class family, she has neither the economic means nor the emotional detachment to act independently. Narayan's stance toward Savitri is somewhat ambivalent. Even though he clearly disapproves of her husband's behavior and sympathizes with Savitri's predicament, he would appear to agree with both the low-caste wife and the Brahmin priest that she belongs back at home. If, as it seems, the novel supports the view that women are unsuited to renunciation and detachment, then it also suggests that they are not ready for independent action.

Malgudi's very rootedness in its small-town ethos has made it an all-India symbol or, more accurately, as Meenakshi Mukherjee has described it, a symbol of "Hindu upper-caste pan-India."[53] As such, *Malgudi Days* has been made into a nationwide television serial in the national language of Hindi, although it comes from the Tamil-speaking South and was written in English. Narayan's works have remained popular in and outside India, where, as we noted at the outset, they are considered quintessentially Indian. As Swaminathan becomes Swami in the English title, and Narayanaswami becomes Narayan to his English, pan-Indian, and worldwide readership, so is the new Indian national Subject shaped seamlessly to soothe nationalist anxieties and later, trimmed to fit global expectations. But some conflicts cannot be smoothed over altogether, occasionally giving Narayan's sleepy, self-contained world surprisingly sharp edges—and the greater authenticity for them.

Raja Rao: Kanthapura *(1938)*

Its author's first and most famous novel, *Kanthapura* is a mythified and idealized story of an organic village society that is caught up in and transformed by the Gandhian independence movement.[54] In order to narrate his story in the tradition of village storytellers through the ages, Raja Rao adopts the voice and persona of a female character, an old Brahmin widow who remains nameless throughout. In order to convey the sense of a collective subject, he makes her speak in the first-person plural and the second person, thereby including the entire village in her account of the action, and addressing her readership as if they too were fellow villagers. Although the central force in *Kanthapura* is the freedom struggle, there is no direct British opponent as also in the novels by Anand and Narayan discussed earlier. The absentee owners of the coffee plantation are British, but they employ Indian managers and Sri Lankan Tamil workers; and the British colonial administration employs the Muslim officer Badè Khan as the undercover policeman to police the village when the Indian National Congress begins organizing in it. Like the first novels of Anand and Narayan, *Kanthapura* acknowledges the rifts within Indian society, rifts that must somehow be closed if the independence movement is to be successful. Instead of directing its attention outward, the novel focuses on threatened social hierarchies and structures of power in the village with the advent of the political organizing, focusing particularly on the hierarchies of gender and caste, with a view to creating a cohesive society that can act in concert to end colonial rule. Rao is anxious to make the point that the villagers cannot simply wait for the Mahatma to save them, but must take responsibility for their collective condition by acting to transform themselves and their society from within. However, Rao's utterly Brahmin worldview severely limits the extent of the transformation he can imagine in the novel; further, his anxiety to endow his villagers with collective agency serves to mask the actual subject(s) of the novel's action. This reading considers the subjects and the nature of action in the plot, and the extent of the social transformation it envisions.

At the very outset, the Indian National Congress enters the village of Kanthapura by way of religion, through a nationalist storyteller who comes to a gathering of the devout Brahmin women of the village to recite *harikathas*. Traditionally, *harikathas* are stories of the miraculous exploits of the young God Krishna, particularly in his youth, but these *harikathas* are stories of Gandhi as an *avatara* of Siva, already semideified as a *mahatma*.[55] These stories prepare the way for Gandhi's party and its nationalist message, first carried from house to house by the upright, idealistic Moorthy. A Brahmin son of the village studying in the city, Moorthy has heard Gandhi speak and, like thousands of other college students, has followed his call to drop out of school and return to the villages to spread the word among the masses. The village is rigidly stratified by caste, and Moorthy must swallow his own deeply ingrained notions of caste purity in order to enter the homes of the untouchables, drink the water they offer him, and involve them in the movement. Rao also shows him, like Gandhi, unsettling gender hierarchies by involving women centrally in the struggle, particularly Rangamma, a young Brahmin widow.

The movement begins close to home, with the women picketing the government toddy shops, whereby the colonial state benefits from the men's addiction and impoverishment. As it spreads to protest the treatment and working conditions of the migrant workers from the British-owned coffee plantation, the villagers are forced to challenge their own class hierarchies, gender norms, caste prejudices, and xenophobia. Their worldview is progressively widened from the confines of family and caste to Kanthapura as a whole and even, hazily, beyond, to the region and the nation. Leading activists like Moorthy and the widow Rangamma even begin to develop an international worldview, becoming aware of different tendencies within the Congress and also of socialism and the Soviet Union.

In his famous foreword, Raja Rao seeks to locate his novel in the tradition of the *sthala-purana*, or "legendary history"—as an ancient story firmly rooted in place.[56] Narratives of nation always seek to represent themselves, and the nation itself, as having been in existence from time immemorial, no matter how newly conceived they are, and Rao's narrative presents his historically and geographically bounded conception of Kanthapura as a microcosm of village India. However, his narrative's changing worldview cannot be contained within the timeless vision of the *sthala-purana*. When Moorthy breaks the rules of caste purity, he is excommunicated by the Brahmin priest, and grief kills his widowed mother. As the novel ends, the village activists have been uprooted and driven from Kanthapura with no prospect of return. When they refused to pay their taxes, their lands were sold, and they were driven out of their native village. Moorthy himself is estranged from them, and has moved to the city after his release from jail, having become disenchanted with Gandhi's methods and gravitated toward Nehruvian socialism after the Gandhi–Irwin pact.[57] The novel does not develop the differences between Nehru and Gandhi, or even note that Nehru was a Congress leader. However, the uneducated villagers remain entirely behind Gandhi, while the educated young Moorthy leaves the village and is drawn to the urban, secular, Left.

In *Myths of the Nation*, Rumina Sethi points out that while Rao uses Moorthy to register the breach between the communists and Congress socialists on one hand and the Congress moderates and right wing on the other, he "subsumes the [socialists] within Gandhism," smoothing over their differences by having Moorthy describe Nehru as "a Bharata to the Mahatma."[58] The relationship of Nehru *vis-à-vis* Gandhi he sets up thereby is an entirely non-threatening one, that of the reverential younger brother in the *Ramayana* who refuses to rule the kingdom in Rama's stead while Rama is in exile. Nevertheless, in a letter to Ratna, the young widow, in the short closing chapter, Moorthy addresses a number of key questions that haunt the village narrator's vision of a future Gandhian *Ramarajya* (reign of Rama).

> . . . what is the goal? Independence? Swaraj? Is there not Swaraj in our States, and is there not misery and corruption and cruelty there? Oh no, Ratna, it is the way of the masters that is wrong. And I have come to realize bit by bit, and bit by bit, when I was in prison, that as long as there will be iron gates and barbed wires around the Skeffington Coffee Estate, and city cars that can roll up the Bebbur mound, and gaslights and coolie cars, there will always be Pariahs and poverty. Ratna, things must change. (180 181)

Although the future is uncertain, the village women keep the faith and look forward to a *Ramarajya*, oft-promised by Gandhi, when all of India will return from exile, as Rama and Sita returned from their years of forest exile and their victorious war with forces of evil. Resolution in the novel is deferred to this mythified future. But in its present, it is unclear what forces could deliver the *Ramarajya* promised to the faithful but naïve villagers, or even whether it is a *Ramarajya* that India as a whole needs. The novel is ambivalent as to whether Gandhi's model of village self-sufficiency alone can deliver better lives for the villagers of Kanthapura, and even less clear how or whether Nehru's model of a secular social democracy might combine fruitfully with Gandhi's Hindu vision of a twentieth-century theocracy, however benign. Rao's own social vision remains wholly Hindu and Brahmin, in spite of his focus on changing gender and caste norms. Brahmins remain firmly in control of the movement's leadership throughout, even though members of the lower castes take as many risks and make as many sacrifices. And as Tabish Khair notes, Rao frames his highly textualized, highly Sanskritized Brahmin definitions, traditions, and worldview as "universally Indian," implicitly rendering any other Indian viewpoint invalid.[59] The only Muslim in the village is the hated policeman, Badè Khan, an outsider who is sent as an agent of the British to monitor and quell the Congress organizing. Badè Khan becomes the generic policeman: when another policeman is sent to Kanthapura, he too is called Badè Khan, and when the women, preparing themselves to withstand police violence, think of the police charging them, they imagine "Badè

Khan after Badè Khan, short, bearded, lip-smacking, smoking, spitting, booted Badè Khan" (117).

Although women are profoundly and permanently changed by their involvement in the movement, the central female characters are all Brahmin women. Whether or not their family relations will be revolutionized remains unknown, because their families are split up in the village turmoil. When, early in the struggle, the women form a women's Congress group, their husbands begin to complain that their wives are no longer waiting on them as they should. One of them beats his seven-months-pregnant wife. When another complains that his wife isn't serving his meals on time, Rangamma, their leader, tells her to be more regular in her cooking, and all the women join in admonishing her, "We should do our duty. If not, it is no use belonging to the Gandhi-group" (105–106). Whatever else the women do outside the home, they must continue to do their duties. Later, when the police are beating the women, Ratna encourages one of the other women thus, "Be strong, sister. When your husband beats you, you don't fight back, do you? You only grumble and weep. The policeman's beating are the like." And the women answer, "So they are."[60] The Gandhian model of karma/action being advanced here is that of the performance of one's socially ordained duty, both individual and national, and an acceptance of the personal consequences—whether it is a beating from one's husband, arrest by the British Raj, or expulsion from one's beloved village.

Just as gendered structures of power persist through the villagers' mobilization, so too do structures of caste. Some of the most memorable parts of *Kanthapura* deal with Moorthy's overcoming the high-caste injunctions on caste purity. Going house to house to spread his Gandhian message, Moorthy enters a pariah's house and even takes water from a pariah's hands. His Brahmin instincts all rise in his gorge, but he suppresses them, although he is later convinced by a friend to drink Ganges water in self-purification. Nevertheless, he stands up to orthodox excommunication, and even to the broken-hearted death of his old mother, in his commitment to overcome the caste barriers to village unity by drawing both lower castes and outcastes into the struggle. However, caste categories remain intact, even at the height of the struggle. One of Raja Rao's most colorful uses of language to evoke the intimacy of the village grandmother's speech has been his use of one-word nicknames to typify the characters: thus, Nose-scratching Nanjamma, or Waterfall Venkamma, or Corner-house Moorthy. But tellingly, the only descriptive phrase given to the outcastes is their outcaste status itself, "pariah": Pariah Madanna, Pariah Rachanna, Pariah Lingayya, and so on: their caste status continues to be their most important—in fact their only—narrative marker. Although the village outcastes are increasingly shown to identify themselves with and sacrifice themselves for the struggle, facing imprisonment and eviction with the others, they never emerge from behind the veil of their outcaste status to become individualized characters. And the leadership—hosting and moderating meetings, making strategy decisions, launching and calling a halt to campaigns—remains firmly in the hands of the upper castes. Although caste barriers are temporarily lowered when they become an obstacle to mass mobilization and unity under Gandhian leadership, they are not overturned altogether. The transformations occur within the category of Brahmin, so that there is the old feudal orthodoxy of priest and landlord (the "bad" Brahmins) and the new, enlightened leadership (the "good" Brahmins). But the category of caste itself ultimately remains intractable, as it was in Gandhi's own vision, and the social structures of the village are naturalized even as they are sought to be reformed.

What the movement promises the villagers is transformation of a static, stratified society, in a new spirit of initiative and unity. They come to learn that this is not a transformation that will be delivered by a leader, or lived vicariously through him: when Gandhi is imprisoned, and after him their own Moorthy too, they realize that they themselves must take the responsibility to act. However, at the end of the novel there is a reversion to passivity. Driven out of Kanthapura, their lands auctioned after their refusal to pay tax, the villagers learn that Moorthy has been radicalized in prison and, disenchanted with Gandhi's capitulations in negotiations with the British, has moved toward socialism under Nehru's leadership. Moorthy's words, twice removed from the villagers (bracketed from the readers by virtue of their having been written in a letter to Ratna, which she then reads to the narrator), question the real goal of the struggle—is it national independence or social justice? He goes still further to question the entire power structure that produces "Pariahs and poverty." This long letter from Moorthy is the fourth-to-last paragraph of the novel, but directly following it is the narrator's highly mythified eulogy about the coming of Ramarajya, as if seeking to recuperate any status Gandhi may have lost, and giving over sole power and responsibility for *Swaraj* to the Mahatma: "They say the Mahatma will go to the Red-man's country and he will get us Swaraj. He will bring us Swaraj, the Mahatma. And we shall all be happy."[61] The narrator's need to reaffirm the theocratic idyll of *Ramarajya* after the loss of Moorthy and Ratna to socialism and the city bespeaks disquiet beneath the surface certainty.

K.R. Srinivasa Iyengar notes the disaffection with Gandhi on the part of Moorthy and intellectuals like him, but concludes his discussion of the novel by asserting a continued unquestioning devotion to Gandhi on the part of the masses, for whom "Gandhi can do no wrong...and they accept the [Gandhi-Irwin] truce contentedly and await further developments patiently. In the old woman's heart there are neither regrets nor recriminations, only an abiding sense of fulfillment."[62] However, as we have noted above, that fulfillment is in fact projected into a mythified future. In the present, Moorthy and his like attempt to push Congress to the Left, while all that is left for "the masses" is to accept the decisions of their leadership and wait patiently for *Ramarajya*. In fact, the novel has registered a widening rift between rich and poor, educated and uneducated, city and country; everything that has tied the villagers to their particular place and their past in this *sthala-purana* appears to have been unsettled. In spite of the desire to reaffirm the Gandhian vision, the romantic evocation of *Ramarajya* is followed by an altogether more troubled ending. In the closing lines, the old narrator, herself in exile, goes to Kanthapura's river to seek the blessings of Siva and the village Goddess:

> I drank three handfuls of Himavathy water and I said, "Protect us, mother!" to Kenchamma and I said, "Protect us, father" to the Siva of the promontory, and I spat three times to the west and three times to the south, and I threw a palmful of dust at the sunken wretch [Range Gowda, the corrupt village headman], and I turned away. But to tell you the truth, mother, my heart it beat like a drum. (182)

What further dislocations the drumbeat heralds remain unknown, but in the closing section, the prerogative to act has clearly been transferred from the hands of the villagers themselves back to the city and the central leadership of the Congress. After a whole novel in which the author makes the point again and again that the villagers must act by and for themselves, rather than wait passively for their leaders to act for them, the final paragraphs would seem to enact an abrupt reversal. While it is undeniable that the novel's lasting power lies in its portrayal of the inner transformation of the villagers, in the end it fails to promise any thoroughgoing social transformation. Caste and gender hierarchies remain intact and power remains in the hands of a high-caste leadership. Raja Rao's self-proclaimed *sthala-purana*, consciously intended to articulate an ideal of rural self-rule with a firm foundation in place, paradoxically ends with physical displacement and no hope of return.

Ultimately, the collective national subject and the self-empowered mass action idealized in the novel come into conflict with the realities of Congress' high-caste leadership, the internal political divisions within the nationalist movement, and the resistance of the village and communal power structures to thoroughgoing social change. Thus, the poignant last sentence of the novel is also its most resonant, evoking as it does the sad recognition that for all the faith and courageous collective action of the villagers, the decisions that will most powerfully affect their futures are being made elsewhere, and by others.

Celibacy and Deferral

The nationalist Gitas produced between 1910 and 1940 by Tilak, Gandhi, the Gandhian reformer Vinoba Bhave, and the conservative Congressman C. Rajagopalachari, were all written in prison, asserting moral and spiritual freedom and self-control from a place of physical confinement, exhorting Indians to self-discipline from a space of enforced inaction, projecting national sovereignty into an imagined future.[63] Celibacy was encouraged by a line of nationalist figures from Bankimchandra's "Children" to Swami Vivekananda to Gandhi himself. The personal fulfillment of a householder's life represented a normality that was to be put on hold for the duration of the struggle. In the tradition of asceticism, individual desires were to be sublimated into the impersonal desire for national liberation.

Literary texts also created spaces of freedom and projected them forward, either into a mythified imaginary (as in Venkataramani's Meenakshipuram) or into a post-independence future. They valorized action and inaction successively, in keeping with the Congress policy of Struggle-Truce-Struggle.[64] Those texts which were unable to reconcile internal conflicts similarly projected their resolution into the future. However, in the historical present, they featured struggle, self-denial, celibacy; marriage and consummation were deferred in domestic plots and nationalist romances alike. This kind of deferral features prominently in several of the novels and stories set in the run-up to 1947, during the Quit India Movement and the later 1940s, and published in the aftermath of independence, among them Bhabani Bhattacharya's *So Many Hungers* (1947), Venu Chitale's *In Transit* (1951), and R.K. Narayan's *Waiting for the Mahatma* (1955). Thus in N.S. Phadke's *The Whirlwind* (translated from the Marathi by the author, 1956), set during the Quit India

Movement, the Gandhian hero exhorts peasants who have been mobilized into action to go home and cultivate their gardens until the leadership are released from prison: "…we shall come amongst you and organize 'village kingdoms.' You will have to wait, but don't lose your patience." When an elderly villager asks him when he is getting married, he jokes, "Grandma, [D]on't you see I'm wedded to the Congress?" He returns to a life of service in his ancestral village, refusing to give in to the charms of Meera, the beautiful city girl who offers herself to him. He loves her, but "check[s] the impulse to take her in his arms." The novel closes with Shyam alone, back in the village, "eyes closed…fingers holding [a] blue envelope, still unopened"—a letter from Meera, it is to be presumed, and a promise of future fulfillment.[65]

Chapter Three

Colliding and Colluding Codes:
Post-Independence Alienation, 1947–80

The moment of independence, so long awaited, was necessarily followed by further deferrals for the individual citizen of the new Indian nation-state. Part I of this chapter, "Dreams Deferred," considers in brief four factors that marked the novel in English in the first decade after independence: the trauma and disillusionment of Partition; a polarization of gender roles that represented a period of setbacks for women after their active participation in the independence movement; a literary turn inward, particularly by young urban writers; and a preoccupation with "Indianness" as a measure of authenticity by the literary–cultural establishment. Part II discusses a series of early novels by Anita Desai, spanning nearly two decades from the early 1960s to 1980, examining the alienation of her mostly female protagonists and their progressive struggles to engage with a larger collectivity. Besides being one of the most prolific of the Indian English novelists who came of age after independence, Anita Desai wrote some of the most important and psychologically complex Indian English novels of the 1960s and 1970s. I suggest that Desai's early novels challenge the success of the nationalist synthesis, which would often seem to compound the pressures upon women, its constituent social and cultural codes now in collision, now in collusion. The very retreat into interiority points to a failure of action in the new nation as formulated by the dominant nationalism. Rather than sidelining her as a bourgeois "woman novelist" or dismissing the alienation in her novels as a lack of "Indianness," I contextualize the alienation of Desai's protagonists within a gendered post-independence framework. For many women in the post-independence period, karma is simply defined as selfless performance of domestic duty, and as such is seen to offer little of the potential for personal liberation and social transformation that it held out during the independence movement. And yet at a time when nationalism is seeking to consolidate itself, there is little space for critique: the self is to be identified with the nation.

Part I: Dreams Deferred

The Moment of Consummation
The Bride's Book of Beauty: Sringar, published in August 1947, was a lavishly produced and illustrated guide to ancient Indian beauty preparations, cowritten by Mulk Raj Anand and Krishna Hutteesing (Prime Minister Jawaharlal Nehru's

sister).[1] Its publication at the moment of Independence was a sign of the times. It seemed that the long period of waiting was over and the union of the patriot and the nation was at hand, that beauty and pleasure could at last be celebrated after years of self-denial. *The Bride's Book of Beauty* displayed an unabashed nationalistic pride in the superiority of a Hindu ideal of beauty, and shamelessly celebrated a male point of view, in which the woman exists to adorn herself for the man. The aesthetics of *sringar* derives from the erotic mode of *bhakti*, in which the relationship is that of deity and devotee. The book's cosmopolitan strand of Indian nationalism rejected both Brahminical asceticism and Victorian middle-class morality. However, its advocacy of frank enjoyment of the body conflicted with the sexual purity and self-denial enjoined upon middle-class Indian womanhood. Enlightened as its authors considered themselves to be, the book participated in the ongoing nationalist project of modernizing Indian women, making the contradictory demands that they become more like European women while remaining "essentially Indian." More than anything else, *The Bride's Book of Beauty* was an expression of long-deferred (male) nationalist desire on the verge of taking state power and a promise of the pleasure that was to attend its consummation.

But there was to be no joyous union: the moment of independence was attended by the bloody Partition of India and Pakistan, a traumatic upheaval of massive proportions, in which an estimated six million people were uprooted and made into refugees, as large numbers of Hindus and Sikhs were driven from their homes in what became East and West Pakistan and equally large numbers of Muslims were similarly forced to flee from those areas that were designated as Indian. It was some time before people were able to write novels about Partition, because the trauma, the scope of the violence, and the dislocation were too great. The experience was too disillusioning, too incomprehensible. For this reason most of the literary outpourings, especially those in the immediate aftermath by people who lived in regions directly affected, were expressions of grief that attempted to relive and thereby relieve the trauma and violence through personal memory, but could account for the Partition only in terms of sin and madness.[2] Reasons of state also delayed the development of sustained counternarratives of Partition. Both the new nation-states developed rationales for Partition compatible with their respective national narratives, and although the Indian National Congress, which had stood for Hindu–Muslim unity and tolerance of difference, had agreed to the Partition, Indian national history took recourse to a politics of blame, putting the responsibility for Partition on the Muslims and their leader, Muhammad Ali Jinnah. Especially in the first two decades after independence, it would have been difficult to produce a novel whose perspective on Partition differed from the official national version. As hostilities increased between India and Pakistan, it was no longer possible to travel between the two countries or even to communicate with friends and family members across the national boundaries. Many of the women who were raped or abducted during the Partition and who were subsequently "recovered" became wards of the state at "rehabilitation" centers where they were rendered voiceless through being spoken for by the state. "Recovering" them whether or not they wanted to be recovered, the Indian nation-state effectively denied agency to these women, constructing them as Indian citizen-subjects according to its own exigencies. It was not until the mid-1990s, half a century later, that accounts and sustained analyses of these experiences were to be published.[3]

Besides the rift between Indian and Pakistani national narratives, ideological rifts within India appeared to be equally unbridgeable: less than five months after Independence, with the "infant" nation still traumatized by the violence of the Partition and the communal riots that continued in its aftermath, Mahatma Gandhi, "Father of the Nation," was assassinated at the hands of Nathuram Godse, a hard-line Hindu nationalist who saw Gandhi's conciliatory approach toward the Muslims as responsible for the Partition, an unforgivable violation of the Motherland. Godse felt that, if allowed to live, Gandhi would further "'emasculate' the Hindu community and destroy the Hindu nation."[4] In a tragic irony of history and the laws of karma, the unrepentant Godse went to the gallows with a copy of the *Bhagavad-Gita* in his hands.[5] With the Congress (now the Congress Party) struggling to cope with the mass violence and dislocations of Partition, the loss of Gandhi, with his tremendous popularity, his moral stature, and his political gift of negotiating compromise, was a tremendous blow. Under such circumstances, national narratives were obliged once again to defer any celebrations of the long-awaited "union"—the actual rifts were too much in evidence. There was a new nation on paper, but all its promise remained to be fulfilled.

Few Indian English novels could begin to look squarely at the events of the summer of 1947 again for two decades or more, when the crisis in the dominant national narrative made it possible to consider alternative versions of history. One important exception was Khushwant Singh's novel *Train to Pakistan* (1956), and another was Attia Hosain's *Sunlight on a Broken Column* (1961). This novel of an elite, feudal Indian Muslim family's complex and varied relationships to the nationalist movement is set in the 1930s but leaps over the events of the 1940s leading upto Partition, leaving a fourteen-year caesura in their place between 1938 and 1952. Perhaps trauma, loss, and conflicting national narratives erase the possibility of Hosain's young female protagonist putting forward her own version of Partition, even though the novel was written in Britain, where its author moved in 1947 and remained for the rest of her life.

R.K. Narayan's *Waiting for the Mahatma* (1955) addresses the theme of deferred desire, the historical event of Gandhi's assassination, and the making of a reluctant citizen of the new India. Along with *The Dark Room* (1938), it is one of two novels in Narayan's *oeuvre* that are generally considered anomalous, because of the disjuncture between Narayan's comic tone and focus on "little" people on one hand, and the high seriousness of the national historical events and the near-deification of Gandhi on the other. The significantly named Bharati, an orphan taken in and named by the Mahatma himself, has worked side-by-side with him as a Congress volunteer wholly dedicated to the national cause. Sriram, the callow youth who falls in love with her, must wait five years until Gandhi gives them permission to wed. It is at the moment when the Mahatma finally gives them his blessing that he is killed by an assassin's bullet. Here Narayan's novel ends abruptly, without the comforting resolution characteristic of his other works. Sriram and Bharati must embark on their married life without Gandhi's guiding hand. Although Sriram is the reluctant citizen of Narayan's story, it is Bharati who loses the most and gains the least. Her superhuman capacity for hard work and self-sacrifice appears to be no more and no less than what is expected of her as an Indian woman. For Sriram, personal fulfilment was deferred for the duration of the independence struggle, but for Bharati self-denial would seem to be the indefinite prescription for the success of her marriage—indeed, the very definition of her femininity.

Scenarios of deferred desire in early post-independence novels often project a successful marriage only at the expense of the woman, requiring the modern Indian woman to sacrifice her personal freedom in order to smooth the transition to "modernity" for the nation as a whole. Novels like Venu Chitale's *In Transit* (1950), Bhabani Bhattacharya's *Music for Mohini* (1952), and Rama Mehta's *Inside the Haveli* (1977) all feature an urban, educated bride whose liberal, English-educated father marries her off into an orthodox family that still lives as a joint family in its ancestral home. After her liberal upbringing and modern education, the bride must make a painful adjustment, but she suffers uncomplainingly, succeeds in earning her mother-in-law's respect, and slowly brings about reforms. In *Inside the Haveli*, it is not until the next generation that women can be expected to enjoy the freedom that the heroine has to give up.[6] One of Bhabani Bhattacharya's characters describes the instrumentality of such a marriage in nationalist terms: "We who're so wed, serve some real purpose. It's as though we made a bridge between two banks of a river... Our new India must rest on this foundation."[7] Women themselves cannot be represented as actors; rather, their continued self-sacrifice for the nation is posited as the necessary precondition for future action on the part of others. This would appear to be their postcolonial karma.

Gender and Nation After Independence
As women struggled for agency in the post-independence period, the woman in the Indian English novel became a sign of the nationalist synthesis under strain. The post-1947 position of Indian women was complicated by a powerful convergence of historical forces that both defined and confined the space in which Indian women could act. In nationalist discourse, the figure of Woman continued to serve as self-sacrificing mother of the nation, bearer of Tradition, and bridge between old and new. And yet in the universalist post-independence ethos, with equality of gender, caste, and creed enshrined in the Indian Constitution, and with women defined as already free and yet with their social and domestic situations substantially unchanged, demands for women's rights found little support. The 1950s and 1960s were a time of setbacks for women's issues and "a lull in feminist campaigning,"[8] the prevailing attitude being that women who had fought alongside men for freedom were now free—as Indians. What need, then, had they to complain? Their duty was the same as that of every Indian: to work selflessly for the greater good of the nation.

As we have seen, men of the emergent Indian middle classes during the colonial period coped with the hierarchical imposition of colonial "modernity" upon Indian "tradition" not by creating a real synthesis but by developing a gendered opposition between the private and the public, the home and the world. Male cultural nationalism compartmentalized reality into inner and outer realms, naming the inner realm female, and a space where Indians were already free; hence nationalism's subsequent silence on issues of domestic social reform.[9] According to this formulation, the economic and material dominance of the Western world in the outer world cannot threaten the sovereignty of the cultural and spiritual inner world, where an essentialized idea of tradition reigns supreme, presided over by the Indian woman, symbol of purity and Indianness. For women themselves, however, the illusion is maintained at great personal cost; the model works only by freezing the figure of Woman into what R. Radhakrishnan has called "the pure and ahistorical signifier of interiority."[10] The Manichean polarities of colonialist discourse now consigned men to Production, women to Reproduction, men to Doing, women to Being, men to Nation, women to AlieNation.[11]

In Indian English novels after Independence, particularly in the 1960s and 1970s, certain themes begin to emerge again and again, prominently and problematically. Spiritual duty and self-realization clash and overlap clumsily with family duty and social responsibility, shifting uneasily across each other as if endlessly unresolved. When religious and nationalist imperatives conspire or conflict with each other, neither speak in terms that are enabling to women. Women find themselves trapped in the interstices between national, social, religious, moral, and sexual duties. Men are able to separate the public and private spheres—at a cost to themselves, certainly—but women, embodying nationalist "difference," have to bear the burden of both without the freedom of either. The woman becomes the shock absorber between the inside and outside worlds, occupying what poet Meena Alexander has called "a fault line, a site of potential rupture" between incompatible constructions of reality.[12] As a result, writers seeking to create female subject-agents frequently found themselves reproducing nationalist stereotypes, while those attempting to resist the constructions of the dominant nationalist discourse found that they simply did not have the language to do so. The discourse either constructed their heroines in its own terms, or it destroyed them.

The Turn Inward

Beginning in the 1950s and accelerating in the 1960s, the Indian English literary scene saw the emergence of a new literature of interiority. In *The Twice-Born Fiction* (1971), Meenakshi Mukherjee observed that the "public preoccupations [of the thirties and forties] were followed, in the next decade, by a concern with one's own self that was basically a private search...the shift of interest from the public to the private sphere may be regarded as a characteristic of the fifties and the sixties."[13] Writers appeared to fall silent on national issues, beginning to explore the complexities and tensions of their own psyches, turning away from the violent, turbulent, schismatic half-century in which the independence struggle had dominated the literary scene along with every other area of life. Indeed, this shift was not restricted to fiction in English; in the early 1970s, introducing a collection of writing in translation from a number of Indian languages, critic Adil Jussawalla wrote, "The last ten years have seen Indian writing get more and more subjective."[14] Introducing a collection of new Hindi short fiction from the 1960s, Gordon Roadarmel sees them "reflecting greater disillusion with political, social, and individual relationships" than works of the generations before them: "Major religious, social, and political problems are not of primary concern. Instead, these writers tend to turn inward, portraying loneliness and estrangement, social disruption, urban anonymity, bureaucratic indifference, and a general loss or absence of individual identity."[15] Most of this new writing was by members of the English-educated urban middle classes of the first generation after independence.

The conceptual multivalence of the philosophical concepts in the nationalist Gitas was narrowed in practice as the Congress Party could no longer be all things to all people. After independence, the Gita came to represent not only "the official Hindu belief system,"[16] but also the semi-secular scripture of the nation itself. While the Gita interpreters of the freedom struggle had been activists, frequently writing and teaching in prison, one of the most prominent Gita interpreters of the post-independence period was the Vedanta philosopher Sarvepalli Radhakrishnan, who became president of India under Nehru in the mid-1950s. At the "Moment of Arrival" of the Indian nation-state,[17] nationalism was geared toward building and consolidating the modern, industrial nation-state. Karma was now a work ethic, a secularized, peculiarly Indian brand of existentialist stoicism.

As novels began to explore the interiors of the social body and the individual mind, some sought refuge and identity in Orientalist models of tradition, representing the East–West conflict in stereotyped formulations, in which the "East" inevitably—and almost automatically—won, the alienated Indian protagonist ultimately accepting his or her fate as Indians are expected to do. However, others also rehearsed the themes, symbols, and images of the nationalist discourse, but in a way that did not merely reproduce them, but attempted to problematize them as well. For example, writers like Anita Desai and Arun Joshi attempted to explore more complex personal predicaments in which neither "traditional" nor "modern" solutions presented themselves ready-made.[18] In the works of these new writers, an obligatory national code of ethics, with its secular–religious notions of sacrifice and duty—as expounded in nationalist renditions of the Gita—was often questioned and represented as stifling and oppressive. Their protagonists, caught in crushing double-binds, a kind of death-grip of national duty and social custom, were driven through alienation to madness and self-destruction. These novels turned away from sloganeering to the isolated individual voice. Themes of renunciation and disillusionment accompanied by the Gita's exhortations to nonattached action recur again and again as protagonists struggle with themselves, each other, and society, and attempt, with varying results, to use the Gita as their guide.[19] The Gita and its ideals of nonattachment and selfless performance of duty figure prominently in an astonishing number of Indian English novels of this period, not merely in a passing reference or quotation, but as a central theme. To name just a few: *The Dark Dancer* (1959) by B. Rajan, *Cry, the Peacock* (1963) and *Voices in the City* (1965) by Anita Desai, *The Cat and Shakespeare* (1965) by Raja Rao, *The Vendor of Sweets* (1967) by R.K. Narayan, and *The Foreigner* (1968) by Arun Joshi. The nationalist Gita had become so embedded in the national consciousness that, whether or not writers referred to it explicitly in their works, they often found themselves using its terms in their attempts to reconcile their dilemmas of action.

In a period of aggressive nationalism, either when the movement is seeking state power, or the newly formed state is seeking to consolidate itself, the nationalist discourse permeates all areas of life. In the aftermath of political independence, then, during the height of the Cold War, different worldviews no longer interpenetrated creatively, throwing up innumerable new possibilities. The arena of action narrowed into sharply opposed polarities in a postcolonial throwback to colonialist categories of thought that privileged rationalism and action, and invested them with state power and legitimacy.[20] The national idea, which had represented itself as a broad, inclusive vision of "unity in diversity," began to shrink into a more monolithic concept in the late 1960s and 1970s as the Congress Party sought to secure increasingly centralized state power.[21] In terms of the relationship between the individual self and the nation, one was either a patriot, wholly identified with the nation and its symbols, or one was a traitor: there was little middle ground. This was especially so for the Indian English novel, whose loyalties were already suspect. As a result, the Indo-Anglian novel—as it was more commonly called at that time—began to stagnate, robbed of "authenticity," unable to find an acceptable voice, form, or subject matter that was at once uniquely its own and indisputably "Indian."

"Indianness" and Alienation

In *Women Writing in India*, Susie Tharu and K. Lalita historicize post-independence women's literary texts in terms of both the emergence and consolidation of the independent Indian nation-state and also the relationship of gender and nation, identifying major tendencies in post-independence Indian literary criticism. They point out that critics of early post-independence texts and, to a certain extent, the writers themselves, read and judged these texts in terms either of the demands of the nation, on the one hand, or of "critical tendencies dominant in the West," on the other. Critics used often-repeated terms such as "alienation" and "Indianness" normatively, as the measure of a writer's patriotism and the appropriate expression of citizenship.[22] Tharu and Lalita are discussing pressures on writing in the Indian languages as well as in English, but during this period the pressure was all the greater for writers in English which, as the language of the former colonizer and the collaborationist bourgeoisie, was widely considered alienated, inauthentic, and un-Indian almost by definition.

The isolation felt by writers in English was so great that the Calcutta-based Writers' Workshop was formed in the late 1950s in order to promote and defend Indian creative writing in English as legitimate Indian literature. In an essay in the English-language journal *Quest*, Workshop founder P. Lal insisted that for those Indians who wrote creatively in English, the language came naturally. He added that the Workshop made no special claims for English as the only language capable of providing an "all-India" flavor. However, they did argue that English was "a pan-Indian elite language" and, as such, "involved certain responsibilities" for those fluent in it.[23] Lal was responding to an essay entitled "On Caged Chaffinches and Polyglot Parrots," which had referred to Indian English literature as "a nightmare of sterility," and to Indian writers in English as opportunists and social climbers. English in India was imitative and prescriptive, it said, used "not to suggest feelings but chart courses of action"; it could never be a language of the Indian imagination.[24] Post-independence Indian English writers reacted to such criticism with a defensiveness that they have never since managed to shake off, and which Meenakshi Mukherjee has recently called "the anxiety of Indianness."[25]

The pressures of "Indianness" meant that Indian literary critics' approval of the patriotism of a given literary text was often bestowed or withheld based upon the degree to which it appeared to draw upon "traditional" Indian—in fact, high

Hindu—concepts and sources. Thus, for example, one Indian English critic defended Anita Desai's *Cry the Peacock* as "Indian" simply because it quotes from the Gita, regardless of the role of or attitude toward the Gita within the novel.[26] A character's alienation and isolation from the larger society would be ascribed to the corrupting influence of European existentialism. Depending on the position of the critic, it would be used as proof either of the novel's universalism or of its lack of a properly Indian sensibility. For example, Nirode's angry nihilism in Desai's *Voices in the City* and Sindi Oberoi's curious lack of affect and obsession with the nonattachment of the Gita in Arun Joshi's *The Foreigner* have been discussed both as imitations of French existentialists and as alienated from the "Indian ethos." However, although many post-independence Indian writers themselves fully acknowledge the influence of the French existentialists,[27] I see the alienation in their novels as arising chiefly from specifically Indian conditions that frustrated action during this period.[28]

In fact, Indian English novelists who turned inward during the doldrums of the 1960s and 1970s were not rejecting their social responsibilities, but struggling to find an authentic voice in which they could express themselves as modern Indians, attempting to come to grips with their own predicaments. The reasons that they could not do so lie in the ambivalence at the very roots of Indian nationalism, and thus, rather than merely being the irrelevant, existential posturing of a small, privileged class, their struggles for personal self-expression can also be seen to register a conceptual dissonance within the Indian nationalist discourse.[29] Even today "Indianness," or the lack thereof, continues to be wielded as a not-so-subtle weapon to silence and marginalize dissent. Indian English poet Eunice de Souza quotes poet Nissim Ezekiel: "… there are aspects of life in India from which one should be alienated, and dissent and criticism are not to be confused with alienation. [If so] then one is forced to conclude that 'roots' may be a plea for conservatism and insularity."[30]

Part II: Post-Independence Alienation in Anita Desai's Early Novels[31]

Anita Desai was one of the most prolific of a new generation of Indian English novelists of the 1960s and 1970s who appeared to fall silent on national issues, exploring an interior world rather than the public arena of the Gandhian Age. Born of a Bengali father and a German mother, and raised and educated in Old Delhi, Desai earned a Master's degree in English Literature from Miranda House before getting married and raising four children of her own. She has written eleven novels spanning much of the half-century since Independence, beginning in 1963 with *Cry, the Peacock*. Her fifth novel, *Fire on the Mountain* (1977), won the national Sahitya Akademi award for the best Indian novel in English. Since then, three of her five subsequent novels have been short-listed for the Booker Prize, giving her a large international readership.[32] It is her early work I am most interested in examining here, leading up to her 1980 novel, *Clear Light of Day*.

Anita Desai's work has been widely read and well received both in India (where she tends to be read as a "woman writer"[33]) and abroad (where she is read as an "Indian" writer), and she remains one of the most established of the Indian English novelists writing today. Nevertheless, some critics have charged that the alienation they see in her novels can be laid to insufficient "Indianness" in her sensibility.[34]

Others have characterized her dismissively as a bourgeois, middle-class woman novelist who is cut off from the pulse of the people or as an alienated Westernized writer who presumes to represent India to the world.[35] Even appreciative critics have noted her inwardness and narrow social scope, and her style and subject matter as feminine, poetic, and the intensely subjective work of a hypersensitive woman.[36] In fact, Desai herself appears to have confirmed some of the above statements in a 1975 essay on Indian writing in English:

> Now for the problems this [writing in English] is supposed to have created for me. I think I have simply sidestepped them—again, not deliberately, but unconsciously and intuitively—by not writing the sort of social document that demands the creation of realistic and typical characters and the use of realistic and typical dialogue. By writing novels that have been catalogued by critics as psychological, and that are purely subjective, I have been left free to employ, simply, the language of the interior.[37]

Here Desai uses the word "free" to refer to the withdrawal of her novels from the external, social world. Their classification as psychological novels has freed her from the expectations placed upon the works of other writers. But at the same time it has allowed for their dismissal in the terms of the larger social arena. Freedom *to* use the language of the interior is thus also freedom *from* the public sphere. We shall see that for women, the interior, the private sphere, becomes a prison as well as a refuge. Anita Desai's novels, particularly her early ones, have indeed tended to shy away from the broad political canvas. But in so doing they reveal a great deal about post-independence Indian social and political life, particularly on the vexed relationship between national and personal identity, and on the pressures of the dominant Indian nationalism upon women.

In a 1989 talk on Indian writing in English, Anita Desai said that the need to apologize for and defend writing in a particular language can drive a writer into an artistically fatal isolation.[38] This statement may help to shed light on Desai's own early writing during the 1960s when all creative writing in English had to be defended and apologized for, or else turned in on itself, into isolation. In *Voices in the City* (1965), the passive, self-destructive Monisha writes, "I am turned into a woman who keeps a diary…I do not like women who keep diaries."[39] She presents herself as keeping a diary not because she has deliberately chosen the diary as the most effective or satisfying form of expression but because external conditions have restricted her to that form.[40] This situation, of being forced into a form one has not chosen, forced to speak to oneself, forced into employing a form of communication that by definition fails to communicate, can testify simultaneously to the situation of women, the situation of writers who seek to explore reality in their own terms, and the situation of Indians writing in English during the period of ascendant state nationalism, in which the ideal woman was Mother India; criticism or reformulation of the national self was unacceptable; and Indians writing in English found themselves rejected as un-Indian. The inhospitable intellectual climate forced them into a self-defeating isolation.

Writing in the 1960s, the young Anita Desai felt strongly the lack of support and guidance from a tradition of women writers.[41] In a 1992 review of *Women Writing in India*, she applauds the anthology's valuable contribution to such a tradition, and questions the contradictory messages that a home/world dichotomy sends to women. Referring to Partha Chatterjee's work on the nationalist compartmentaliza-tion of the public and private spheres, she comments:

> There is a school of opinion that says the feminist question did not "disappear" under nationalism but was "resolved" by it. Nationalism asked that in the material field Western ideas should reign, and in the spiritual field Indian; a balance was required between "the inner and the outer, the home and the world." A balance or an irrationally divided personality?[42]

The Desai of the 1960s, however, had not yet arrived at this kind of overt critique of the nationalist discourse; rather, her protagonists themselves became victims of this "irrationally divided personality," of these contradictory, conflicting expectations of women, often losing their sanity to them, and sometimes even their lives.

In the 1980s and 1990s, studies of the reconstruction of gender as part of the middle-class nationalist project in both colonial and postcolonial India constituted one of the most dynamic areas of the recent scholarship on the colonial construction of Indian nationalism. However, in the 1960s and 1970s, writers and critics alike lacked the language with which to give voice to a feminist critique of nationalism, and in any case, the political climate did not permit such a critique. In the symbolic language of a creative writer, the impossible conflicts that entrapped Desai's heroines sought to articulate the then-inarticulable, to give voice to a conflict that could not be heard. It is now possible to place her early work within a longer and broader tradi-tion of Indian women writers, and to recognize her courageous questioning of the sacred codes of Indian nationalism and her scrutiny of a woman's often-futile strug-gles for selfhood and agency in the early post-independence period.

In approaching Desai's work I am chiefly interested in examining the *internaliza-tion* of the response to the dominant national identity reflected in and refracted through the personal identities, internal conflicts, and family relationships of central characters in her novels. Their withdrawal from the public sphere into darkness and silence speaks volumes on the relationship between the individual and the nation, and particularly of women's vexed relationship to the nation. I see the central conflicts for the protagonists of Desai's early novels as symptomatic of the disjunctions between nationalist discourse and lived realities in the post-independence period. However, the challenge to the nationalist synthesis remains unvoiced, as Desai both resists and reproduces the dominant structures and symbols of nationalism.

Her short story, "Games at Twilight" is typical of how this internalization works in Desai's fiction, and how conflicting codes place her characters in double-binds.

"Games at Twilight"

A group of brothers and sisters clamor to be let out to play on a hot summer afternoon, stifling after having been kept inside by their mother for the hottest hours of the day.[43] The older siblings call the shots, of course, and Hide-and-Seek is chosen. One panicky little boy, Ravi, scrambles to hide before he is tagged "it." He is afraid of the dark, but manages to squeeze through a crack in the locked door frame of a dank garage, shiver-ing with excitement and fear, congratulating himself on his winning hiding place. He is sure that no one will be able to find him, and he is right. He hides huddling in the dark for a long time, confident of victory as the other children's shouts die down outside, and then hides a little longer, just to be perfectly sure. As one of the younger children, he has never won any of their games before. Then suddenly he remembers that he must come out and touch the den, "home," before he can win. He bursts out of hiding and runs desperately, furiously, to the den, screaming, "I won, I won, I won." The other children are amazed and bewildered. They have finished playing Hide-and-Seek and forgotten all about him long ago. They allow Ravi to join their new game, at the end of the line, if he will stop crying like a baby. They are playing a miserable funeral game now ("He had wanted victory and triumph—not a funeral"). Ravi refuses to join them and flings himself face down on the grass in humiliation and despair, "silenced by a terrible sense of his insignificance." No matter how well he plays their game, by all their rules, he does not receive any recognition. Even if he wins, they will not notice. The rules require him to hide, so that the better he plays, more completely is he hidden. If he refuses to play, he will be excluded from the group, and if he plays, it will always be on other people's terms, which guarantee his continued suppression.

This bleak little story raises a central preoccupation of Anita Desai's work, and can be read as paradigmatic of her relationship to the Indian nationalist discourse. "Games at Twilight" stages Ravi's predicament as the age-old children's game, Hide-and-Seek. It is notable that the protagonist is a dependent younger sibling, one who is perpetually left out and left behind. It is also significant that the story's action, staged as a terrifying game, takes place mostly enclosed in the dark, with the protagonist finally emerging at twilight, when it is neither light nor dark, rather than at the midnight or dawn of a new day commonly used to stage national independence.[44] The winner can be the player who succeeds in hiding well enough not to be found, but only if s/he does not become so marginalized as to be unable to claim victory at the Center. If a player is so insignificant that his or her presence is never missed, then there is no benefit in continuing to hide. The trouble with hiding too successfully is that one may never be found, and thus may be excluded from the game altogether.

For many of Desai's protagonists, the Interior becomes both a cage and a refuge: a woman's place, where she is both confined, cut off from the world, and able to speak with authority, her authenticity unchallenged. This inherently ambivalent position gives rise to one of the central themes and characteristic double-binds in Desai's early novels: the simultaneous struggle to engage and the pressure to withdraw. When a character is denied a dynamic engagement with the world on her own terms, she is forced into alienation. And when she attempts to engage, the struggle threatens to destroy her, so that she often has no choice but to withdraw into a "safe" isolation. The tension between escape and engagement, rejection and return, nonattachment and desire, alienation and commitment, runs throughout Desai's work. Examining four of her early novels, we shall see how her protagonists attempt to grapple with the nationalist Gita's ideal of nonattached action.

Terms of Engagement: Four Desai Protagonists

Cry, the Peacock: Fatal Detachment
In *Cry, the Peacock* (1963), Desai's first novel, Maya is a sensitive, sensual, childlike wife, secretly haunted by a childhood horoscope that had prophesied violent death

for either her or her husband after four years of marriage. Her cultured, Anglicized Brahmin father presided over her sheltered childhood, and her unimaginative husband Gautama dominates her young adulthood. Maya desires passionately to live and love; but her sensibility and sensitivity is denied and derided by her dry, cerebral lawyer-husband, whose middle-class family, dedicated nationalists all, lead admirably and exhaustingly practical, busy, useful lives. Maya and Gautama live in different worlds, between which there is mutual incomprehension. "In his world there were vast areas in which he would never permit me, and he could not understand that I could even wish to enter them" (104), Maya moans after her husband has shut her out of a social group of his male friends. Conversations between the two always seem to end with her frustrated and plaintive cry, "You don't understand," conversations in which the very terms of the discussion are alien to her.

Gautama condemns Maya's sensuality and her desire to engage with the world as excessive attachment, while he complacently preaches a rationalistic and rationalizing interpretation of the *Bhagavad-Gita's* doctrine of nonattached action. He warns her paternalistically of the error of attachment, quoting from the Gita itself: "Thinking of sense objects, man becomes attached thereto. From attachment arises longing and from longing anger is born. From anger arises delusion; from delusion, loss of memory is caused. From loss of memory the discriminative faculty is ruined and from the ruin of discrimination, he perishes." Cut off from the world in a kind of doll's-house existence, Maya longs to experience life in all its materiality, and finds her husband's patronizing words a rejection of life itself. She lashes out at him with bitterness:

> How it suits you to quote those lines of a dry stick—an inhuman dry stick. Oh, you know nothing, understand nothing… Nor will you ever understand. You know nothing of me—and of how I can love. How I want to love. How it is important to me… Love has no importance for you. It is merely—attachment. (112)

But whenever Maya ventures to discuss her way of seeing, and her love of life, Gautama uses the charge of insufficient "Indianness" to silence her, accusing her of being an "Occidental."

Maya's longing to engage fully with the world is negated by her husband. He admonishes her with quotes from the Gita in order to pacify her, to make her accept her lot: "Why not create [a world] inside oneself, to detach oneself into when the world around one grows either too boring or too hectic?" Maya cries, "I don't care to detach myself into any other world than this" (117). He prescribes detachment when she needs to engage, action when she has been given no skills with which to act. At the same time, he denigrates attachment because he himself cannot cope with physical closeness or emotions, and he dismisses Maya's ability simply to be, rather than to do, because he can imagine no other way of being and knowing than that of action and rational positivism. Gautama uses the Gita as a weapon, in order to dismiss Maya and her way of being and perceiving as a delusion. Here he has taken the place of her father, who named her Maya (illusion, delusion; also compassion, pity) and raised her as a sheltered plaything. Both men have betrayed Maya, her father by giving her expectations of life that have been dashed by married reality, and by sheltering her from priests and prophets of fate while suggesting that she accept her fate rather than try to change it or make her own. Gautama's betrayal consists of preaching detachment to mask a total lack of understanding and to justify excluding her from his masculine spheres of action. He preaches action while expounding an inexorably logical theory of karma as cause and effect, which denies the possibility of all independent agency. Thus, for Maya, karma comes to mean, not action, but its impossibility.

Gautama appears to be a successful product of modern India, an honest, socially conscious man who has risen to prominence through his own efforts, rather than through caste or class privilege. He is patriotic but not religious, believing in the Hindu religious tradition in its philosophical aspect, rather than in its spiritual or devotional aspects. But Gautama is only half a man. He accepts life in all its dreary routine, rather than trying to transform and revitalize it. In his dry rationality, he cannot experience love, emotional or physical closeness with a woman, or sensuous perception. His narrowly intellectual interpretation of the Gita is symptomatic of the impoverishment of Hindu multiplicity as interpreted by modern Indian nationalism. For Gautama, the Gita serves as a coping mechanism that allows one to retreat into detachment in order to escape the emotional storms of life. Gautama uses the Gita to suppress and deny his wife's sense of self, preaching self-denial to a woman whose ego is dangerously underdeveloped, detachment to a woman whose links with the world are already so tenuous that she is becoming unhinged.

In spite of knowing that Gautama does not understand her, Maya comes to admire and depend on his steadying solidity. It is true that she has been pampered and sheltered. It is true that he must work hard every day to support her. The detachment described in the Gita is indeed calming. And Maya herself often believes that she is spoiled, neurotic, and hysterical, as Gautama calls her. But in fits of sanity she believes in herself and in her own perceptions; she knows that she has desires that will never be fulfilled, and that she longs to live in a way that Gautama could never accept, much less comprehend.

Together, Maya's father and husband so completely deny her any form of agency that she drifts into madness, ultimately grasping at engagement only through a desperate act of violence. In her fevered attempts to use Gautama's own logic to find a way to survive her prophesied fate, she becomes detached from reality altogether.[45] She convinces herself that if one of them is to die, it ought to be her husband, since he clearly does not care for life as she does. "The man had no contact with the world, or with me. What would it matter to him if he died and lost even the possibility of contact?" (175). The double tragedy that ensues is a consequence of the tragic disjunction between their two ways of seeing and understanding the world. Maya pushes Gautama off the roof, and he falls to his death, ironically ensuring her own final cut-off from the world as well.[46]

Ultimately Maya has almost completely internalized Gautama's view of her. He has consistently dismissed her reality as illusion and caused her to withdraw into a separate reality. She says at last, "my very name means nothing, is nothing but illusion." In the closing chapter even the narration disowns her by shifting from first person to third, leaving Maya completely isolated. She is seen as a pathetic, helpless child, through the eyes of her efficient, responsible, self-sacrificing mother-in-law, "the mother" (she is given no other name) for whom work, giving, and ceaseless activity (she has "great faith in activity") leave no room for the kinds of personal desires that rack her daughter-in-law.

Cry, the Peacock is riven with impossible rifts between the public and the private, the material and the spiritual, male and female, reason and passion, duty and desire. Gautama and Maya embody these Orientalist dichotomies in modern nationalist thought, dichotomies that have become part of its conceptual makeup. We see the discrepancies between Maya's Anglicized upbringing and her traditional marriage, as she is caught between the nationalist exhortation to action and her lack of preparation for practical action in the world. Maya is completely isolated, since her father has abandoned her to her fate and counseled her to accept it. Her brother, Arjuna, broke away from the overprotective influence of their father, mixed defiantly with lower-caste and Muslim boys as a child, and eventually "escaped" to the United States where he became a union organizer and completely cut himself off from his family. It is interesting here that Desai figures Arjuna's action as escape. Because Maya was a girl, such avenues of escape were not open to her, who remained her father's darling in the gilded cage of the family mansion, until, at her father's suggestion, she married Gautama, a friend of his, "almost a protégé" (40). Gautama's weapons are a combination of secularized religious dogma and rational positivism. He uses nationalism reinforced with religion and duty compounded with *dharma* to exhort Maya to accept her lot. For Gautama, sensuousness is condemned as self-indulgence, and spirituality is required to be sterile and disembodied, rather than passionate and wholehearted. What Maya needs is not self-denial but self-realization, not nonattachment but engagement. However, her desire is perceived as a threat, to be contained and conquered.

Gautama trivializes Maya's sensibilities to the extent that she becomes totally detached from reason and the material world, while his identity as a modern Indian citizen—active, dutiful, eminently rational—renders him utterly unable to comprehend her or take her seriously. He can deny all responsibility for her inner turmoil by labeling it as her problem, diagnosing moral and mental deficiency on her part. And to a certain extent, both Maya and the narrative itself participate in this internalization of her conflicts. Several critics also see Maya's social and political conflicts as psychological problems belonging to her alone. To them, Maya is simply a pampered, neurotic rich girl suffering from a father-fixation, while Gautama is a sensible, hardworking citizen. Jasbir Jain, for example, in a study of Desai's recurrent themes and their development, asserts that Maya's problems are illusory: "Maya's unhappiness... is not related to the reality of her circumstances; it is a product of her consciousness."[47] Jain sees Maya's failure to achieve the detachment of the Gita as her downfall, and Gautama's adherence to the Gita's ideals as his strength: "Maya turns to Gautama's advice of detachment. But detachment is difficult to attain and attachment leads to self-destruction... Gautama aspires as near the goal of the Gita as is humanly possible." Being an utter rationalist, he "relates the karma theory to logic not to faith."[48] In my reading, however, Gautama's dry rationalism is his problem, and in large part, Maya's as well, while Maya's very attempt to achieve the detachment he prescribes, so alien to her own nature and needs, ironically leads to her self-destruction.

Cry, the Peacock is an exploration of the desperate effort of a young woman to survive, in an environment where she is not in a position to make herself heard or understood. The point of the exercise is not to allocate blame to either one; the novel certainly shows Maya to be as overwhelmed by her emotions as Gautama is divorced from his. The success of Desai's execution must be measured in the degree to which the reader is able to be drawn into Maya's consciousness, and the perverse reasoning that eventually rebounds on her, removing her from the world and the reader to a third-person narrative that presents her from the point of view of her capable mother-in-law. Ultimately, the novel's tragedy lies in the polarization and disjunction of Maya and Gautama's worlds, and in the power of the outer, rationalist world to devalue the inner world of sensibility and emotion.

Voices in the City: *A Yoga of Not-Touching*
In *Voices in the City* (1965), sensitive, well-read Monisha has been married into a "respectable, middle-class Congress family completely unsuitable to [her] tastes and inclinations." Why her father agreed to the match nobody is quite sure, except that perhaps he thought that she "ought not to be encouraged in her morbid inclinations and . . . it would be a good thing for her to be settled into such a stolid, unimaginative family."[49] In the household of her husband Jiban, whose name ironically means "life," Monisha has no life of her own. There is no privacy, no silence, no opportunity for Monisha to be alone with herself; again ironically, since her life is so circumscribed. Through her narrow-barred bedroom windows she sees only other windows, other bars, and thinks of "generations of Bengali women hidden behind the barred windows of half-dark rooms, spending centuries in washing clothes, kneading dough and murmuring verses from the *Bhagavad-Gita* and the *Ramayana*, in the dim light of sooty lamps" (120). She too turns for help to the Gita, and reads from chapter two—Gandhi's favorite verses—about the *sthitaprajña,* the person of steady wisdom, free from all attachment, satisfied in the Self by the Self alone.

In his *Anasaktiyoga* Gandhi wrote: "Do your allotted work but renounce its fruit—be detached and work—have no desire for reward, and work . . . the only universal prohibition (is) desire for fruit: Desirelessness is obligatory."[50] Gandhi distinguished between the disciplined ascetic and the sensual man: "Whereas the ascetic is dead to the things of the world and lives in God, the sensual man is alive only to the things of the world and dead to the things of the spirit" (104). Ironically, in order to cope with the unbearable closeness of life in her husband's family, Monisha attempts to use the nonattachment of the Gita to withdraw into a kind of living death. "Allow us just this," she prays silently to the world, "to stand back, apart, in the shadows and watch the fire and the flames, the sacrifices that are flung into it, the celebration, the mourning, and permit us—*not to take part.*" Monisha sees the only escape from her claustrophobic existence in casting away all involvement, totally withdrawing into herself, into darkness. As she massages her mother-in-law's feet, the image of the dutiful daughter-in-law, she uses a Vedantic method of distancing oneself from one's body:[51]

> She thinks I am touching her feet. But I am not. I do not touch her, nor does she touch me—there is darkness in between. They will never reach through it to me.

Darkness, silence, and isolation thus become both prison and refuge for Monisha. Her progressively more complete withdrawal both encloses her within herself and relieves her from the constant pressures and demands of her life in the joint family. Of the family she writes, "They have indoor minds, starless and darkless. Mine is all dark now. The blessing it is" (139). Here is a seeming paradox: darkness has become freedom to Monisha because it represents a total lack of contact with the world. But the drab indoor world of the family is neither dark, nor illumined, but a kind of living death. Complete withdrawal is preferable to the enclosed half-life, where the individual has no time or space for herself. And yet her diary is evidence that she desperately wants to reach out and communicate; she has been forced into isolation.

One afternoon, when itinerant musicians come into the family courtyard to perform, Monisha leans on the rails of the upper balcony with the other women of the household listening to the ravaged female singer, who sings throatily of love, betrayal, and the intense pains and pleasures of life. All the women respond with corresponding waves of emotion to the songs, all but Monisha who alone is "untouched." She begins to understand that she fears the "raw passion" evoked by the musicians. Then the realization breaks in upon her that life has never really touched her.[52]

> Why am I so sad? Why am I so afraid?...I have lost touch...They put me away in a steel container, a thick glass cubicle, and I have lived in it all my life...I am locked apart from all of them, they cannot touch me, they can only lip-read and misinterpret. (239)

As the singing comes to an end, Monisha feels that her whole life has been to no purpose. "What a waste, what a waste it has been, this life enclosed in a locked container, merely as an observer." She is suddenly "on fire to experience desire, to experience feeling." She runs into the kitchen and struggles along the empty corridor to her room carrying a heavy tin, a red funnel, and a box of matches. "Now that action had seized her in its maniac grip, she seemed to have seized the very secrets of action itself" (241). All at once she is caught in the "embrace" of the oil and the flames. As the heat and the smoke and the searing pain envelop her, she begins to fight it, realizing too late that "it was not what she wanted" (242). Denied productive engagement with the world, Monisha deeply fears and desires life, feeling, action. Action she gets, with a vengeance: frustrated action turned in upon herself.

It is rare to read an account of an Indian woman's death by burning that does not invoke either the figure of the sati or, since the second wave of the Indian women's movement, the victim of a dowry murder. In neither case is the victim able to present her viewpoint, although in the latter, at least, women are generally speaking *for* other women, while in the former, men are talking to other men, and only ostensibly *about* women.[53] *Voices in the City* is unusual in that it refrains both from comparing the passive Monisha to a sati in any crude or simplistic way, and from giving others the sole power to make meaning of her death. Monisha's withdrawal, her yoga of not-touching or allowing herself to be touched, has been so complete that the sensation of burning momentarily seems to her like real living. By the time the pain changes her mind, it is too late. She fights the flames, screaming "No!" until she loses consciousness. *Voices* neither glorifies nor justifies Monisha's act, neither sanctifies nor sanitizes the stark materiality of the pain and its accompanying lucidity. Desai gives her the opportunity to explain herself by permitting the reader to enter her consciousness until the very moment of death.[54] However, in the aftermath of the suicide, after a scene in which Desai does not draw a veil over the horrific sight of the burned body, Monisha's act does prove to be redemptive for her alienated brother Nirode, who is awakened into a new responsibility for life by his beloved sister's death, her ultimate failure to communicate.[55] Although in a state of heightened consciousness he feels that he understands the impulse behind her suicide, no one (but the reader) will ever know the whole truth.

Through Monisha's tragic death we see that her recourse to the Gita's yoga of nonattachment, interpreted as withdrawal from life, becomes self-deluding and self-destructive, rather than a means of self-realization. We also see the glaring discrepancies between her pre-independence hopes and the post-independence *status quo*, and the disillusionment and cynicism that results. Every character in the novel, male and female, struggles in his or her own way to engage with this post-independence reality, to find ways of acting while maintaining their own integrity.

Anita Desai rarely reduces her observations of choices, actions, and their consequences to one character. Her composite protagonists together build up a picture of choices and responses, being two, three, or more siblings or friends who can make different life choices based on gender, social or class position, or simply personality. There is no pressure in her work to consolidate a unitary protagonist. In *Voices in the City*, each of four siblings who come of age in the 1950s and 1960s responds differently to the overwhelming pressures of city and family. The eldest brother, Arun, escapes the conflict by leaving India to study abroad. It is clear, as he leaves, that he will never return. The youngest sister, Amla, escapes through her vivacious, optimistic nature, which refuses to dwell on the horrors of life. But Nirode and Monisha, the brother and sister in the middle, experience all its hypocrisies and disillusionments with full force.[56] Nirode, almost Monisha's psychic twin, is an angry, sensitive young man and an underpaid writer, living from hand to mouth in the urban jungle of Calcutta, his protective mechanism a cynical nihilism as his sister's was a psychic withdrawal.

Monisha's younger sister, Amla, who has come of age since independence and just completed a commercial art degree, cannot see why Monisha did not rebel if she was so dissatisfied with her parents' match for her. Amla herself is pragmatic and self-assured, and has no trouble speaking her mind. Rather than brooding, she gets out and acts. Monisha's passive behavior, indeed, her whole mode of being, is incomprehensible to Amla. There is a parallel incomprehension on the part of nationalist feminists of the older generation, whose lives were given meaning and purpose by the independence movement.[57] Monisha's eccentric aunt Lila cannot understand her niece's lack of drive and political commitment, and the younger generation's ungrateful disaffection.

> You belong to such a uniquely free generation . . . At last we have won our freedom and you can do as you choose . . .
>
> When we were young, we believed, we stood on the rooftop and shouted to the world that we would come and conquer it! But the young don't do that any more. How sad to be so realistic, so cynical, so without dreams . . . (145–146)

Amla resents her Aunt's idealistic speechmaking, so unconnected with the difficulties actually being faced by the post-independence generation of women. "It isn't that," she retorts. "Perhaps it is just that we believe we should do things first, then shout about it." Forced to look back for a moment on the unhappiness and disappointments of her own life, Aunt Lila admits gruffly, "Perhaps we didn't achieve so much after all... but we did win freedom, remember that! We gave your generation your freedom, and it is your heritage to do with as you please. I envy you" (146).

Monisha's death is not the end of the story: *Voices in the City* begins and ends with her brother Nirode. After his beloved sister's suicide, Nirode has a sudden vision of the meaning of her gesture, however tragically misplaced. He sees that it was an effort to live, to burn with a brilliant flame, and he himself is fired with a resolve to realize that effort in his life, so that her own ultimate gesture will not have been in vain. His final vision is of Calcutta, of his mother, of life itself—as the Goddess Kali, divinity, destruction, creation, the entire spectrum of reality rolled into one. Life includes it all, and must be embraced in its entirety if it is to be lived. In this final image, we again see Anita Desai resisting the oversimplification of the either/or and straining toward a much more complex reality. P. Lal of the Calcutta Writers' Workshop acknowledged this complexity in a review of *Voices in the City* written at the time of its publication: "[P]art of the greatness of *Voices,* and some of its failure, comes from its urgent desire to possess and express the vast vision, to contain multitudes and contradictions. Anita Desai is a compulsive over-reacher."[58]

In her early novels, Desai is more withdrawn, more claustrophobically internal, as she turns away like a sensitive plant from the hurly-burly of the larger society and concentrates on her portraits, in minute detail, of intricate, labyrinthine workings of the human mind, often the human mind descending into madness. In this she is reminiscent of Dharma the artist in *Voices in the City*, who withdraws from the horrors of Calcutta, filling his canvasses with scientifically accurate enlargements of insects drawn in unnerving and excruciating detail. Desai's insistent interiority in her earlier novels reflects a distaste both for the kind of social novel that refuses to let individuals speak for themselves and a social structure that does not give individuals privacy but manipulates them into representatives of a social type, so that, especially for women, they are turned into symbols and spoken for by others, while they are shut silently behind a phony façade. As if compensating for the silences of isolation and failed communication, Desai seems to fill every available space with words, words that seem to come tumbling out and crowding into every available opening in the obsessive overwriting produced in a fevered brain condemned to talking to itself. Perhaps, just as Dharma eventually realizes that he needs to get back in touch with city life if he is to restore vitality and a sense of proportion to his art, Desai the artist senses that she too must find a way to reconnect with the destructive, yet life-giving public sphere.[59]

Where Shall We Go This Summer?: *The Impossible No*
Questioning the notion that women's writing is "always and essentially resistant," Rajeswari Sunder Rajan has noted that women's "resistance is not always a positivity; it may be no more than a negative agency, an absence of acquiescence in one's oppression."[60] Several of the urban, middle-class heroines of Anita Desai's early novels struggle to achieve even such negative agency, which Sita in *Where Shall We Go This Summer?* (1975) describes as "the impossible No." Sensitive, idealistic Sita has found herself pregnant, for the fifth time. Middle-class married life, for Sita, is a

brutal, grinding rat race, not the "solidity and security" she had hoped for when she married but "dull tedium and hopeless disappointment." She longs to withdraw from society with her unborn child, to shelter it from the cruel world, to protect it from life. "I want to *keep* it—I don't want it to be born."[61] She longs for a magic that will prevent it from being born. Never once does she consider abortion; she simply sees herself at a point in her life where she must have the courage to say No, even if she is bound to be defeated in the process, rather than to take the easier path of acquiescence. She is desperate to find a great "No" that will give her a positive way to reject the "real world." Must rejection always be seen as the act of a weak person? Must acceptance of life with all its evils always be the socially approved choice? Against the inevitability of this child's birth, Sita holds out a wild, irrational hope that she can will it to remain unborn. She returns, as if into a cocoon of magic and illusion, to Manori, her childhood island home, which has lain empty for twenty years since 1947, when her father (a charismatic, saintly nationalist leader, full of contradictions, known as the second Gandhi) died and Sita was swept away in marriage by the eminently sensible Raman.[62]

The great, inaccessible figure of the Father is almost synonymous with the Nation, neither of whom will take responsibility for Sita after her marriage, which was simultaneous with national independence. The father's betrayal of trust is a recurrent theme in Desai's novels. In the upbringing of his daughter, the enlightened father gives her expectations for her future, which he betrays in his marriage choice for her; and after marriage, he dies or washes his hands of her. In each of these first three novels, he is simply "father" or—even more impersonally—"the father." In *Where Shall We Go This Summer*, Sita's naïve faith in her father is explicitly associated with the expectations of nationalism, which are crushed after marriage and Independence. She has grown up as a motherless child, her mother rumored to have left her husband and children and run away to the holy city of Benares in an act of renunciation, disappearing without a trace. After her own marriage, Sita tried in vain to locate her mother. Her father, in contrast, though long dead, has left "not merely traces, but what could be called monuments" (88).

All the expectations of Sita's girlhood have been shown to be hollow in wifehood. Her father is dead and gone and all his ideals have come to nothing. She retreats to her father's home, only to find, as she has really known all along, that she must return to the city. The islanders of Manori think nothing of this undistinguished daughter. They remember only the Great Father, and his other, dutiful daughter, Rekha, Sita's placid, demure elder sister (or stepsister—it is rumored that they share only their father, but that Sita and her brother Jivan have a different mother), who is so differ-ent from Sita in every way. Rekha loses her individuality along with her name when she becomes a symbol of pure Indian womanhood as the All India Radio Nightingale, always singing *bhajans* (Hindu devotional songs from the *bhakti* tradi-tion). A similar female figure recurs in Salman Rushdie's novel *Midnight's Children*, in Saleem's sister, who is lost to him forever when she becomes Jamila Singer the Bulbul-el-Din (or Nightingale of the Faith), a national monument, symbol of the purity of the Nation and the Faith. It is interesting to contrast the critical rendering of the subsuming of individuality into a national symbol on the part of Desai and Rushdie with novelist Bhabani Bhattacharya's entirely unproblematized portrayal of such a figure in his *Music for Mohini*. Mohini also represents pure Indian woman-hood and sings for All India Radio. However, in Bhattacharya's novel she is the idealized protagonist who literally must be wedded to tradition in order to enable India to enter the modern age with its Indian "essence" intact.[63]

As much as Sita tells herself that her desire is sane, even noble, the world tells her that it is crazy, self-indulgent, and irresponsible. Even the two children she has taken away with her long to be back with their father in the city, and in the end it is her sensible daughter Menaka who "betrays" her by summoning her father to the island to take them all back to Bombay in time for Menaka's medical school applications. All that is left of the charmed childhood is a crumbling old house, alcoholic servants, and disillusionment. In the end, Sita succumbs to the necessity of return to another bout of motherhood and the never-ending round of middle-class existence, not because her feelings have changed, but because the family has a force and a life of its own and lays claim to her. She does gain a new understanding of her natural instinctive desire to hide and protect the new life within her, but she is unable to explain it to her husband. It will remain forever unspoken, as she forces herself to laugh with her husband, "gulping down the words of explanation…in painful swallows" so as not to upstage him (151). Ultimately, Sita must suppress her individual self and her own personal insights. She is not allowed to reject the world, or her role as a wife and mother; she has no choice but to return. The baby is growing inexorably within her, and she cannot help but admire her husband's dogged good sense and capability as she lets him shepherd them all home. After she has gone, the islanders all agree, "she was plain…She was mad…We will only remember *him*, the father…Who is she?…let her go" (157).

In each of these three early novels, Desai's protagonist is caught between the two halves of a paradox, an ironic impossibility that nonetheless encapsulates her situation. In *Cry, the Peacock*, Maya's impossible predicament was encapsulated in her deranged rationalization of Gautama's interpretation of the Gita: because he was utterly detached, she reasoned, death would mean as little to him as did life. The irony was that her very action to save her life condemned her to life-imprisonment. In *Voices in the City*, Monisha was condemned to confinement without privacy. Consulting the Gita, Monisha practiced detachment and withdrew from life completely. Later, burning with the desire for life, she burned herself to death. Her attempt to detach herself prevented her from living and her attempt to engage killed her. Sita's predicament was her unwanted fifth pregnancy, the life struggling to be born that could not be, but had to be. The paradox lay in her desire to protect the child's life by preventing it from being born. Desai quotes a poem by Cavafy to sum up Sita's impossible desire to "say the great No":

> He who refuses does not repent. Should he be asked again, he would say No again. And yet that No—the right No—crushes him for the rest of his life.[64]

Sita had to return, "gulping down" her words. She was both denied and crushed by the great No. She can find no acceptable way to detach herself from the world.

Each of Desai's young protagonists has attempted action, but been denied it, whether through engagement, detachment, or rejection. Instead, they are faced with impossibly polarized choices. Although Anita Desai herself would be the last to suggest that her work is in any way representative of anything but itself, her heroines scream into the gulf between nationalist ideology and reality in the post-independence period, and fall into the predicaments in which the colonially constructed nationalism has placed women. Desai's truth-telling is not restricted to women, but applies to the nationalist formulation as a whole, which produces such "irrationally divided personalities" as her characters Gautama and Maya, Raman and Sita. Protagonists in Desai's novels struggle to find a way out of a paralyzing duality and a constructive way to engage with the larger social organism, failing which, they must themselves be destroyed.

Fire on the Mountain: *The Ashes of Disillusionment*
In spite of continuities of theme with Desai's earlier novels, *Fire on the Mountain* (1977) in several different ways marks a culmination and a transition in Anita Desai's work. It won the prestigious Sahitya Akademi Award and inaugurated a new phase in her career—and, as it turned out, in her writing as well. Unlike her earlier female protagonists, the protagonist in *Fire on the Mountain* becomes thoroughly disillusioned; when her strenuous efforts to achieve and maintain detachment are exposed as a self-deception, she is forced to face this knowledge squarely.

Nanda Kaul, a widow and a great-grandmother, is enjoying the seclusion of her hill station home, savoring the reclusiveness of her old age after a lifetime of the heavy responsibilities of home, husband, and children. But it seems that a woman is never free of family responsibilities, even in old age, the traditional stage of renunciation in Hindu life. When her daughter writes to announce that she is sending her granddaughter Raka to live with her for an indefinite period of time, Nanda Kaul reacts with feelings of violation. When the child arrives, Nanda Kaul finds with alarm that all her carefully cultivated detachment is falling away from her. It seems that her nonattachment had merely been the mirror-image of attachment. Her great-granddaughter, however, appears to be a new and different breed of girl, almost autistic in her indifference; *her* nonattachment appears to be innate. She loves nothing better than to clamber alone up and down the craggy hillsides like a mountain goat, threading her way unconcerned through rubbish chutes, latrines, and the contaminated debris from an animal research laboratory, while the older woman tries in vain to look up and away, to contemplate eagles and kites as they seem to soar above the nasty realities of life.

The reader becomes increasingly aware of Nanda Kaul's growing attachment to Raka and of the troubled past that she has been attempting to escape through nonattachment. At the end of the novel, as Nanda receives the news by telephone of the murder of her old friend Ila Das, she is suddenly confronted with the awareness of the denial of a lifetime, and is thoroughly disillusioned about the nature of her own self-deception.[65] Her nonattachment has been rooted in a need to shut out unpleasant truths about the hollowness of her marriage, her husband's lifetime infidelity, and her powerlessness to do anything about it. Ila Das, as a less-privileged single woman, was forced to act to support herself, and chose a path of social work that brought her into conflict with vested interests and resulted in her murder. Now reality stares Nanda in the face, and she can no longer evade it. Nevertheless, although utterly disillusioned about her past, she still feels helpless to act. Young Raka, however, has no such problems: she quite literally burns it all down. Her instinctive reaction to hypocrisy, powerlessness, and delusion is much more direct (if no less destructive): she simply sets the entire hillside alight in one purifying conflagration. "Look, Nani," she whispers, as her great-grandmother loses hold of the telephone and hangs her head, speechless: "I have set the forest on fire."[66]

In "The Seed of Destruction" an essay written in the aftermath of Prime Minister Rajiv Gandhi's June 1991 assassination, Anita Desai spoke of the inevitability of the violence of political disillusionment gathering force and breaking out in an unstoppable wave of destruction. She argued that the Congress model of the nation-state had sown the seed of its own destruction with its corruption, elitism, manipulation of the masses, social injustice, and increasing centralization of power, and that the ever-present tensions and simmering frustrations of the masses threatened to erupt and explode at any moment:

> The climax has been reached, predictably bloody and awful, and a period of catharsis follows for India. Watching the funeral pyre flame and flicker, one could be forgiven for thinking one saw India upon that pyre, burning, out under a sun half-obscured by smoke and the dust of the open cremation field. Not in the sense that Rajiv Gandhi represented India and with his death it is extinguished, but in the sense that the fires that have been lit are likely to rage further and higher and engulf the entire country. Then, perhaps, a clearing will be made in which a new beginning will sprout.[67]

Behind the sober world-weariness of the older woman, one senses the spirit of Raka, impatient to burn it all to the ground, clear the air and start afresh. For the time being, however, there was only fire and a great deal of smoke.

"Nothing's Over, Ever": Clear Light of Day *(1980)*

The protagonists of Anita Desai's next novel, *Clear Light of Day*, return to face the past and struggle to come to terms with it, rather than persist in their physical or psychological alienation. Rather than allowing themselves to be defined out of the picture, they begin, however tentatively, to redefine themselves in terms other than the normative national models. Increasingly, Desai's protagonists and plotlines are enabled to look backward in preparation for moving forward, to find the strength to engage with the larger public sphere, and to raise questions that her earlier texts were unable to articulate.

Clear Light of Day begins with a deliberate attempt to reopen the past, in full awareness of its pain. Tara, second-youngest of four now-adult siblings, has returned with her diplomat-husband from the United States to visit her childhood home in Old Delhi where her elder sister Bim (Bimala) and her mentally retarded younger brother Baba still live. Their eldest brother Raja has lived in Hyderabad since Partition/Independence, where he went to visit the Hyder Alis (their Muslim neighbors until Partition forced them to flee), and married their daughter. Bold, strong-willed Bim never married, staying at home and arranging for Tara's wedding. She now oversees the family business, looks after Baba, the house, and the Hyder Ali's dog Badshah, and supports herself by teaching History at the nearby women's college. Raja and Bim, once inseparable, are now estranged, as she resents his having abandoned her, as she sees it, with all the burdens and responsibilities that should properly have been his. The timid Tara, who is soon to attend Raja's daughter's wedding, seeks to reconcile the family, to heal the rifts that have divided them all these years, to ask questions of the past, which until recently has been too painful to contemplate.

There are no escapist longings for soaring eagles here; from the outset the cuckoo's domestic note is struck, and the whole novel remains determinedly earthbound, prepared to expose memory's raw nerves. Tara does not recoil as painful memories are repeatedly unearthed. Two motifs recur throughout the novel, a tiny snail, "an eternal, miniature Sisyphus," and a crushed fledgling in its shell, never to be hatched. The snail evokes the tortoise of the Gita in *Cry, the Peacock*, a creature who withdraws into its shell as the *sthitaprajna* or man of wisdom withdraws from the world of the senses. The crushed bird evokes the fetus that Sita was desperate to protect from the world in her escape to the island in *Where Shall We Go This Summer?* But neither Tara nor Bim withdraw from the world. On the contrary, they are increasingly enabled to look clear-eyed upon their shared past and to listen past the roaring silences that swirl around the traumatic events of that summer of 1947.

In *Clear Light of Day*, while the sisters show strength and staying power, their brothers, in different ways, escape and withdraw. Tara and Bim, although temperamentally very different, both struggle—each in her own way—to engage with their personal pasts and the present in order to heal the rifts in themselves and the family. Raja, with his romantic childhood dreams of heroism and splendor, broke out of the enclosed, claustrophobic women's world of his childhood. Although he pursued the ideals of his youth, he has rejected the responsibilities of the eldest son, leaving everything to Bim, and has not returned to Delhi for more than twenty years. Baba was himself born like the snail: timid, vulnerable, reluctant to emerge from his shell, he hardly leaves his room, much less the house, and never speaks. The few times he ventures forth into the world outside the walled family compound, the harshness and cruelty of the world drive him back into the safety of home. His sole activity is endlessly replaying old records on an HMV gramophone.

Tara has always been a timid, unambitious person. As a child, while her elder siblings Bim and Raja memorized romantic poetry, roved and adventured down by the banks of the river Jamuna, and dreamed aloud of becoming heroic men and women of action, Tara stayed at home with their widowed aunt, Mira-*masi*, and dreamed of becoming a mother. Bim loved school and was a born leader; but it was Tara, ironically, who moved abroad and saw the world by marrying the smooth-talking Bakul at eighteen, while Bim stayed on in her childhood home and cared for Baba.

Tara now sees that she married because she had to escape, to flee the nest, but, like a homing pigeon, she is compelled nonetheless to return regularly—not to India, but to her family: "We must come," she tells Bim, "if we are not to lose touch, I with all of you, and he [Bakul] with the country." Bakul intones a diplomat's platitudes about the Wonder that was India:

> The Taj Mahal—the Bhagavad Gita—Indian philosophy—music—art—the great, immortal values of ancient India . . . [W]hy talk of local politics, party disputes . . . such matters as will soon pass into oblivion? These aren't important when compared with India, eternal India.

But by the late 1970s the Gita has come to be associated with all the corruption and hypocrisy of officialdom. Bim retorts that it is best he lives abroad if that is how he feels. If he were a government servant in India, she argues, the escape into a glorious past might not be so easy: "I'm not sure if you could ignore bribery and corruption, red-tapism, famine, caste warfare and all that. In fact, living here, working here, you might easily forget the Taj Mahal and the message of the Gita" (35). But Tara hardly hears their discussion; it is irrelevant to her. She needs to return, not to align herself with India's ancient verities, but because she feels her deepest self to be bound up with her brothers and sister and their family home.

Bakul complains that whenever Tara returns home, she reverts to her old passivity and inertia. He has "trained her and made her into an active, organized woman who looked up her engagement book every morning, made plans and programs for the day ahead..." (21) But Tara's task is not one that demands action as Bakul defines it; rather, it requires a clear-eyed look at her past, the shared pasts of all her family especially during that nightmare summer of 1947, when India was in flames. There is no escape from this task, regardless of whether she moves to the other end of the earth or whether, like Bim, she stays home. Ultimately, the choice to fight or flee has little to do with physical location; if one refuses to look reality in the eye, one will eventually be forced to return and face it. Bim has been as blind as Tara, even though she has stayed in the family home and shouldered all the family responsibilities. And Tara's escape, it turns out, had been a youthful act of self-preservation; now, stronger and more detached, she is better prepared to plumb her childhood guilt and fears.

Ultimately, the changes that take place are subtle but significant changes in perspective. Tara realizes how much her own limited perspective has distorted her vision. Memories of events that have haunted her for years turn out to be based on misunderstandings, dwindling into insignificance when she hears Bim's version of them. Her image of Bim, the shrinking younger sister's image of a bold, all-powerful elder sister, must also undergo a number of modifications as she gains deeper insights into the formative events of her childhood. Just as Bakul's interminable pontifications on the eternal India bear no relation to Tara's current need to understand and repair the rifts within her family, so his "banal untruthful reassurances... about measures being taken... about Mountbatten's goodwill... about Nehru's idealism and integrity" (71) offered no reassurance to Bim on the eve of Partition, when the ideals of the national movement were betrayed. In the summer of 1947, as their parents and Aunt Mira were dying, and Raja and Tara were leaving, everything was left up to her: "there was no one else."

When Bim was a girl she and her beloved elder brother Raja had longed to be romantic heroes, riding white stallions and fighting glorious battles. When Raja escaped his family responsibilities through his elopement at Partition, and Bim was left to bear all the burdens of Baba, the family house, and her father's business, she came to resent her abandonment bitterly. In conventional terms, Bim is a failure, left aging and unmarried in the decaying family home with the specter of her widowed Aunt Mira's tragic end hanging over her. And yet Desai quietly compels the reader to redefine what constitutes a hero and to recognize Bim's heroism in having chosen to reject an offer of marriage in order to assume the responsibility of supporting herself and Baba, and of maintaining the business and the home. When Bim herself comes to recognize and appreciate her own actions, she is able to let go of the resentment she has held on to for so long. Moreover, Desai also enables the reader to acknowledge Tara's triumph in forcing her elder sister to confront their shared past.

Over the course of the novel, the reader's perception of who the protagonist is undergoes a series of changes. First, it would appear to be Tara, the foreign-returned diplomat's wife, then it shifts to Bim, as the daughter who has taken on the responsibility of the eldest son in his absence, and finally there is the recognition that the novel's protagonist is not an individual, but the interconnected web of the family as a whole.

As Tara keeps urging Bim to reopen long-repressed memories and old wounds, Bim's anger and resentment swells until she vents it on the innocent Baba. Overcome with shame, she has a momentary epiphany in which she sees the tattered web of life and love connecting them all, and recognizes the incompleteness of her own love and her need to forgive and be forgiven. However, the fleeting sense of wholeness does not eliminate the need to continue the struggle on the ground. She also realizes how different she is from her sister, how she needs her solitude as much as Tara needs her family. In their parting scene, as Bim tries to get Tara to stop worrying the past and leave it behind, Tara insists on continuing to work toward reconciliation. Finally a tearful Tara wrests an agreement from her: "It's never over. Nothing's over, ever." And as she hurries Tara and her family out of the house Bim settles with Baba into a peaceful silence, accepting this truth at last.

In the closing scene at the concert of Mulk and his ancient guru, Bim has another moment of understanding. A line from Eliot's *Four Quartets*, much loved by her estranged brother, comes to her: "Time the destroyer is time the preserver."[68] For the first time she sees "her own house and its particular history" not as something binding, something to escape, but as containing, linking, nourishing "her whole family, with all their separate histories and experiences." And the soil, the "secret darkness" from which they draw their sustenance, contains within it "all time, past and future." Mulk's guru sings two couplets of Iqbal's in his cracked old voice, and Bim's joy is complete. Iqbal was Raja's favorite Urdu poet. As she embraces truths of the two poetic traditions she heals rifts, not only between herself and her brother, but rifts made by history itself. While nationalist history remains nothing but a destructive force, Bakul's Taj Mahal and quotations from the Gita notwithstanding, Iqbal holds up an ideal that was repressed and banished at Partition, for India as much as for Bim, an ideal of love and dynamic engagement with the world.[69]

*   *   *

Even as they struggled to reject the dominant nationalism, Anita Desai's novels of the 1960s and 1970s found themselves entrapped by its codes. Throughout the colonial and the postcolonial periods to date, individual women's voices have been silenced as the category of Woman has been used in the interests of other, ostensibly greater, categories, such as Religion or Nation. Revisiting women's writing and listening to their individual voices can begin to "ensure that a woman's voice is listened to as such and not as a reverberation of something else."[70] The important recognition in Desai's novels is that the nationalist discourse is not appropriated successfully by women, even the upper-caste, middle-class, and elite women who comprise her female protagonists. Her protagonists fail to constitute themselves as subject-agents of action. For them, the nationalist synthesis is not an enabling formulation but a destructive synergy of patriarchal discourses of power. The problem of action in these novels is an intractable problem of language and definition, as it becomes clear that the terms of social engagement are set elsewhere and for others. Karma remains resolutely colonial for Desai's post-independence bourgeoisie.

Clear Light of Day was published in 1980, the year before Salman Rushdie's *Midnight's Children*. If *Fire on the Mountain* in many ways represented an ending, or at least a turning point, in Desai's work, then coming as it did on the brink of the 1980s, predating the departures signaled by the publication of *Midnight's Children*, *Clear Light of Day* had much to say about the importance of "agreeing to a continuance" rather than succumbing to the urge for escape.[71] As we shall see in Chapter Five, despite Rushdie's undeniable influence on Indian English fiction, writing by women in the 1980s and 1990s shows a remarkable continuity of themes and preoccupations with women's writing in earlier decades. However, *Clear Light of Day* was significantly different from Desai's earlier works; it prefigured several of *Midnight's Children's* defining characteristics—a preoccupation with memory, a recognition that the past is double-edged, and an acknowledgment that, for better or worse, individual lives are bound up in the life of the nation. It has been a nationalist truism that the individual life must be given meaning in the service of the nation. But the reverse lesson—that national history is made meaningful only through the scrutiny of individual lives—is something that Anita Desai's writing has been insisting upon quietly all along. Her novels have always asserted the importance of the individual over the institution, rejecting the lofty-sounding flights of political rhetoric that truncate or deny the reality of individual experience, and upholding the personal voice that is suppressed or excluded in the act of national self-definition.

CHAPTER FOUR

TURNING VICTIM INTO PROTAGONIST?
MIDNIGHT'S CHILDREN AND THE NATIONAL
NARRATIVES OF THE 1980S

The Indian English literary scene in the late 1970s was in the doldrums. In *Indian Literature*, the official Sahitya Akademi publication, the Annual Review of 1980 summed up the contemporary Indian English literary scene as "mediocre and... meretricious."[1] As late as 1981, a critic could still refer to Indian English fiction as a "vestigial curiosity."[2] The novel in English seemed to be stagnating, in terms of both content and form, engaged neither in social movements nor in literary experimentation. The Indian nation had been in crisis since Indira Gandhi's 1975 State of Emergency. By 1980, nation and novel had reached a state of impasse: both the unitary model of the modern nation-state and the narrative of the modern Indian English novel needed rethinking. At this particular historical moment the pressing problem of action for the English-educated classes, so long self-defined in relation to the Indian nation, was how to reformulate that relationship creatively. This was the problem addressed by Salman Rushdie in *Midnight's Children* (*MC*).[3] It broke both deadlocks simultaneously, being at once eulogy and elegy for the unitary model of nation state that had failed to deliver the promises of the Indian freedom movement, and also a literary and conceptual model that opened up new possibilities for reimagining and representing enabling relationships between self and nation. The task of this chapter is to examine just how *MC* sets out to turn alienation into agency.[4]

Midnight's Children as a Breakthrough

The 1981 publication of Salman Rushdie's *Midnight's Children* was a watershed in the post-independence development of the Indian English novel, so much so that the term "post-Rushdie" has come to refer to the decade or so afterward, in which a wave of novels appeared, by established as well as by young writers, that were clearly influenced by *MC*. Unashamedly self-centered, Rushdie's novel celebrates the creative tensions between personal and national identity, playing up and playing with both their polarity and their unity, recognizing, like its protagonist Saleem Sinai, that if the individual is "handcuffed to history"[5] whether he likes it or not, he can make a virtue out of that necessity. Sparks fly between the private and public realms, making artistic fireworks where there had previously been deadening dichotomies. *MC* neither denies nor seeks to transcend polarities, but embraces them as artistic method, rejecting nothing, celebrating the resulting chaotic multiplicity, even if it crushes the protagonist himself into a billion pieces. *MC* brings heresies into the open and transforms them into prophecies. What had been the Indian English novel's problems now suddenly became its trademarks.

The number of new Indian English novelists published throughout the 1980s testify to *MC*'s tremendous influence, not merely on superficial would-be imitators (of which there were several), or on the metropolitan demand for Indian fiction (which has since been considerable), but also on the fundamental conception of the national narrative. My central claim in this chapter is that *MC* enacted a discursive reconfiguration of the relationship between Self and Nation. I seek to demonstrate how it did so, and also why and how it opened up new spaces for a new crop of writers in English. *MC* declared that there were as many valid versions of Indian identity as there were Indians. This concept proved to be liberating for many Indian English writers, allowing them to break the polarized stalemate between self and nation that had caught the Indian English novel in a kind of ideological and artistic holding pattern for two decades. The 1980s and 1990s were distinguished by an Indian English literary explosion as writers found themselves free to speak in a multiplicity of voices and write in a multiplicity of modes.

In asserting the literary influence of *MC*, I do not assign it a uniquely privileged status or make an exaggerated claim for its centrality, although it clearly had an important influence on Indian English fiction in the 1980s. Rather, I employ it as a literary marker of the post-Emergency crisis in the Indian national idea, both expressing and embodying the crisis, both celebrating and mourning the idea. The formal and conceptual breakthroughs that Rushdie's novel achieved set the tone for the 1980s and ended a certain stagnation of both form and content that had characterized the Indian English novel of the previous two decades. I explore how both *MC* and the increasing fragmentation of the times, primarily brought on by the crisis of the dominant model of nationalism, influenced other Indian English writers and enabled them to enter imaginatively into new relationships with the nation. I also suggest the limits and limitations of that influence.

When *MC* was published in 1981, winning that year's prestigious Booker Prize (and subsequently, the prize for the best of twenty-five years of Bookers), it was hailed both in and out of India as a literary masterpiece, and almost immediately became a kind of benchmark against which both writers and readers began to assess new novels. But it has become virtually impossible to look back at *MC* without seeing the novel through the filter of the events of the past two decades. It is hard to remember, or even to acknowledge, the enthusiasm with which its publication was greeted in India—not because of its politics (there were always quarrels with that), or because of the accuracy of its representation of Indian history (it did not even pretend to that), but because of its exuberance of language and style, its combination of hilarious comedy and scathing political satire, its triumphant overconfidence, and, not least, its very success. When Rushdie toured the country in 1983 in a "triumphal homecoming," people flocked to see him.[6] At the British Council in Delhi, fully 700 people arrived at a reading where no more than 300 had been expected and the organizers had to set up loudspeakers on the lawns outside.[7] According to a 1988 article in the Indian weekly, *Sunday*, "copies of pirated editions (of *MC*) flooded the pavements before the paperback edition reached India."[8] In 1984, Shyamala Narayan wrote: "Publishers claim that the novel has sold 4,000 copies in hardcover, and 45,000 in paperback (in addition to the pirated editions); these sales figures are unprecedented for an Indian-English novelist."[9] "*MC*'s commercial success certainly helped to pave the way for future Indian English writers, as publishers in India became more attentive to the domestic market for fiction in English, and publishers in Britain and the United States became more receptive to new writers from India."[10]

Nowadays, critics both inside and out of India are much more cautious, less likely to embrace Rushdie or claim him for India; he tends to be discussed as a diasporic writer, and his influence on the Indian literary scene is often criticized as having negatively influenced a group of already elite, alienated, or expatriate Indian English writers, and intensified the neglect of Indian-language writers.[11] Of course, chief among the events that have so radically changed critical perceptions of *MC* and its author since 1981 was the 1989 Iranian *fatwa* against Rushdie for his novel *The Satanic Verses*. Its intellectual and political fallout was disastrous, both for Rushdie himself and for the dialogue between the "West" and fundamentalist Islam, always strained, now more polarized than ever (ironic, this, for a writer whose stated aim was to open up space on the very horns of a dilemma). And at least as important as the *fatwa* to our changed view of *MC* has been the deepening crisis of the nation-state and the worldwide rise of myriad Indian and other subnationalisms throughout the last two decades. To take a few landmark events in one rather prominent Indian family as an example: when *MC* was written, Indira Gandhi, demonized in the novel as the Widow, was still very much alive; she was assassinated by her Sikh bodyguards in 1984. Her son Sanjay, whom she was grooming as her successor and who figured as the "labia-lipped" goon squad leader in *MC*, was still alive; but he was killed in a plane crash in 1980, after the novel had been completed. Her son the airline pilot Rajiv, who was never meant for the limelight, and who received barely a mention in *MC*, succeeded her as Prime Minister and was himself assassinated by the Tamil Tigers in 1991. Historical events have indeed proven stranger than works of fiction, even one with Salman Rushdie's own fantastic mix of ingredients, and the megalo-maniacal claim by protagonist Saleem Sinai that the elimination of his family from the face of the earth was the hidden purpose of the entire Indo-Pakistani war of 1965 no longer seems so very far-fetched.

It may also be useful to remember that the publication of *MC* preceded the contemporary critique of nationalism and the social and political fragmentation of the large, totalizing nation-state. It preceded the worldwide explosion of simmering ethnic and religious nationalisms, from Ayodhya to Kosovo. It also preceded the end of the Cold War, and the rise of the New World Order and the global economy of the 1990s. And as for scholars of nationalism and postcoloniality, in 1981 Partha Chatterjee, Eric Hobsbawm, Benedict Anderson, and Ernest Gellner had not yet published their works on nationalism, colonialism, and the nation-state. Frederic Jameson and Aijaz Ahmed had not yet had their now-famous exchange about whether the Third World novel is necessarily a national allegory. Still years away from its now-widespread "dissemiNation" was Homi Bhabha's *Nation and Narration*, and scholars were not yet speaking of nations as acts of the collective imagination and "India" in quotation marks. Rushdie's beloved Bombay was still a tolerant, cosmopolitan city years away from the riots and bomb blasts of 1993, from the nativist Shiv Sena government of 1994, and from changing its name to Mumbai in 1995. Rushdie as a Bombay Muslim, albeit a thoroughly secular one, could in 1981 identify affectionately with the elephant-headed god Ganesh, the scribe of the epic *Mahabharata*, [12] as a chubby, endearing deity, the epitome of auspiciousness, and one who brings all newly begun enterprises to a happy conclusion; while less than fifteen years later in *The Moor's Last Sigh*, Rushdie could no longer represent him as a benign figure. In 1981, the world was certainly a fresher place in which to entertain notions of self and nation, although perhaps also a more confined one.

There has been a flood of critical writing attempting to account for different aspects of *MC*'s success and literary influence. Critics have written of the multiple literary influences on *MC*, and on Rushdie's postmodernism, his narrative art, and his deconstructive use of history.[13] Critics in India have noted, first and foremost, that nothing succeeds like success, and that the novel's commercial success outside India created a metropolitan demand for Indian writing in English and a corresponding new confidence and productivity on the part of writers in English within India. For example, *Sunday* magazine characterized *MC* as "a confident novel," one that "offered no explanations, proffered no apologies, sought no compromise." This confidence was seen as a "refreshing departure from the past," when Indian writers were "far too apologetic about writing in English." Professor Vrinda Nabar of Bombay University recalled the 1960s, when "there was a strong feeling against English and writers were criticized for using it."[14] Indian critics who might have tended to dismiss the expatriate Rushdie as a cocky, elite, alienated outsider found themselves prepared to be charmed by him (albeit sometimes grudgingly), at least until the controversy over *The Satanic Verses* erupted. But much of this criticism is descriptive or impressionistic, without closely examining the underlying conditions that contributed to the success. Many Indians were annoyed by the terms in which *MC* was hailed, exemplified by the *New York Times* reviewer's phrase, "a continent finding its voice"—as if the region's millions had been silent through the millennia until Rushdie came along to speak for them. And more relevant to my purpose, Indians have been critical of the weight, following *MC*, given to the narrative of nation—as if there were no other way for people to tell their story—thereby silencing or sidelining other voices using other terms.

I mentioned in the introduction that Rushdie has referred to Indian English writing as "the bastard child of Empire,"[15] which is precisely what Saleem Sinai was in *MC*; so at one level his protagonist can be seen *as* Indian writing in English, claiming centrality for himself. Rushdie himself was doing the same when he asserted in the same essay—characteristically over-aggressively—that the best prose writing in India since independence has been in English, which has by now become an Indian language. Moreover, against all evidence and internal assertions to the contrary, he argues in his usual hyperbolic fashion that Indian English writing has not just a place for itself among other Indian literatures, but a preeminent place. Rushdie needed to lay claim to India—and further, to centrality within it—in order to feel a sense of engagement, just as Saleem needed to feel an egotistical sense of mission in order to allow himself a new kind of engagement with India. Rushdie's act of claiming must also be seen in another light: he returned to India in the late 1970s at the age of thirty-something, in the aftermath of Indira Gandhi's Emergency, a time when large numbers of expatriate and emigrant Indians (many acting against their instinct not to wash dirty linen in public) had expressed their outrage at Gandhi and the Congress Party's betrayal of the secular social-democratic ideals on which they, as the first post-independence generation, had been raised. In *MC*, Rushdie reaffirms and seeks to reclaim those ideals, even as he recognizes that their time may be past, and that he and his generation may be out of touch and out of time.[16]

Midnight's Children's Conceptual Conjuring

Philosopher of Action Jerome Segal describes alienness as "the experience of one's own incoherence," as "the experience of something as one's own and also, at the same time, as not-one's-own."[17] He further defines agency, alienation's opposite, as "a web of relations that constitute the presence of the self in the activity," a "structural connectedness between the person and his or her action."[18] It would follow, then, that coherence, ambivalence, and structural correspondences would be essential elements of Rushdie's conceptual conjuring in his quest to turn alienation into agency. Meaning is all-important in the definition of a happening as an action and the human subject as an agent. If a human subject does not have the ability to make meaning of an event, to give it (and thereby him/herself) coherence, it becomes not an action, but merely a happening, and the actor not an agent, but merely the acted-upon.[19] Identifying with Meaning itself, Saleem stands to lose everything by its loss, and thus making sense of the crisis takes on the proportions of a life-and-death struggle. "I must work fast," he pants as he introduces himself and underscores the urgency of his literary endeavor on the very first page of the novel, "…if I am to end up meaning—yes, meaning—something. I admit it: above all things, I fear absurdity" (9). While Saleem is all too aware of his impotence and impending demise, his prophetic awareness does not lead him into fatalism or disillusionment. Instead, it spurs him on, not to struggle for his personal survival, but to reach toward the meanings-within-the-loss-of-meaning of the national idea that he embodies.

In *MC*, Rushdie's reconfiguration of the relationship between the individual self and the nation opened up space that proved to be very enabling for new Indian English writers in the 1980s. The novel's publication was a watershed for the Indian novel in English, coming at a time when the dominant Congress model of nationalism was cracking up. Many critics have commented upon *MC*'s influence on the Indian English novel, and several studies have analyzed the use of history and memory in the novel, its identification of self with nation, and its struggle to overcome duality. Few, however, have discussed how such elements of the novel combined to influence Indian writing in English.

In an early interview, Rushdie characterized *MC* as more a political novel than a historical novel, and most of all, as a novel about the nature of memory, "about one person's passage through history," in which the individual's version of the truth was presented as at once coherent and suspect. This personal view of history, Rushdie explained, allowed him to discuss and explore the nature of "the relationship between the individual and history, between private lives and public affairs."[20] Without denying historical necessity, *MC* reconceptualized the dichotomy between personal and national identity in a way that made a new kind of social engagement possible. Rather than merely forcing the self into the image of the nation, Rushdie comically and mock-heroically insists on creating Nation in the imaginative image of Self. He takes on History, too, in the same way. The individual must either acquiesce to history's grand narratives or be destroyed—swept aside, or crushed underfoot. Rushdie's protagonist Saleem Sinai must also eventually succumb to the relentless march of History, but not before he tells his own story on his own terms.

MC opened up space—conceptual and narrative—for play. Nevertheless, Rushdie's project is not merely postmodern free play, or flirting dangerously with a fashionable crisis of meaning, as Kumkum Sangari has argued in her influential essay, "The Politics of the Possible."[21] Rushdie certainly does not seek to avert his—or our—eyes from the threatening loss-of-meaning implicit in the crisis of nation, but neither does he seek to trivialize it. Sangari suggests that through "double-coded" works like *MC*, "the crisis of meaning in the West" is imported into the "non-West." I recognize Sangari's concern that Rushdie's novel and others like it are all too easily appropriated into the academic discourse of poststructuralism as "texts of a near-canonical Euro-American postmodernism." However, the crisis that Sangari fears was already built into the epistemological categories of nation and history within which Rushdie was working, and these categories were already deconstructing them-selves through their own inner conflicts. The crisis of the nation was inherent in the underlying formulations of the Nehruvian nation-state, and is one that *MC* recognizes, but surely cannot determine.

Interpenetration of Self and Nation
Born at the stroke of midnight, August 14–15, 1947, baby Saleem Sinai receives a letter of congratulations from Prime Minister Nehru himself, worded with all the promises and truth-claims of the newly independent nation. Confidently identifying Saleem's life with the life of India itself, the letter links the unlimited potential of the newborn infant both with that of the nascent state, with all its future glory lying before it, and with the India of timeless antiquity, tales of whose past glories inspired and unified the nationalist movement:

> You are the newest bearer of that ancient face of India which is also eternally young. We shall be watching over your life with the closest attention; it will be, in a sense, the mirror of our own. (122)

"In what sense?" asks narrator-protagonist Saleem thirty-two years later as, battered by history, castrated by a prime minister, thoroughly disillusioned and "fullofcracks," he struggles desperately to preserve his version of India's history and his own before he completely falls to pieces. In what sense can it be said that his life and the lives of all the midnight's children—those 1,001 babies born within an hour of the moment of independence—has mirrored that of the nation? And writer-storyteller Saleem answers his own rhetorical question, mock-heroically, pseudo-scientifically, in rhetorical terms, in "adverbs and hyphens":

> I was linked to history both literally and metaphorically, both actively and passively, in what our (admirably modern) scientists might term "modes of connection" composed of "dualistically combined configurations" of the two pairs of opposed adverbs given above. This is why hyphens are necessary: actively-literally, passively-metaphorically, actively-metaphorically and passively-literally, I was inextricably intertwined with my world. (238)

The device of the "modes of connection" enables writer/narrator Saleem/Salman to grant his postcolonial protagonist multiple methods of engagement with the larger social realm and gives his characters room to move in ways that would be impossible within a unitary, social–realist structure, saving him, disillusioned as he becomes, from alienation and despair ("I was inextricably intertwined..."). Unlike a realistic novel that privileges action and the actual, *MC* recognizes the passive and metaphorical modes as well, expanding the stage of action fourfold (at least), and giving both formal and metaphysical realization to the fervent prayer quoted in Rushdie's essay, "Imaginary Homelands": "For God's sake, open the universe a little bit more."[22]

Rushdie's playful handling of previously implacable categories opens up possibilities within language where there would seem to have been none, thus delivering a measure of discursive room-to-move. Says protagonist Saleem Sinai, "Setting my face against all indications to the contrary, I shall now amplify...my claim to a place at the centre of things." This is exactly what Rushdie's modes of connection enable him to achieve in *MC*. Saleem and his age group have no agency in the active and the literal modes, where he is perennially the victim, the one-to-whom-things-are-done; it is only in the metaphorical and, interestingly, in the passive realms of reality that he and his compatriots are controlling Subjects. " 'Passive-metaphorical,' 'passive-literal,' 'active-metaphorical': the Midnight Children's Conference was all three; but it never became what I most wanted it to be; we never operated in the first, most significant of the 'modes of connection.' The 'active-literal' passed us by" (238–239). Powerlessness and lack of choice continually characterize Saleem's predicament, yet he doggedly persists in positioning himself, the bestower of meaning and form, at the center of his story—as indeed he is, in the role of author-narrator. Even though Saleem is supremely the person to whom things have been done, it is Rushdie's magic that, "against all indications to the contrary," transforms victim to protagonist.

But there is also another child born at that stroke of midnight, a child whose life was to have been Saleem's life of upper middle-class privilege, but for the hand of fate that robbed him of his birthright and relegated him to a life on the streets of Bombay. That child is Shiva, archrival and polar twin, the only other one of the midnight's children who has powers as great as Saleem's. And a third child triangulates these two, whose powers are almost-but-not-quite as great as theirs: Parvati-the-Witch, who is to bear the child who will be his-and-not-his, Parvati who loves him, Parvati who saves his life but to whom he cannot return the favor.

In *MC*, women are seen to be the powerful practitioners of yet another mode of connection, the passive-aggressive. In spite of their seeming lack of control in the public sphere, they loom large in Saleem's family life, feeding all their repressed sorrow, guilt, jealousy, and bitterness into him like mother's milk, as did his Aunt Alia, who "fed us the birianis of dissension and the nargisi koftas of discord," and whose kormas, "spiced with forebodings as well as cardamoms," wrought a terrible vengeance upon his mother. Saleem's postcolonial condition gives him an intimate connection with the passive modes of interaction with the world. Women's status within a patriarchal structure and the weapons of the weak that they wield mirror the weapons that the postcolonial subject can wield in the uneven struggle for self-determination. As the women do in the private sphere, so does Saleem in the universe of his narrative, namely, elevate the passive mode into equal significance with the active, and the metaphorical into equal prominence with the literal.[23] The Manichean dynamics of the neocolonial Indian nation-state maintain its sovereign subjects in a female/passive relationship to the Center even as the nationalist rhetoric exhorts them to work and action.[24]

R.S. Pathak describes "the interplay of personal and national histories" as "the most significant feature of *Midnight's Children,*" the inextricable intertwining of "the public and the private strands" as giving the novel its coherence, and "the interaction of historical and individual forces" as having "made the narrator what he is." Given that Indian history has been mutilated by the British, Pathak sees Rushdie's re-creation and reappropriation of Indian history and his charting of the "interlocking and interdependent relationships of history and the individual" as restoring a "much-needed sense of dignity" to the individual.[25] Pathak also points to Rushdie's savage satire and entertaining comedy as a winning combination, as does Thakur Guruprasad, who echoes similar sentiments in ascribing Rushdie's disarming charm to his having "conjured up a…new genre" that combines "fairy tale with savage political indictment," through "a fictional family story intertwined with dismal political history in a comic strain."[26]

In an early review of *MC,* Anita Desai hesitated to call the novel "historical," because of Rushdie's insistence upon the interpenetration of the individual and the national, his belief that "…while individual history does not make sense unless seen against its national background, neither does national history make sense unless seen in the form of individual lives and histories."[27] *MC* does not deny the nation's power over individual lives, neither does it subordinate individual to nation, but it acknowledges and makes creative capital of both their polarity and their unity. In the same review, Desai, in whose novels of the interior the protagonists are often helpless victims of history, spoke of the novel's purpose as "wholly serious" and its subject as tragic, "the tragedy of individual lives harried and wrecked by history, and of history harried and wrecked by individuals." However, part of the novel's appeal lies in its refusal to accept the relentless march of history as inevitably tragic. Rather than the individual being altogether obliterated by the nation-state or matters of state being subordinated to the individual, it is the interesting space-in-between that is explored, and thereby what is patently the stuff of tragedy made comic. Rushdie does not deny the dichotomy between the private and the public; rather, he demonstrates how the two partake of each other in curious and often unexpected ways and how the possibilities of a situation may differ depending upon how it is perceived: baby Saleem was handcuffed to history, force-fed by events (passive-metaphorical), yet as the narrator, he can turn this around. History is *both* violent menace and nourishment for baby-to-be Saleem: "He, too, has to swallow all his past, all that made him—or, put another way, it feeds him" (107–108). Rushdie's triumphant technique in *MC* is simply yet supremely the discursive room-to-move gained by putting it another way.

Both Saleem's privileged relationships—to his audience as the omniscient author-narrator of his text, and to the midnight's children as the medium by which they are enabled to speak to each other—can be compared to the relationship of the Indian National Congress (and, after independence, the Congress Party) to the Indian people as a whole. He compares his narrative position to a "hover" at the apex of an isosceles triangle, balanced and grounded by the earthy Padma at his feet forming the base, as he ranges back and forth between past and present.[28] Bipan Chandra et al. describe the Indian National Congress as "the apex national organization that was to guide the destiny of the Indian national movement till the attainment of independence," drawing a similarly hierarchical relationship to the "masses."[29] After Saleem's brain becomes the *lok sabha*, the Indian Parliament, he begins to have a strong sense of social responsibility, but also perhaps an overdeveloped sense of his own importance to the success of the Midnight Children's Conference, very much like his mentor Prime Minister Jawaharlal Nehru, who presides similarly over the Indian Parliament. Nehru's niece, the novelist Nayantara Sahgal, describes his sense of mission on the eve of independence: "he resembled a knight in quest of the Grail, or an artist dedicated to the completion of his task... On the night of August 14... [i]t was as if he had taken upon himself the entire burden of the new freedom..."[30]

Action and Engagement

What does Rushdie achieve by the creation of his larger-than-life, tragicomic hero and how might this feat be said to have enabled a new kind of social engagement for a new generation of writers? Perhaps the success or failure of this engagement may be judged by the degree to which his protagonist Saleem is able to engage with the public sphere; if so, we may chart his progress through the novel. Or perhaps the success or failure of a character who starts life with the optimistic faith that his country's achievements will be his own, tests the truth claims of a nation that has promised to deliver self-determination to the greatest and least of its citizens.

MC is an ironic, quirky, but deadly serious critique of quiescence, of withdrawal, of forgetting. Being pulled forcibly from his roots by his parents' relocation to Pakistan begins the process of disconnection for Saleem. Across the political border he can neither receive signals from nor broadcast them to the midnight children, and thereby becomes isolated within his own head. He succumbs first to a fatalism that allows him to accept all that is done to him. When he is struck by a flying spittoon in the Indo-Pakistan war of 1965, he loses his memory altogether, and with it, six years of his life. The narrative picks up in the midst of West Pakistan's foray into what was soon to become Bangladesh, to quell the Eastern rebellion. Saleem is no longer the youthful "I" but is presented at a third-person remove as "the buddha"—referring both to an old man, prematurely aged by history, and one who—like the Buddha who found enlightenment under the Bo tree—has withdrawn in spirit from the world of pain and sorrow.

Here Rushdie depicts the buddha's "not-living-in-the-world as well as living in it," as an act of weakness and submission; as indeed it is for the former Saleem, who has become a man-dog, silently and obediently carrying out the function of a canine tracker for a Pakistani military intelligence unit, tracking down rebels—"undesirable elements"—and destroying them. Saleem's state of amnesia prevents him from taking moral responsibility for his actions. "Emptied of history, the buddha learned the arts of submission, and did only what was required of him" (350). The historical Buddha, of course, returned to the world and engaged in nonattached action to eliminate sorrow from the world. As an escape from responsibility, Saleem's "nonattachment" is clearly a perversion of that nonattachment.

In an 1983 interview, Rushdie explained that his "comic inversion" of the relationship between the individual and history enabled him to discuss the problematics of that relationship in modern India. His protagonist Saleem begins his life with supreme confidence in his centrality and agency, but his unbounded optimism is besieged and eventually destroyed by disillusionment. Rushdie charts the disillusioning "series of retreats" that lead Saleem and the reader from his youthful omnipotence at the moment of independence to his premature impotence and decrepitude at the age of thirty-two.

> Saleem believes that there is a relationship (between the individual and the nation), Saleem has a thesis, as it were, and the book tests the thesis. It turns out to be a destruction-test, because by the end of the book, it is clear that the thesis doesn't hold up: he's not in charge. And he can't stand it—at the moment at which he begins to be faced with the facts of life, he performs a series of retreats, whether into a kind of catatonic state, or into quiescence or acceptance, or finally, into the pickle factory.[31]

Throughout the novel, withdrawal is always achieved at a price. Saleem the man-dog leads his unit into the Sundarbans, steamy jungles of the subconscious, where his own mind leads him tortuously and inexorably through fevered, shifting nightmare landscapes toward a recognition of his identity and the responsibility that he must take for his actions. As he runs from the conflicts of the psychic battlegrounds, he is drawn into the depths of his insanity, an experience that may lead him toward a recognition of the truth of his situation, but is fraught with its own dangers—madness and the risk of never being able to return.

Even when the poison from a forest snake awakens him to himself and to the realities—and the dangers—of his predicament, he still cannot remember his name. It takes Parvati-the-Witch to name him and recall him fully to himself. After Shiva, who was also born on the stroke of midnight, Parvati was the child born next-closest to midnight, the Third who embodies a point of meeting for the polarized pair. It is Parvati's magic that conveys him safely back into India, but again, survival exacts a price. To survive, Saleem is made invisible, and carried into Delhi crouched inside a basket. But, ironically, the invisibility that saves him also carries the risk of robbing him of his very essence. What saves Saleem from the enervation that accompanies invisibility is anger, a righteous anger on behalf of India's oppressed people that brings with it an exalted sense of mission: a mission no less than that of saving the country. However, like the self-appointed leaders of the Indian nationalist movement, he is to betray the people he claims to represent. He fails to overcome the isolation that followed his rejection of Shiva, his nemesis and polar opposite, and his loss-of-connection with the midnight's children. Far from saving the country, he is sucked down into the vortex of its crisis. In the attempt to restore his own fortunes by contacting his despicably toadying uncle Mustapha, who is a high official in the Indira Congress bureaucracy, he abandons Parvati and his adopted family in the communist magicians' ghetto. He returns, but what might have been is derailed by the squashy-bellied Youth Congress leader and his goons as the slum is razed. He falls victim, like so many others, to "the Widow's" 1975 State of Emergency, in which he is tortured and made to reveal the names and addresses of all the surviving children of midnight, the hopes and possibilities contained within that moment of history. They are then given a fiendishly efficient operation—a "sperectomy"—which not only ensures their irreversible sterilization but also removes all hope.

For Saleem, it is a time of endings. For his son, however, and for the legion of bastard children whom Shiva has implanted in wealthy women across the nation, it is the beginning of a new chapter in India's history. Saleem's success in writing down his story—which is, in so many senses, the story of his generation—may or may not ensure that it is passed on and remembered. Against the evidence even of the narrative itself, the powers of Saleem's son and, by extension, of the new generation, project the hope that the times have bestowed upon them what it will take to survive and move forward collectively—even to create new myths.[32]

Rushdie's narrative, which so fiercely advocates political engagement and social responsibility and so firmly condemns quiescence as betrayal, characteristically shows his naïve protagonist's progressive withdrawal and eventual destruction to be both beyond his control and of his own making. Saleem's family, and his own sense of connection with the pulse of India, was destroyed by internal divisiveness as well as the will-to-power. In his bitter disillusionment and loss of his sense of centrality, he withdraws into himself, destroying himself and betraying his fellow Indians. Rushdie explains the social and political withdrawal of writers of his generation in terms of a profound disillusionment with the myths of the secular-socialist nation, myths that failed to deliver either material or spiritual results to a generation of believers. Yet at the same time, he paradoxically reaffirms those very myths, even as he pronounces their obsolescence; both author and protagonist are bedeviled by duality and ambivalence.

Duality and Ambivalence

Rushdie, as well as Saleem his creation, is a child of midnight, formed and raised by the secular ideals of the Nehru Congress in the days when Independent India itself was young. As a student of history and a left-leaning social democrat, he has recognized intellectually the limitations and ambivalence of the Indian inheritors of the colonial state, and *MC* subjects them to a serious critique. As an antidote to the paralyzing polarities of endlessly contending dualities, Rushdie poses the notion of multiplicity—many Indias, many versions of truth, and an infinite capacity for regeneration. Nevertheless, ambivalence remains, because of his continued emotional investment in a unitary idea of India, the India of his lost innocence, and his own inability, despite everything, to conceive constructive possibilities in its demise.[33]

As Homi Bhabha points out in his introduction to *Nation and Narration*, the idea of the nation is by definition ambivalent, shifting as it does between modern ideologies and premodern cultural systems, shuttling as it does between the secular and the religious, the public and private spheres; and the ambivalence of the nation is mirrored in the very form of the national narrative.[34] It is significant Bhabha uses Tom Nairn's term, "the modern Janus," for the nation, since the Indian English novel was, sometimes with dubious distinction, dubbed "Janus-faced" by Indian critics in the 1970s.[35] In the early post-independence context, the term was used to describe the dual literary heritage of Indian English, but could also be used in its sense of "two-faced," to cast aspersions on its insufficient "Indianness," because of its dual parentage. This view, preceding the contemporary critique of nationalism, failed to consider the ambivalence inherent in nationalism and the nationalist discourse itself, which itself has a dual parentage regardless of which modern Indian language it speaks through. Another sense of Janus-faced, however, is "sensitive to dualities and polarities," and this is the spirit in which Rushdie writes, sensitive to the dualities inherent in postcoloniality, accepting—even flaunting—them rather than attempting to deny or conceal them, and elevating condition into method in his metanarrative.[36] Bhabha's use of the Janus metaphor aptly characterizes *MC*'s narrative approach, that of turning "the two-faced god into a figure of prodigious doubling," so that the condition of ambivalence is transformed into a dynamic process.[37]

M. Keith Booker has identified one of the central themes and strategies of Rushdie's fiction as "embracing contradiction," both constructing and deconstructing dual oppositions "by demonstrating that the apparent polar opposites are in fact interchangeable and mutually interdependent."[38] I think that Rushdie's approach to duality in *MC* functions as theme, as form, and as a method that enables a shift in post-independence nationalist discourse by exposing and enacting the radical ambivalence of the Indian nation. However, as Booker also notes, Rushdie constructs and inhabits his opposing dualities only to expose their limitations; duality as method enables him to expose dualism as prison. I see Rushdie's reproduction, reconfiguration, and critique of nationalist dualities as creating new possibilities for postcolonial narrative discourse in the 1980s, but also as raising doubts about the outcome of the swirling embrace of polar opposites: will it be perpetual motion, fusion, or fission?

Rushdie portrays Saleem as a victim of the paradoxes of Indian nationalism, among them the splits between idealism and pragmatism, the elite and the masses, centralization and federalism, rationalism and spirituality. As Krishna, in the *Bhagavad-Gita*, exhorted the doubt-torn Arjuna to rise above the pairs of opposites, so that he might see clearly and act, so Rushdie's hero longs for a Third Principle that can overcome the dualities within and around him and break through to another level of truth. At meetings of the Midnight Children's Conference (or M.C.C.[39]), through which the children meet telepathically, the idealistic young Saleem as convenor and central switchboard operator implores the squabbling midnight's children to overcome their differences. Their miraculous powers, so full of possibility, are powerless to prevent the apparently inevitable conflicts that break out among them:

> "We," I cried passionately, "must be a third principle, we must be the force which drives between the horns of the dilemma; for only by being other, by being new, can we fulfil the promise of our birth." (255)

But Saleem himself—like the Indian nation and the Indian English novel—has internalized the very dualities that he seeks to unite. He is as yet unaware of his own mixed parentage, ironic evidence of the dual cultural heritage of the Indian nation-state. And as he finds out, his own continued privilege is predicated upon the disinheritance of Shiva. Even though Saleem desperately seeks to avoid Shiva, it would seem that the enmity between the two of them is inevitable: "Shiva and Saleem, victor and victim; understand our rivalry and you will gain an understanding of the age in which you live" (432). And the enmity of Shiva and Saleem ("knees-and-nose, a nose and knees"), polar opposites, split selves, drives the novel to its tragic climax and its ambiguous conclusion.

When Saleem excludes Shiva from the *lok sabha* (people's assembly or Parliament) of his mind because he is afraid that Shiva will "insist on claiming his birthright" (282), he closes off the option of regaining the harmony that the children had shared in the early days of the M.C.C. It is this active rejection on his part, as much as the passive-literal act of being taken across the border to Pakistan, that is responsible for his loss of connection with the midnight's children. Instead of accepting Shiva as an equal member of the group, even as equal to himself, Saleem perceives him only as a threat to his own preeminence (which, indeed, he is) and relegates him to the realm of an eternal Other. The possibility of a Third Principle is forever closed off for Saleem, as the polarization of knees-and-nose takes hold:

> he became, for me, first a stabbing twinge of guilt, then an obsession; and finally, as the memory of his actuality grew dull, he became a sort of principle; he came to represent, in my mind, all the vengefulness and violence and simultaneous-love-and-hate-of-things in the world . . . (298–299)

Still, Parvati-the-Witch, who always believed in Saleem, remains open to the possibility of reconciliation. Even as Saleem dreads the return of Shiva, the principle of destruction, Parvati is able to see him as a principle of Creation as well; after all, he is the father of her child—Saleem's son-who-is-not-his-son—and the father of many more throughout the land. Parvati the witch, perhaps the mediator/medium who can transform a vicious circle into a triangle, welcomes the return of the repressed: "Maybe he will come when he has time; and then we will be three!" (389)

Even though neither Saleem Sinai nor his creator are able to find a way to transcend Manichean dualities in their own lives, Salman Rushdie is able to break their stranglehold in the realm of language. He accomplishes this simply, just as he opened up more breathing space for the Self in his deadlock with the Nation. Can anything capture the essence of duality more simply and ineluctably than the children's game of Snakes and Ladders?

> . . . implicit in the game is the unchanging twoness of things, the duality of up against down, good against evil; the solid rationality of ladders balance the occult sinuosities of the serpent; in the opposition of staircase and cobra we can see, metaphorically, all conceivable oppositions, Alpha against Omega, father against mother; here is the war of Mary and Musa, and the polarities of knees and nose . . . but I found, very early in my life, that the game lacked one crucial dimension, that of ambiguity—because, as events were to show, it is also possible to slither down a ladder and climb to triumph on the venom of a snake. . . . (141)

Beyond realizing the ability of each opposed half to turn into its opposite, Saleem begins to recognize that, rather than becoming paralyzed and alienated by seemingly irreconcilable dualities, an individual can aspire to partake of both (either/or becoming and... and). He invokes the spiritual image of the *paramahamsa*, "symbol of the ability to live in two worlds, the physical and the spiritual" (223). The *paramahamsa* symbolizes divinity and spiritual freedom, the creative ability to live in the world and rise above its dualities, at once engaged and detached.[40] Rushdie also employs as an antidote to Manichean dualism the traditional Indian conception of the multiple levels of correspondence between microcosm and macrocosm:

> As a people, we are obsessed with correspondences... It is a sort of national longing for form—or perhaps simply an expression of our deep belief that forms lie hidden within reality; that meaning reveals itself only in flashes. (300)

But the older Saleem, despite everything, remains earthbound like his grandfather before him, who was struck on the nose with a frozen clod of earth when, "foreign-returned," he attempted to pray. The cause? "Altered vision"—he "saw things differently"(11). From the moment he returned to his native Kashmir from medical study in Germany and found himself unable to pray, Saleem's grandfather Aadam Aziz finds himself knocked into a place in which he is able neither to believe or disbelieve in God. Throughout the novel, however, where real life continually breaks the bounds of reason, Saleem tells the reader, "believedon'tbelieve. But it happened anyway."

While Saleem is able to communicate with the midnight's children, he is able to inhabit two worlds; but when the powers and possibilities of the M.C.C. are cut off, his connections with both are severed. In his disillusionment, he bids farewell to his hopes: "If there is a third principle, its name is childhood. But it dies; or rather, it is murdered" (256). Fear and cynicism murder it; it is blocked in the closing-off of possibilities, the hardening of the mind and heart, the loss of the ability or desire to put things another way.

Finally, *MC* accepts the dual legacy of midnight, a legacy split at the very root. Saleem does not come without Shiva, and Shiva would not be Shiva were it not for Saleem. There is an acceptance of ambivalence, of the degree to which polarized opposites partake of each other, so much so that one cannot exist without the other, one feeds the other. Even as Saleem-the-narrator finally succumbs to the cracks and is trampled into dust, Rushdie-the-author triumphs. He has succeeded in creating a space between the horns of the dilemma, not by transcending them or denying them, but by reconfiguring them. For his generation are privileged *and* cursed "to be both masters *and* victims of their times."

Fragmentation and the Whole

Writing on the fragmented self in *MC*, Kathleen Flanagan recognizes divided selves in Rushdie's works as "the products of crises of faith in political and religious institutions," and stresses the importance for Rushdie of the individual's responsibility to society. She makes the important point that Saleem's act of writing down his story combines for him both "public good and private need" as it connects self to society by making the individual a "speaking subject" who recognizes his private acts as having public consequences. She further points out that Rushdie draws attention to the disjunction between the individual and the official views of history through what she calls the child Saleem's "ridiculous" and socially destructive self-centeredness. Taking from Lukacs a developmental view of Saleem's consciousness, she argues that he must progress from seeing "himself as the center of the state to seeing himself as a responsible part of the state." Although he desires to place himself at the controlling center of an "ordered reality," he is forced to recognize the power of "the fragmented forces of society" and the "preeminence of the social and the historical over the private." In Flanagan's Lukacsian argument, Rushdie's child-narrator starts with the problem of seeing history in isolated parts, and only as they relate to him as the center of his childish universe. His problem, according to Flanagan, is that he should be seeing these parts "as aspects of the historical process and integrat(ing) them in a totality" if his knowledge is ever to be brought into line with reality, and that he must come to terms with the self as "decentered, yet responsible" *vis-à-vis* the state.[41]

It is here, in the insistence that Saleem's "absurd" self-centeredness must be decentered in order for him to mature into a truly responsible member of society, that I part company with both the teleology and the spirit of the argument. For while Saleem's childish megalomania is of course absurd, it is also quite clearly privileged in the novel. At the same time as Rushdie parodies and undermines the overcentralized nation-state that seeks to control and speak for all its "children," he also romanticizes the Congress Party ideal of "unity in diversity" in which the center provides a forum through which all the children can speak to one another. While the progression of the novel may certainly be seen as a movement from an immature megalomania to a more realistic, downsized sense of self, it is also a movement from idealism to disillusionment; from dynamic growth to castration and impotence, premature aging, and death; from a deep sense of connectedness with the pulse of India to alienation, betrayal, and insignificance. Saleem's irrepressible megalomania was precisely what post-Rushdie novelists found so attractive and inspiring. The lesson they drew was not that he needed to be cut down to size, so that he might learn to become a humble, socially responsible pickle-factory worker. Rather, they saw that, in spite of the fact that his story was just one story among millions, it was his own story, and therefore truer for him than any other. It was possible for an insignificant fragment to speak in his own voice from the center of his universe. Ironically, however, even as Rushdie's novel may have inspired a myriad of speaking subjects, his elite narrator Saleem recognized that it was only at the expense of his own sense of wholeness that the subaltern voices of the other midnight's children could begin to be heard. For Rushdie, as for Saleem, fragmentation presents both the terrifying prospects of chaos and also the productive possibilities unleashed by the breakdown of the controlling center. But as a true child of his time he is unable, in spite of everything, to fully accept that breakdown.

An interviewer once reported that Salman Rushdie kept on his writing desk a little sculpture of an unpartitioned India. Even as he wrote of the realities of a divided subcontinent, he couldn't help but persist in holding on to India's geopolitical wholeness as both an idea and an ideal. His protagonist Saleem shares some of his creator's nostalgic idealism. Once a kind of radio who was able to tune in to voices from all over India, and more importantly, the instrument through which they were enabled to tune in to each other, Saleem has been drained of his powers, has aged prematurely, and is cracking apart. He hastens to record his memories before it is too late. And he seals his last chapter of pickled memories not a moment too soon, for now he is breaking into millions of fragments and his particles are being scattered and trampled into the Indian dust. And for Saleem, the vicissitudes of whose life are a mirror of his country's, whose battered, misshapen body is a grotesque caricature of the national map, fragmentation is something to be resisted to the end, even as he accepts its inevitability and indeed its desirability.

In 1957 Saleem was confidently in control—the prime minister, so to speak, of the "*lok sabha* of my brain," as he called the diverse, clamorous gathering of 581 ten-year-olds who convened inside his head. His idealistic quest for meaning and purpose drove him to declaim earnestly and endlessly to his agemates ("we must think...what we are for"), while his birth at the very stroke of midnight had given him greater powers than any other (except, of course, *his alter ego* Shiva, the cynical, streetwise gang leader who mocks him as a "pampered rich boy," and whom Saleem strives to shut out of his head, at his own cost). "I was not immune to the lure of leadership," he acknowledges with rueful hindsight (227). But then, while few of the children had his privilege, few had his larger sense of purpose or his powers. It was undeniable that the powers themselves had been apportioned unevenly, but was it equally undeniable that, without Saleem, the children would have been unaware of the larger national arena, and unable to communicate with each other? Was the M.C.C. an institution of tremendous promise, or was it rather the vehicle of the children's eventual undoing?[42] Was Saleem, as its founder, their savior or their betrayer? Was the breakup of the M.C.C., of Saleem, of India itself, the end of possibility, a tragedy to be averted at all costs, or was it, on the contrary, an opportunity to be welcomed? Like many others in *MC*, the answer to all these questions is—well—both. And yet, from Saleem/Salman's personal perspective, it comes down quite clearly on one side.

As Saleem's bedeviled body begins to disintegrate, he naturally resists. Who in his position would not have striven to remain whole?

> O eternal opposition of inside and outside! Because a human being, inside himself, is anything but a whole, anything but homogeneous; all kinds of everywhichthing are jumbled up inside him, and he is one person one minute and another the next. The body, on the other hand, is homogeneous as anything. Indivisible, a one-piece suit, a sacred temple, if you will. It is important to preserve this wholeness...
> ...Uncork the body, and God knows...The consequences for the sphere of public action...are...no less profound. (236–237)

The individual body, once intact and indivisible but now falling apart, ironically allows expression to the myriad voices that it contained, controlled, suppressed, denied. It also allows the fragments to take on lives of their own.[43] "Midnight's other children...are pressing extremely hard. Soon the cracks will be wide enough for them to escape" (179). Rushdie's narrative accepts the inevitability of the fragments breaking through, yet persists in holding on to an idea of the whole. Saleem's cracking up allows the voices to escape and be heard, and yet without Saleem they might not have been able to hear each other in the first place. From the first page of the novel, the cracks signal the beginning of the end for Saleem as a unitary individual. He already more than half acknowledges the absurdity of his enterprise, yet persists stubbornly, ultimately succeeding in "pickling" all thirteen chapters of his story before the forces of disintegration prevail.

During the Quit India Movement of 1942, Aadam Aziz, the patriarch, is infected with the optimism disease, the blind nationalism that prevents him from seeing the incipient divisions within nation and family, from failing to anticipate Partition, and from responding to his wife's deep dissatisfaction. Later, the narrator/protagonist Saleem Sinai suggests that "the urge to encapsulate the whole of reality" is another Indian disease. Lifafa Das tries to put the whole world in his peepshow. Nadir Khan's painter friend had drawn ever larger paintings, trying to "get the whole of life into his art." In the end he had committed suicide, saying, "I wanted to be a miniaturist and I've got elephantiasis instead." Saleem Sinai worries, "Am I infected too?"[44]

Richard Cronin asserts that Saleem's urge to encapsulate the whole of reality is "a disease to which only those like Rushdie who write about India in English are vulnerable," and that "it is only because he (the young Saleem) is an outsider that India seems one to him" and "he can aspire to encapsulate the whole of it."[45] Cronin calls Kipling and Rushdie, in the same breath, impudent "trespassers" in India. Further, he claims that, for Indians who write in a regional language, a regional identity "unavoidably" takes precedence over an Indian identity. Cronin's essay is full of categorical statements. First, if the young Saleem had a unitary conception of the nation, so did many of the educated Indians of his generation in the post-independence Nehruvian era. Second, Rushdie's conception of the nation, while still holding emotional allegiance to the Nehruvian model, at the same time questions it deeply. Third, if Saleem is an "outsider" because he is from a wealthy family and does not speak Marathi or Gujarati in cosmopolitan Bombay, then legions of the Indian urban middle classes are outsiders as well.[46] Fourth, the meaning of "reality" for Rushdie here is clearly not restricted to the unitary Indian nation—in fact, it is the very multiplicity of India, and beyond India, the multifaceted nature of reality itself, that he is attempting to convey.

MC mocks its own melodrama but makes literary fireworks out of events that persistently refuse "to remain life-sized." Like India, Saleem Sinai finds himself cracking up into tiny pieces, like the pieces of his grandmother that his grandfather fell in love with and the pieces of his father that his mother tried to love; but, like Partition, it seems that his eventual fragmentation is inevitable. The urge of the work is to resist (however vainly) fragmentation and compartmentalization, providing a strong contrary current of inclusiveness (like the epic *Mahabharata*, of which it is said that what is not in it, is not). Thus the text thrives on and is driven by a contrary dynamic, a dialectic that simultaneously undermines and privileges its totalizing urges, recognizing their obsolescence while refusing to let go of their emotional power. In this dynamic polarization lies the explosive success of the novel—and perhaps, also, Saleem's ultimate fate. In the end, which is sanity and which the disease, the desire to embrace reality and to swallow the world whole, or the tendency to fragment, to compartmentalize oneself and the world into internally homogeneous, manageable, bite-sized pieces? Or is it both?

*　*　*

In the crisis of the long-dominant Congress model of nationalism, polarized political forces intensified their struggle in a swirling death-grip, and it would seem that there was nothing beyond the dualities of endlessly contending extremes. One can only hope that in the fragmentation of the national ideal of unity-in-diversity, of the Midnight Children's Conference, deep fissures in the once-impermeable national membrane allow entry to new ideas, as well as to old, long-suppressed ones; flames curl up through the cracks and set the nation ablaze, destroying but possibly also illuminating. Only time will tell what will arise out of those ashes, time that Saleem and his generation may not have; he can only bequeath to his son-who-is-not-his-son his version of the national narrative that has formed him.

With his final words, the disintegrating Saleem prophesies his fate and articulates the postcolonial condition of his generation:

> Yes, they will trample me underfoot...reducing me to specks of voiceless dust... because it is the privilege and the curse of the midnight's children to be both masters and victims of their times, to forsake privacy and be sucked into the annihilating whirlpool of the multitudes, and to be unable to live or die in peace. (463)

Even though Saleem Sinai is cracking into as many pieces as there are Indians, as there are stories to tell, he has successfully told his story—imperfect, unreliable, distorted, to be sure—but nonetheless triumphantly his own. Is he doomed? Yes, inevitably. But stubbornly and against all the odds, Victim transforms himself into Protagonist, simply through the telling of his own story.

"Post-Rushdie": National Narratives of the 1980s

When *MC* was first published, Rushdie's refusal to censor or sanitize his story, his unembarrassed washing of dirty linen in public, was refreshing to the world of Indian English writing, which had trodden so carefully for so long, walking a tightrope between "Indian" authenticity and "English" correctness.[47] Unafraid either of public censure or government censors, Rushdie sought to embrace the sights, sounds, and smells of the India of his dreams and memories in all their multiplicity. Had he been living in middle-class Indian society rather than metropolitan London, he might have been more circumspect. But then, surely, the novel would have lost much of its dynamism.

In an early review, written before *MC*'s success in India, Anita Desai expressed the belief that Rushdie's message would fall on deaf ears in the unselfcritical intellectual climate of post-independence India. She wrote, somewhat bitterly, "it is tragic to think how unlikely that it will be published, distributed or read in a land that prefers to avert its eyes from the intolerable reality and gaze upon *maya*, the shimmer of illusion." But in fact, as noted earlier, the Indian sales of the novel were unprecedentedly high, heralding a new spirit of freedom and a desire to experiment with subject, language, and narrative strategy. Desai, whose novels of the 1960s and 1970s were preeminently novels of interiority, told me in a 1992 interview that *MC* had given her the courage and artistic room to move into the public sphere in her own fiction.[48] Rushdie's playfulness actually created discursive space for her where there had been none before.

Many Indian English writers of the 1980s found that Rushdie's paradigm allowed them a new freedom of both form and content. His narrative sleight-of-hand juggled multiple modes of engagement between the individual and the national narrative, teased apart the cracks within and between the master discourses, and conjured up space for (relatively) free play—or at least the illusion of it—in a terrain where there had previously been a polarized paralysis. New writers found his acknowledgment of multiplicity and his hybridity of language particularly liberating. It enabled them to tell their personal stories in their own voices as *national* epics.

Over the course of the 1980s, a wave of Indian English novels followed *MC*, clearly influenced by it in language, style, and structure. Some prominent new novelists of the 1980s whose work is indebted to Rushdie include Namita Gokhale (*Paro: Dreams of Passion*), Amitav Ghosh (*The Circle of Reason* and *The Shadow Lines*), Upamanyu Chatterjee (*English, August* and *The Last Burden*), I. Allan Sealy (*The Trotter-Nama* and *Hero*), Boman Desai (*The Memory of Elephants*), Shashi Tharoor (*The Great Indian Novel* and *Show Business*), and Nina Sibal (*Yatra*).[49] Of course these novels did not represent the only tendency within Indian English writing during the period, but the Rushdie-inspired personal-narrative-as-national-epic was certainly an important one, and it brought a new vitality to what had become rather a stagnant tradition with little experimentation and few new names. Rushdie-influenced works by new novelists have variously been seen to include one or more of the following features: (1) a multigenerational, mock-epic family saga, complete with family trees, maps, and a long list of *dramatis personae*, that tells the story of the protagonist's family as a national history; (2) a rejection of the traditional, social realist novel: larger-than-life allegorical characters and events in the tradition of magical realism; (3) both a fluency in standard English and a confidence with the language that allows the unembarrassed creative use of various kinds of Indian English; (4) a sprawling, rambling style, full of digressions and humor; (5) the use of myth, oral tradition, and different versions and ideas of history; and (6) a playful irreverence for the sacred cows of nationalism and religion. Aside from these similarities, however, there is a broad range of tendencies among these post-Rushdie novels, even if one were to focus on their conceptions of the relationship between the individual and the nation and the action made possible thereby.

Less commonly noted is the opportunity these novels give to members of marginalized groups or national minorities to place themselves centerstage in the drama of national history, rather than feeling the pressure to subsume themselves in the mainstream, official version. For example, Parsis and Anglo-Indians are two groups whose "Indianness" is often called into question, but Parsis like Boman Desai (*The Memory of Elephants*, 1988) and Anglo-Indians like I. Allan Sealy (*The Trotter-Nama*, 1988), range back over the centuries in their novels to celebrate the long and colorful histories of their respective communities in India.[50] In Sealy's comic, digressive, mock-heroic mode, his protagonist is able to present the checkered past of his "glorious" Anglo-Indian ancestors and to poignantly acknowledge their marginalization in post-independence India. Boman Desai draws on *MC*'s notion that there are competing histories that are equally valid—for the individual, at least—and that the individual has moral authority and willpower, if not political power. In *The Memory of Elephants*, Desai's protagonist gains access to the collective unconscious of his contentious family in particular and the Parsis in general, but although he is able to tune in to them, he has no control over the events he sees. However, just before he is forced to relinquish his dangerous powers, he is able, just for a moment and by a tremendous effort of will, to bring all his ancestors together and hold a united family tableau in his mind.

Besides giving new novelists the courage to tell their own stories *as* Indian stories, *MC* also gave them permission to be ironic and ambivalent about their relationship to the nation-state. Upamanyu Chatterjee, in his first novel, *English, August: An Indian Story* (1988), is able to portray Agastya, a disaffected young protagonist in the Indian Civil Service who suffers from prolonged boredom, cynicism, and indecision in his provincial posting. It is interesting to note the centrality in the novel of the Gita, to which Agastya repeatedly returns, neither as a spur to action nor as a guide to equilibrium, but to sound the depths of his own restlessness and deep ennui.[51] And Shashi Tharoor, in *The Great Indian Novel* (1989), is able simultaneously to allegorize the story of modern India in terms of the epic *Mahabharata* and to question the very notion of using the authority of tradition to offer certitudes in the seeming chaos of the present.

Despite its conceptual freshness and vitality, *MC* remained very much emotionally committed to the narrative of nation. In the end, it could only reconfigure the ideological categories, not step out of them altogether. If the new trajectories set in motion by Rushdie's reconceptualization of the relationship between self and nation were to remain within the self-as-nation framework, it might be that they would eventually mire themselves in the same dualities as did earlier novels of the 1960s and 1970s, with the possibility of alternative realities remaining just that, a possibility—a spectacular, but ultimately illusory, authorial conjuring trick. Is the discursive space in which they function merely in the realm of virtual reality, or do they posit alternate realities that in fact create new possibilities for public discourse?

Some of the new Indian English writers of the 1980s used the nation as a framework to define themselves against, either as a peg on which to hang their identities or a boundary to demarcate their own liminal positioning. Thus they tended to gravitate toward two extremes, either a romantic clinging to the ideal of Nation, or its opposite, a fashionably disillusioned individualism answerable to no one. To put it differently, either an obsession with the need to belong to a nation-state, or a defiant declaration of one's alienation. In a thoughtful review of Salman Rushdie's *East, West* in the *Indian Review of Books*, Sanjay Iyer argues that the Rushdie-inspired narratives of nation have been privileged to the extent of obscuring other Indian novels that work out of different paradigms:

> In privileging the experiences of nation and post-colonialism, Rushdie, as a literary giant, has powerfully set the terms for inclusion in this countercanon (of Third World Literature). The result is apparent to us every day, in the spate of novels that *do* take the personal as national...The price of this has been the marginalization of countless works that are not obsessed with national experience.[52]

I would agree that the continued conflation of self and nation eventually ceases to be productive during a period when the Indian nation-state has quite clearly shown itself to be in a prolonged political and epistemic crisis. It is important to recognize that Rushdie's model in *MC* is not the only one operating in the contemporary Indian English novel, and no longer even the dominant one.

In the 1980s the new narratives of nation burst forth in a dazzling display of artistic pyrotechnics with a new confidence in self, language, and form. Their energy was based on a celebration of the simultaneous identity and duality of self and nation, a recognition of the creative potential of ambivalence. But ultimately life must be lived, and it cannot be lived for long on the fence—on the hyphen, as it were.[53] The energy that breaks forth from the crisis of the nation must eventually be redirected. When allegiance to an idea is lost in disillusionment, new allegiances must be affirmed (or old ones reaffirmed) and new commitments made, in order for life to go on. In the meantime, of course, life goes on anyway, and the interregnum is characterized by "a great diversity of morbid symptoms."[54]

The first wave of exhilaration that produced a score of epic national/personal narratives directly inspired by *MC* may well have run its course. As long as post-Rushdie narratives remained ideologically bound to Nation, they were forced to follow the contours of its crisis and recuperation. If they were not to trickle out into what Saleem Sinai dreaded most, meaninglessness and flippant indeterminacy, they would have to find ways to frame action, despite ambivalence, in or out of the confines of the national narrative.

Rather than taking Indian English writing down a slippery slope into global capitalism, with its postmodern free play and radical indeterminacy, many "post-Rushdie" novels would seem to be moving beyond ambivalence to new commitment. For instance, in Mukul Kesavan's first novel, *Looking Through Glass* (1995), the protagonist starts out as a disengaged young photographer who looks at history and politics only through the lens of his camera, but moves progressively closer to his subjects until his point of view merges altogether with theirs. Sudden and involuntary time-travel magically plunges him into the politically turbulent period of the Quit India Movement of 1942 and forces him to live a Muslim Indian version of history from the inside. This was a period when Muslim points of view began to be erased first from Congress Party politics and later from official Indian histories, and Kesavan dramatizes this erasure by allegorizing it, Rushdie-style: overnight, hundreds of Muslims literally disappear. *Looking Through Glass* carries many of the hallmarks of the post-Rushdie Indian English novel: its portrayal of the vexed but intimate relationship of the personal and the political, the ambivalence of its protagonist, its challenging of official histories and parallel presentation of alternative versions, the magic realism of its time travel, its "literalization of metaphor,"[55] and its valorization of political engagement.[56] In the tradition of *MC*, it does not allow itself to become mired in disabling ambivalence. But we have seen that *MC* simultaneously challenges and reinforces the dominant model of Indian nationalism, and is ultimately unable and unwilling to step out of the framework of the nation. *Looking Through Glass* is equally caught up with national history, challenging the official nationalist version both by applying a corrective lens and by progressively removing the lens between history and life; it does not reject the national altogether, but replaces nationalist politics with a more local allegiance to people and to places.

Just as the narrative of nation may marginalize other kinds of narratives, marginalized groups attempting to lay claim to the nation may themselves be written out of their own texts by the very terms in which the nationalist discourse is framed. Rajeswari Sunder Rajan observes in an essay on Nina Sibal's novel, *Yatra*, that women writers who have attempted to employ the narrative of nation find themselves condemned to rehearse a story that excludes them.[57] In general, national minorities and women, who have found that the exclusive discourse of nation cannot be made to tell their story, have been less likely to employ the narrative of nation. Protagonists of post-independence literary texts—particularly, but not exclusively, female protagonists—have become deadlocked when they have attempted to live out the conflicting demands of the nationalist synthesis. As we shall see in Chapter Five, novelists like Shashi Deshpande and Githa Hariharan, writing in the 1980s and 1990s, share many of the same conflicts and concerns with women writing earlier, in the 1960s and 1970s; with the crisis of the nation-state, however, they can begin to turn away from its language and forms to look for other ways of telling their stories.

Midnight's Children ends with the recognition that Saleem is at the end of a line. Nehru's promise has been drained of all possibility for him personally and perhaps even for India itself. Saleem recognizes that the country will have to fashion new ideals to inspire its people and move forward, but that will have to be the task of a new generation: "New myths are needed," he declares, "but that's none of my business."[58] Another post-Rushdie first novel, Amitav Ghosh's 1986 *The Circle of Reason*, ends with its orphan protagonist's return to India. The rationalist discourse that reared him has finally been discredited and consigned to the flames. He has been forced to live a life on the run from his own native land, and now he is free to return and make a new beginning. But it is clear that he will not be able to make it anew; he will have to work with the fragments he has. As one character says, "Nothing's whole any more. If we wait for everything to be right again, we'll wait for ever while the world falls apart. The only hope is to make do with what we've got."[59]

CHAPTER FIVE

"RETURNING" IN THE 1980S AND 1990S: THE PROMISE AND PERILS OF WOMEN'S AGENCY

With the crisis of the nation-state in the 1980s, we have seen that a number of Indian writers—overwhelmingly male—were able to open up the discursive space to present different perspectives on the nation by acknowledging their ambivalent relationship to it. As influential as Rushdie's model was, many Indian English novels in the 1980s and 1990s appeared to be untouched by it. As we noted in chapter four, this was particularly true of "domestic novels" written by women, which have maintained a continuity of conflicts and concerns since the early post-independence years. If, as I have suggested, Rushdie's conceptual breakthrough in *Midnight's Children* was to reconfigure the relationship between Self and Nation, it would appear that this reconfiguration was not generally a productive strategy for women.

We have also seen that the discourse of Nation was gendered from the start, and that the figure of Woman had always played an important symbolic and instrumental role in smoothing over the cracks in the national "synthesis"; further, that under colonialism, (male) nationalism designated the home as its sovereign space, and enshrined Woman in it as the guardian of an unbroken "Indian" tradition. Indian male frustrations and anxieties over capitulations to colonial power in the outside world were systematically displaced into the domestic realm, the home. For the individual woman, then, the language and forms of the nation have not enabled her to speak with her own voice, but made her a mere conduit for the national narrative. In this period of crisis for the long-dominant model of the nation-state, many different forces, both internal and external, rushed to fill the vacuum of power, providing opportunities for some, but additional pressures for others. Women writers in general had been caught in a coercive relationship with nation too long to find a further exploration of that relationship liberating. Rather, they used the crisis of nation as an opportunity to move away from its confining discourse. The new problem, however, was where they were to go.

During the 1980s and 1990s, action in Indian English novels by women, no less than in other literary and cultural texts, was repeatedly figured as a "return." In domestic novels by women that deliberately turned away from Nation as Home, the problem of action was twofold: what women were to return *to*, and how, upon their "re-return," they were to configure their relationship to a larger collectivity *differently*. Here the operative meaning of karma dictates that actions imperfectly performed or understood are doomed to be replayed as endless repetition. Thus we find female protagonists of domestic novels returning from marital to parental homes in an attempt to recover a new sense of self. I discuss three novels by Shashi Deshpande and two by Githa Hariharan, all of which configure action as a married woman's return to her father's house and a return to the master texts of a patriarchal tradition. I consider not only the liberating potential of such returns, but also their pitfalls, particularly in a period when ascendant forces of the religious Right have been enacting returns of their own.

Projects of Return and Recovery

Representations of women's situations in Indian English novels do not appear to have changed dramatically over the past thirty years. The female protagonists of so many Indian English women's novels of the post-independence period have been driven repeatedly into the darkness of interiority, madness, or self-destruction. Faced with a domestic crisis, their choices, especially if they are married women, are quite limited: return to their father's home, suicide, or some form of adjustment to the situation. Does this lack of change indicate unchanged ideologies and rationales governing women's choices and actions? Or does it indicate the lack of significant improvement in women's material realities? After all, repetition suggests a lack of meaningful change, and a lack of agency with which to effect change.[1]

The differences between the novels of the 1960s and 1970s and those of the late 1980s and 1990s may lie more in their characters' changed perspectives than in their material realities. If contemporary Indian women have more self-confidence, and more social and economic alternatives than their counterparts of a generation ago, what kind of new choices do they make, and perhaps more importantly, how do they justify these choices to themselves? Do "traditional" prescriptions for women suppress or sustain them? I have found that they do both, as women ambivalently both draw upon and problematize these codes.

As we saw in Anita Desai's early novels, alienation or escape was a recurrent theme in Indian English novels of the 1960s and 1970s. Many novels of the 1980s and 1990s have been preoccupied with the complementary theme of "return," in several senses of the word. In an intellectual and political climate that rejects the once-dominant Nehruvian secularism, return can mean attempts to return to a polity based on "Hinduism," variously interpreted. Return may be conceived as a healing process, one that involves revisiting a traumatic past that has been repressed or denied. The 1980s and 1990s saw returns to the long-suppressed trauma of the Partition, both in literary–cultural and person-to-person efforts that were both cathartic and healing, and in new historical analyses of the events leading to the Partition that were independent of the nationalist versions that had long dominated the field. New feminist and historical scholarship returned to colonialist and nationalist histories to recuperate subaltern perspectives and write new "histories from below."[2] Return may involve an attempt to tread an earlier path-not-taken, or a renewed assault by forces that have been defeated in the past, as in the resurgence of Hindu nationalism in the 1990s.

The fiftieth anniversary of independence in 1997 was naturally the occasion for critical reevaluation of the successes and failures of the past half-century. Contemporary critiques of nationalism in the past two decades spurred postcolonial scholarship to return to the colonial period with the important but theoretically challenging goals of attempting to rethink what-might-have-been, of retrieving an uncolonized consciousness that was not warped by Europe, and of identifying a uniquely "Indian" modernity.

In the postcolonial context, return often involves new readings of canonical literary or historical texts, a "writing back" by those who have been silenced in the colonial past. Canonical texts include those written by the former colonizer and the indigenous elite, but may also include indigenous high-culture texts that have been canonized by colonialism and nationalism alike. To the extent that such texts have provided the ideological underpinning of Orientalist representations or nationalist stereotypes, postcolonial writers return to them to confront and critique the ideas and assumptions that govern them. To the extent that these texts may yield other forms of knowledge or perspectives that were suppressed under colonialism, some postcolonial writers return to them as repositories of a lost or devalued cultural heritage.

In the late 1980s and early 1990s, instead of turning away from Hinduism at a time when the Hindu Right was in the ascendancy, some intellectuals and feminists attempted to reclaim a differently defined Hinduism. In a 1990 essay, Madhu Kishwar argued that it was important to reassert the tolerant, decentralized, nonviolent characteristics of Hinduism in the contemporary climate of intolerance toward minorities and women.[3] Because the Right had staked a claim on an exclusive, monolithic interpretation of Hinduism, she insisted that it was up to those who had a more liberal view of the Hindu way of life to articulate that view rather than to concede the entire field. Similarly, the novelist Shashi Deshpande, locating her characters very specifically within their regional high-caste Hindu milieu, lays claim to her Hindu cultural heritage, among others, but in her distinctively feminist and secular terms.

According to Shashi Deshpande, contemporary women writers return to the epics and Puranas "in search of some truths about themselves and their condition"—to ask new questions of these stories, rediscover themselves, and retell their own tales.[4] Because the stories have been passed down orally in an unbroken tradition, Deshpande sees the ideological influence of mythical figures on Indian women as all the more powerful. However, she argues that the old myths contain "complex, questioning characters in which we find ourselves," whereas in the crude stereotypes of the popular movies, they have been "shorn of their complexities," and the good woman "is always so selfless that she negates herself to the point of extinction." She further notes that since the female figures in mythology are the creations of men, it becomes difficult for contemporary women to imaginatively reappropriate them: "we have so internalized them that they are part of our personal, religious and Indian identity...we do not start with a picture of ourselves on a clear slate."

When contemporary female protagonists compare their twentieth-century lives to those of mythical heroes and heroines held up as models for human behavior, they appear to be both questioning the absolute validity of these models and seeking guidance for the difficult choices before them. This is a different articulation from the uses of mythical models in the novels of the 1950s and 1960s, in which nationalist texts idealized and glorified them, and "alienated" texts rejected them. Again and again, even while amply documenting the divergences between their own lives and those of the epic models, the women in the novels of the 1980s and 1990s ultimately find direction and support from the values they exemplify, deciding to align their own desires with these ancient social and personal ideals, reinforcing rather than rejecting them or even refashioning them into new formulae based on contemporary realities.

<h2 style="text-align:center">Shashi Deshpande: A New Traditionalism?</h2>

Shashi Deshpande won the Sahitya Akademi Award in 1988 for *That Long Silence*, which was published by Virago Press in London. All her previous work, however, had been published in India, and *That Long Silence* was her fifth novel—she had been writing since 1970.[5] Subsequently, *The Dark Holds No Terrors*, first published in 1980, has been reissued by Penguin Books India, followed by three more novels, *The Binding Vine* (Virago and Penguin India, 1993), *A Matter of Time* (Penguin India, 1996 and The Feminist Press, 1999), and *Small Remedies* (Viking Penguin India, 2000). Deshpande was born in Western India in the small town of Dharwar, Karnataka. Her mother was Maharashtrian and her father was the eminent Kannada writer and Sanskrit scholar Adya Rangacharya (or "Sriranga"), so she spoke both Marathi and Kannada and read Sanskrit in a home whose atmosphere was literary and intellectual while speaking and reading English in school. Her settings are decidedly regional, yet her vision is broad and eclectic, as she quotes with equal ease from Camus and Vyasa. She writes exclusively in English, but some of her novels "translate" less easily than others to non-Indian readers, not so much in their themes, but in the particularities of the familial relationships that circumscribe them.

Deshpande's heroines are typically educated middle-class women, sometimes professionals, rooted, like Deshpande herself, in a Western Indian social milieu and a Vedantic philosophical tradition, yet with a secular urban consciousness and a consciously feminist commitment to self-realization. Bringing both the philosophical and the pragmatic to bear upon the conflicts within themselves and their marriages, they often seem to emerge from their personal crises having fulfilled the requirements both of traditionally defined social duty and of modern, liberated women. Although their consciousness is self-avowedly secular, they are shaped by the ideals embodied in traditional stories of gods and heroes in the epics—particularly the *Mahabharata*.

In Deshpande's novel, *The Dark Holds No Terrors* (1980), as in Anita Desai's earlier novel, *Where Shall We Go This Summer?*, a married woman with children leaves her husband and home in desperation. In both cases the departure is itself a return, since the woman (Sarita in Deshpande's novel, Sita in Desai's) goes to the only place a married woman can go within a socially acceptable framework—her father's house and the home of her childhood.[6] And in both cases, after a hiatus in which the protagonist reflects upon her marriage and her childhood relationships with parents and siblings, the novels end with the husband coming to reclaim his wife. Beyond these superficial plot similarities, however, there are important differences in how the two protagonists rationalize their actions, and how they resolve their respective dilemmas.

The Dark Holds No Terrors (1980)

The novel opens with a story from the *Bhagavata Purana*. Sarita (Saru), a medical doctor and a married woman with two children, contrasts her unannounced arrival at her father's doorstep with the version of the Krishna-Sudama story "in one of her school texts, showing Krishna and his queen Rukmini running joyously to greet poor ragged Sudama standing at the palace gates" (15). She wonders why the story has come back to her, when it would seem that her own situation is different on every count. In the story Krishna washes Sudama's feet with his own hands, entertains him lavishly, and replaces his hut with a richly furnished house.[7] Saru, by contrast, is a well-heeled professional, and her father receives her "like an unwilling host entertaining an unwelcome guest" (18). The truth is that she and her Brahmin parents have been estranged ever since she married a low-caste man without their approval while she was still in medical school. Saru feels that her mother never forgave her for the accidental drowning death of her younger brother when she was a girl, a death for which Saru has internalized the guilt and carries a tremendous burden of self-hatred. Deshpande suggests from the outset that her problem may lie not so much in her objective condition as in her poor self-perception.

The immediate and ostensible reason for Sarita's return to her childhood home is that she has learned that her mother recently died of cancer and did not even ask for her daughter on her deathbed. The unspeakable reason is the sadistic sexual cruelty that her husband has been inflicting on her every night, cruelty that neither of them mentions in the light of day, and that she cannot find the inner resources to resist. The reason for her husband's behavior, she feels, is the humiliation of not being the primary breadwinner in the family. With the news of her mother's death, the pressures of all her repressed pain and guilt become too much for Sarita to bear. Eventually her father does give her a gift, as Krishna did Sudama, but it is not the one she might have hoped for or expected. His gift is to make her recognize, when she finally brings herself to speak the unspeakable, that she must face her troubles, not hide from them, that for a grown woman, her father's home can no longer be her refuge.[8] Saru must recognize her self-worth, and learn the difficult lesson from the *Dhammapada* that Deshpande quotes in the novel's epigraph: "You are your own refuge; there is no other refuge. This refuge is hard to achieve."

As she contrasts her shamefaced return with the stuff of idealized popular myth, Sarita also contrasts her nuclear family of one boy and one girl with the idealized family of state officialdom: "A family, the right size. The right kind, like the ads. A happy family. Healthy, happy, smiling and in color." Although looks like the ideal, in reality it is not. Just beneath the surface, night terrors seethe. She feels her life to be a mockery of these dominant ideals, and herself to be a mere mask. Her only possible source of authenticity is her profession, for when she is with a patient, she is wholly engaged in the task at hand. However, her professional success as a physician has not given her agency in the domestic sphere, as a wife.

Despite the success of her struggle to get a medical education, Sarita feels numbed by social pressures and paralyzed by the conflicting codes that condition women's action. She is angered by the traditional, housebound women who come to her for medical help at her father's house for "female troubles" that they have left untreated for too long, angry with "their unconscious, unmeaning heroism, born out of the myth of the self-sacrificing martyred woman...they had schooled themselves to silence" (107). Yet she has been suffering her husband's nightly attacks in the same silence. And when her father tells her that she must face her husband and talk to him, there is no one left to turn to, no place left to go. "It's my fault again," she thinks, when her father has left her alone. "If mine had been an arranged marriage, if I had left it to them to arrange my life, would he have left me like this?" (218). Having defied her parents in her marriage to the man of her choice, she is now unable to hold anyone but herself responsible for its failure. Ironically, having married for love and against her parents' wishes has meant giving herself up more completely than if she had married for more pragmatic reasons. She refers back wistfully to the *Mahabharata* story of King Shantanu who, besotted with a fisherman's daughter, agrees to her condition that she will marry him only if he will promise that her son will be the heir to the throne. In contrast, Saru had given her parents no opportunity to negotiate any conditions for her protection. "The fisherman's daughter was wiser. She sent the king to her father and it was the father who bargained with him. While I...I gave myself up unconditionally, unreservedly to him" (66).

More than once, even while fully recognizing that "we can't go back, we have to go on" (82), Saru finds herself wishing that she had lived during a time when there were fewer choices for women. "It was so much easier for women in those days to accept, not to struggle, because they believed, they knew, there was nothing else for them" (70). What price, then, her education, her urban sophistication? Drained of all energy and vitality, Saru reflects dully that she has made every effort to be an efficient, modern woman, and conform to the dreary round of urban middle-class social life.

> I'm not old-fashioned. I take great care not to be left behind. My legs are weary, my heart is numb, my mind a blank, but I keep marching on. I have even cut my hair, though with that I feel I have lost one means of expressing myself...But I cut it because I have to conform, to be like the others. Or else...? (59)

When a friend invites her to speak on medical careers for women at a girls' school, Sarita finds herself offering them hollow platitudes, telling them that "it's all a question of adjustment, really," that if they want to make both marriage and career work, they can do it. What she really wants to tell them is that in fact they can make their marriages work only if they subordinate their career to their husbands', making sure that their job is inferior in status to his.

Sarita recalls yet another Sanskrit story, of the woman "who would not disturb her husband's sleep even to save her child from the fire," a story "telling all women for all time" that their duty to their husband comes first. Again she finds herself wishing that she could really believe that. If she could really put her duty to her husband "above all else..." But this thought trails off, perhaps because it is not possible for her to do this, perhaps because she is not willing to accept its consequences. If she were to put her duty to her husband above all else, would she have to submit silently to his attacks forever? Would she have to give up her medical career? But without her medical career, they would not be able to maintain the standard of living to which they had all become accustomed. What of her duty to herself? All these questions have remained unanswered. But at no point has she considered the possibility of seeking outside help to stop the abuse, whether from a friend, a medical professional, or the law.

As she slips into the familiar, austere routine of life in her Brahmin childhood home, Sarita finds herself replaying the dilemmas of her married life and, quite against her will, returning to childhood memories and the origins of her adult guilt and self-hate. She is slowly forced to recognize how much she is, in fact, like her self-effacing but powerful mother, whose greater love for her brother than for her she still resents so bitterly. Her father tells Sarita of her mother's reconciliation with death, and of how in her last days she would ask him again and again to read her the story of Duryodhana's death from the *Mahabharata*. In spite of the legions who had fought with the Kauravas in the war, Duryodhana, their leader, ultimately had to face death alone. Sarita's mother had said, "That's what all of us have to face at the end. That we are alone" (194).

With the realization that she has nowhere to run comes a vast sense of relief. Sarita is alone, alone as her mother was at the moment of her death. Ultimately, her only refuge is herself, her only strength her own. At first the realization seems a tremendously lonely one. Her initial reaction is a sense of unreality, in which nothing really matters. But almost immediately her ruthlessly critical mind rejects this nihilistic response as "too glib, too easy a way out," until a second revelation comes to her, "the same one, perhaps that her mother had when she had heard Duryodhana's story just before she died."[9] It is an utterly Vedantic understanding of the ultimate unreality of the world of names and forms, real on its own terms, but ultimately illusory, a creation of one's own mind. Sarita sees that "Even if it is an illusion, it is the only reality we know ... Therefore, the only thing is to go on as if it is real, knowing all the while it is only an illusion" (219–220). This formulation helps to give her the strength to act, the "positive way to reject the world" that Arjuna found in the Gita and that Sita in Desai's *Where Shall We Go This Summer?* sought in vain. Along with this recognition comes an understanding that she is playing a number of socially defined roles—"the guilty sister, the undutiful daughter, the unloving wife"—and that although each of them is real in its own sphere, they do not wholly define her. She is able to accept these imperfectly performed roles as parts of her self, because she has the larger understanding that "if she was all of them, they were not all of her. She was these and so much more." Now that she has accepted sole responsibility for what she makes of her life, and knows that she has inner resources beyond the roles that she is socially obliged to carry out, Sarita finds the strength to face her husband.

Interestingly, rather than blaming her abusive husband, she blames her own fear and incomplete understanding: "I have been my own enemy" (221). As the doorbell rings, she summons up all her courage to face her husband, but it is a neighbor, sent for her help in a child's medical emergency. She throws herself into her role as lifesaver, pausing only to leave a message for her husband to wait for her: she will be back. Sarita's actions are justified by Vedanta philosophy, as she equates her choice to reengage with the struggle of life with the battle of the *Mahabharata*, a battle that must be fought, whatever the outcome.

In this 1980 novel, Deshpande's presentation and resolution of Saru's isolated response to her abuse must be seen in the context of its time, when the problem of domestic violence was only just being taken up by the Indian women's movement, whose second, post-independence resurgence had begun in the mid-1970s.[10] Even today few women leave such situations, and many who do leave may find, like Sarita, and like Sita in Desai's *Where Shall We Go This Summer?*, that return is in fact the best—or only—option for them. In a personal account of her return to an abusive marriage, Bombay feminist Flavia Agnes wrote,

> I went back with a very different attitude…I went back as a person and not a nonentity…The vague dream, a faint vision that I had cherished all the while deep down in my heart, has taken shape…There is something positive in it for me as well, not just as a mother but also as an individual.[11]

In such cases, the most meaningful change might be in a woman's new sense of self, rather than in any measurable improvement in her circumstances.

Although the novel's ending does not reveal whether or not Sarita returns to her husband, it does establish that she makes a commitment to deal with their problems. Further, she recognizes that she has a purpose in life beyond her duty to her husband and family, namely, to fulfil her calling as a medical doctor. When Sarita throws herself into solving a medical emergency, she for once is unplagued by doubts: "There were no thoughts in her mind except those of the child she was going to help" (221). Her tortured "I" finds a new perspective and sense of proportion in the recognition of itself as part of a larger Self, and in nonattached action—selfless service. This nonattachment is not an escape, however, but a full acceptance of responsibility for herself and her actions.

That Long Silence *(1988)*
When her husband Mohan is accused of embezzlement in a burgeoning corruption scandal at work, Jaya, the protagonist of Deshpande's Sahitya Akademi Award–winning novel, *That Long Silence* (1988), is forced to leave their well-appointed home in a fashionable section of Bombay and take refuge for a time in an empty flat belonging to her family.[12] Mohan has to leave for Delhi, and her children are away on holiday, so for the first time since her marriage she is alone for an extended period of time. She finds herself calling into question all her choices in life, including her acceptance of the role of wife and her submission to her husband's values, judgments, and priorities. Feverishly, she sets down on paper her own and her family's stories, particularly the frustrations, resentments, and tragedies of the women, and through the act of writing slowly begins to move through crisis toward a new self-awareness.

Jaya rails at the relentlessness of women's responsibilities: "A woman can never be angry; she can only be neurotic, hysterical, frustrated. There's no room for anger in my life, no room for despair, either. There's only order and routine—today, I have to change the sheets; tomorrow, scrub the bathrooms; the day after, clean the fridge…" Kamat was a man with whom Jaya had had a close and unconventional friendship for years, with whom she had been able to talk honestly. She had abandoned him at the hour of his death, because of her fear of scandal if found to have been at his deathbed. Kamat, she recalls, had encouraged her to redirect her very real and justifiable anger into her writing rather than suppressing it, bemoaning her victimhood, and wallowing in self-pity.

> Middle class. Bourgeois. Upper-caste. Distanced from real life. Scared of writing. Scared of failing. Oh God, I had thought, I can't take any more. Even a worm has a hole it can crawl into. I had mine—as Mohan's wife, as Rahul's and Rati's mother. (148–149)

Kamat had accused her of taking the easy way out in hiding behind her duties of wife and mother and had confronted her with her real reason for having stopping writing seriously.

Jaya finally acknowledges to herself that she had succumbed to social pressures that silence women who struggle to write, and taken refuge behind the façade of her socially sanctioned roles. She realizes that she has been blaming her husband for her failure to continue serious creative writing, when in fact the reason has been her own fear of failure. Instead she has written lightweight, humorous pieces for a women's magazine under the pen-name Seeta, in the persona of a middle-class housewife. She also realizes that she must take responsibility for the emptiness of her marriage, because she has detached herself from it, rather than committing herself to a full relationship with another human being. Here Deshpande is critical of nonattachment as an abdication of personal responsibility for actions and their consequences. Jaya cannot dissociate herself from her husband's drift into corruption, and Deshpande's clear implication is that this drift is a larger, nationwide phenomenon, something that has been allowed to happen by a similar abdication of responsibility on the part of middle-class Indians since independence.[13]

After having poured out on paper all the conflicts and tensions that she has suppressed for so many years, Jaya asks herself what she has achieved. Her answer is that she is no longer afraid of "breaking through that thin veneer of a happy family" (191). Recalling her youthful anger upon learning that women were not traditionally permitted to speak Sanskrit, but had been restricted to Prakrit, the vernacular, she now no longer feels outraged at the injustice, but angry with herself: "... I realise what I've been doing all these years. I have been speaking Prakrit myself."

Jaya compares herself to Gandhari in the *Mahabharata*, who, as a new bride, blindfolded herself when she found that King Dhritarashtra, the man to whom she had just been married, was blind. Looking at her son and brother-in-law talking easily with each other, she suddenly sees them not merely in their relationships to her, but as "two persons, at ease with each other, with themselves." She comes to see that rather than using her duties as a wife and mother as a refuge from the world, her duty lies in engaging fully with her husband and children as whole human beings; in having the social responsibility to answer her children's questions about politics; in having the courage to take issue with her husband when she feels he is doing wrong; and in having the perseverance to work at her writing and to take it seriously, regardless of whether or not it is successful. It is this act of seeing anew, rather than any material change in her relationship with her husband, that makes her return meaningful. She feels "[A]s if in releasing them from the slots I'd put them in I'd released myself somehow" (189–190).

After she has spent the whole novel in self-examination, she reunites, disillusioned, with her husband and family (191). Remembering the final words of Krishna's sermon to Arjuna in the Gita, "Do as you desire," she interprets them as follows: "With this line, after all those millions of words of instruction, Krishna confers humanness on Arjuna. 'I have given you knowledge. The choice is yours. Do as you desire.'"[14] Like Sarita, Jaya asks herself, "With whom shall I be angry? And the answer comes, "With myself, of course." Ultimately, Jaya's action is predicated upon a new self-knowledge, her karma a freely chosen acceptance of her responsibilities to herself, her family, and her society. The novel works toward a conclusion similar to that of *The Dark Holds No Terrors*—the Vedantic recognition that the individual herself is responsible for becoming a complete human being. The socially sanctioned roles of wifehood and motherhood can become excuses not to work at fulfilling her own potential and developing her other talents. Rather than using the Gita's call to nonattachment as a coping mechanism that permits her to remain alienated from herself and society, Jaya's sees her challenge as being to realize herself more fully by throwing herself into her duties, both to others and to her best self.

Recognizing that life holds so many choices, Jaya chooses the traditionally sanctioned one—to return to her husband. Her desires, after all, are in conformity with *dharma*. After an entire novel in which the heroine has "broken a long silence," she ends selflessly, like Sita in *Where Shall We Go This Summer?*, choosing to downplay the understanding she has so painfully gained: "... why am I making myself the heroine of this story? Why do I presume that the understanding is mine alone?" And yet, unlike Sita, who was compelled to return, alienated and alone, Jaya returns out of a free and active choice to reengage with her world. Going beyond mere blame, Jaya gives her husband the benefit of the doubt, returning not to any dramatic change in their relationship, but with a new commitment on her part and the hope for long-term change. In the end, the change lies in the new perspective with which Jaya returns and in her hope for change. Without hope, she realizes, "life would be impossible. And if there is anything I now know it is this: life always has to be made possible" (192–193).

Is this a courageous, newly self-assertive Indian woman, made possible through a return to traditional wisdom? Or is it the old, old story of patriarchal norms rationalizing and justifying the *status quo,* where a woman's highest duty and deepest desire is fulfilled through her husband and marriage, where, if there is a problem in the marriage, the woman must locate it within herself? There appears to be a touch of the pat resolution in these two early Deshpande novels, which both end rather abruptly with the heroine finding new meaning for herself in traditional formulae. They also end "on the threshold" of action, after she has reached a new self-understanding, but before she has implemented it in her life. Rosemary Marangoly George looks skeptically upon Jaya's final and not altogether convincing resolution to "pull herself together," noting how tenuously she has drawn her many fragmented and dispersed selves together through the process of writing. The identities of both Deshpande's heroines, Sarita and Jaya, are an amalgam of their various roles, and, as with Desai's female protagonists, they are fragmented and dispersed through their identification or nonidentification with others in their life, mostly extended family members. George notes that "the specter of Kusum," Jaya's impoverished cousin who committed suicide, haunts Jaya and negatively informs her identity as "the only available alternative."[15] However, unlike the early Anita Desai novels that end in self-destruction for the heroine, Deshpande's young heroines are determined to survive. Shashi Deshpande's heroines do tend to be economically more self-sufficient than Desai's. As the primary breadwinner in her family, Sarita could perhaps choose to approach the old formulae with a stronger sense of self, rather than having self-denial thrust upon her, as happens to Desai's heroines. But despite her potential economic independence, she still endures her husband's sadism and has to escape to her father's home; and ultimately, it is her father who convinces her that she must face her husband.

A Matter of Time *(1997)*

A Matter of Time was Shashi Deshpande's seventh novel, and her first to be published in the United States.[16] Quietly, intensely cerebral, it is typical of her work in its lonely Vedantic vision, and its faithful representation of middle-class life in Western India from a woman's perspective. As in her earlier novels, a woman with children whose marriage is in crisis must return to her father's home. But it is here that the differences begin.

In the epigraph, from the *Brihadaranyaka Upanishad*, the sage Yajnavalkya tells his wife Maitreyi that he has decided to renounce the life of the householder. This episode is mirrored in the novel's beginning, when Sumi and her three teenaged daughters must return to her ancestral home after Sumi's husband Gopal unilaterally decides to leave them, abandoning his life as a householder. From the moment Sumi's mother Kalyani greets her with the anguished cry, "No! Not again!," both the readers and the characters are haunted with a persistent sense of *deja vu* at the repetition of an unresolved family past. For Kalyani, too, had once had to return to her father's house with her daughters, after having been abandoned by her own husband, Shripati, as punishment for the loss of their son. (The loss of a husband, father, or male child, and its consequences for the surviving sister or mother, are recurrent themes in Deshpande's work, in this novel as well as in *The Binding Vine, The Dark Holds No Terrors*, and the powerful short story, "My Beloved Charioteer." Sumi's mother, Kalyani, blames herself for her own mother's disappointment in not having had a son, just as, in *The Dark Holds No Terrors*, Sarita was made to feel guilty for her brother's accidental drowning, haunted forever after by her distracted mother's outburst, "It should have been you.")

Deshpande meditates on the limits of individual freedom and agency throughout the novel, as Sumi, Gopal, and their daughters each struggle for emotional and economic independence. Sumi's husband Gopal's renunciation and her father Shripati's abandonment (and the novel explores the fine line between the two) invite comparison with the Upanisadic sage Yajnavalkya, although, as Ritu Menon points out in her Afterword, one major difference is that the two modern men renounce their duties as householders long before those duties have been fully discharged. Gopal's bid for freedom and self-realization at least temporarily curtails the freedom of Sumi and his daughters by forcing them to become dependent on others and to return to Sumi's ancestral home. Each of her daughters reacts differently to Gopal's departure, and Arundhati (Aru), the eldest, is particularly angry, seeking legal recourse to "get justice" and to "make him pay." However, Sumi holds herself aloof from any legal action, making it clear that she has no desire for retribution. Just as Yajnavalkya's wife Maitreyi never condemns Yajnavalkya's action or indulges in self-pity, instead concerning herself with how she, too, may attain enlightenment, so Sumi alone of all her friends and family never blames her husband's abdication of his responsibilities as a householder, but instead turns inward, gaining a new perspective on the past and preparing herself to embark upon a new stage of independent action in her own life.

Who is the novel's protagonist? As in *That Long Silence*, the narrator asks this question, and keeps the reader guessing as to the answer. Four—even five—generations of women inhabit the novel. At the center are forty-year-old Sumi, her three teenage daughters, and her mother Kalyani; and in the background, but very much present, the spirits of Kalyani's educated mother Manorama and Manorama's pioneering teacher Yamunabai. However, even before the novel introduces its human protagonists, it presents and characterizes the Big House, Sumi's mother's family home, giving it the status of an actor in the plot. From the beginning, the house, named Vishwas (Trust) after Vishwasrao, Kalyani's father, and of which Kalyani is immensely proud, is described ambivalently as both impressive and oppressive, providing a sense of continuity but also a certain claustrophobia. No matter how much Sumi seeks freedom, it seems that she is fated to return to the Big House. During a short-lived spell of househunting for herself and the girls, she sketches her ideal house for the rental agent and discovers that he has reproduced her ancestral home. She tries again, but "once again it is the same. It is as if she has no choice but to follow that unseen tracing" (78).

It would seem that Shashi Deshpande's own Big House is her personal and cultural past. Her father was an eminent Sanskrit and Kannada scholar, and although she was educated in English, she has studied Sanskrit and translated some of his work after his death. The Great Tradition of Vedic Brahmanism is a repository of wisdom to which she continually finds herself returning, an edifice that she recognizes as patriarchal, yet hopes to inhabit in new ways, to reappropriate for herself. Wisdom, she has argued, has no gender.[17] In *A Matter of Time*, Gopal observes that people use myths to justify their own personal desires, and yet reflects that there is no rejecting the past: whether people seek to recreate or resist it, they "are always, in some way, giving it a place in [their] lives" (100). Deshpande suggests that in spite of the continual feelings of *deja vu*, that despite the seemingly endless repetition of the patterns of pain and oppression in this family, it is only a matter of time, even if it is not within the timeframe of this novel, before her protagonists, male and female, will be able to reconcile themselves with their pasts and be able to gain individual and collective agency and self-realization.

The novel's ending forces the question of Deshpande's perspective on leaving the father's house. Slowly, Sumi begins to recover from the shock of Gopal's desertion, comes to terms with him, ventures out into the world again, and finds herself able to write a play. She applies successfully for a job at a residential school and is preparing to depart, joyfully anticipating the beginning of her new life. Then, in the novel's penultimate chapter, Sumi offers her silent father a ride on her scooter. For the first time ever, he utters the name of his dead son to her. The expression on his face gives her a sudden epiphanic moment of clarity—and then the bus hits them. Suddenly the character whom the reader has taken to be the protagonist is dead. It appears that she was destined never to leave her father's house. However, her daughters, her mother, and the Big House remain, and by the end of the novel, the demons of the past have been substantially laid to rest for them. The baton passes to Aru, who has just turned eighteen and who takes charge with courage and strength of character. Aru has become very close to her grandmother Kalyani and has pledged to be both daughter and son to her. In caring for her granddaughters, Kalyani is able to rejoin the community of the living. Her husband has made the Big House over to her in his will—after all, it was originally Kalyani's father's house.

A Matter of Time ends with the old and the young woman relinquishing any claims on Gopal. Thus, they set him free to go on a personal pilgrimage of sorts, taking Sumi's ashes to immerse in a river that the two of them had visited together as a young couple. Kalyani and Aru are strong in themselves and each other, and refuse to curtail his freedom with their dependency. Although action is ultimately up to the individual, as it was in her earlier novels, it is also conditioned by family and community histories that cannot be ignored if they are not to doom the individual to endless repetition. Whether or not it is productive for contemporary Indian feminists to return to recuperate their patriarchal tradition, it would seem that Deshpande's female protagonists are driven to do so. For them, there is no other way forward, except by returning first to the father's house, and finding that it is the house of their mothers and foremothers as well.

*   *   *

Of the novels discussed above, Anita Desai has criticized *The Dark Holds No Terrors* as exemplifying a tendency of women's writing in the 1960s and 1970s to find "orthodox traditional society . . . more protective to their feminine identities than the modern one with its so-called 'Western' ways." Desai writes:

> In *The Dark Holds No Terrors*, Shashi Deshpande's heroine Saru leaves her sadistic husband and returns to the Brahmin home of her childhood that she had earlier repudiated because of its life-denying austerity and rigors. Femininity and family were seen as limiting and restricting but also protective and desirable. Tradition was questioned—but accepted.[18]

To what extent is this a valid critique? We have seen that protagonists of Desai's own novels of the 1960s and 1970s attempted to problematize received ideals, and yet were often unable to find workable alternatives, so that they ended in alienation, even self-destruction for their female protagonists. What are the effects of Deshpande's returns in terms of the possibilities they offer for action? In many respects Deshpande's novels would seem to cover the same ground as those of the early Desai, with their themes of light and darkness, acceptance and rejection, engagement and escape. To what extent do Deshpande's resolutions of her protagonists' crises of action indicate any advance over those that were possible for Desai ten to twenty years earlier?

Deshpande's female protagonists work toward the redefinition of their traditionally assigned roles and responsibilities to self, family, and community. Unlike most of Desai's female protagonists, Deshpande's heroines are educated professionals working actively in the outside world. However, while they have more choices in theory, they still find themselves unable to emerge from their personal darkness until crisis forces them to find inner strength and act. Although they may work in the public sphere, the private sphere of family and psyche is more real to them, and can often be crippling. While most of Desai's heroines inhabit different emotional universes from their husbands, Deshpande's characters are committed to developing more reciprocal relationships with their spouses, at least in principle. The challenge for them lies in how to fulfil their responsibilities to themselves while continuing to fulfil their duties to husband, family, and society.

With respect to the nationalist ideal of nonattached action, Deshpande's protagonists redefine the Gandhian model of action as the performance of responsibility both to society and to oneself. However, in her novels of the 1980s, the action confines itself largely to the private sphere and a fairly narrow social sphere.[19] Responsibility to a wider community beyond class and community is limited to individual efforts, such as helping one's maidservant. Abuses such as rape and domestic violence do not seem to be treated as problems for which there could be a collective social remedy, despite the contemporary women's campaigns on those very issues. However, her scope has steadily broadened over the course of the 1980s and 1990s, although her focus has remained on the individual and on personal relationships.[20]

Deshpande's is a lonely vision. In middle-class urban life, the nation is embodied in the new ideals held up to be emulated, ideals which, like the posters of the perfect family in *The Dark Holds No Terrors*, give women expectations to which they feel duty-bound to conform. They will do violence to themselves in order to act in accordance with those ideals. The struggle to achieve a sense of wholeness remains a personal struggle in the private sphere rather than an effort to achieve a social transformation. The female protagonists seek a synthesis between the demands of modern, urban professional life and the traditional demands of husband, home, and family. However, most of the crises appear to resolve themselves by returning the responsibility for fulfilling both sets of demands—modern professional and traditional—squarely onto the individual woman's shoulders.

Is this a new woman, at once traditional, professional, and feminist, whom we meet in Deshpande's novels of the 1980s? In the 1980s, economic privatization colluded with social privatization as the individual and the family became the new focus of both advertising and social conservatism. And once again in the 1980s and 1990s as in the 1880s during the emergence of bourgeois nationalism, the burden of effecting a graceful synthesis among conflicting social and political forces falls on the individual Indian woman, expected to be at once essentially traditional and effortlessly modern in a rapidly changing world.[21] This would appear to be the pressurized world inhabited by Shashi Deshpande's intelligent, overworked heroines, a world of personal responsibility that allows no escape, even through a return to "tradition."

In Deshpande, action is conceived of as duty, as a responsibility that the individual should shoulder willingly. Insisting on the individual's responsibility to herself, to fulfil her own potential, whether emotional, creative, or spiritual, she rejects withdrawal from the struggle of life as the cowardly option. Mental or psychic detachment, however, provides a certain distance from the pressures of multiple and often-conflicting roles, and some of her early characters do use it as a survival mechanism. However, Deshpande's protagonists learn that love cannot be partial—it must be unconditional and wholehearted. As Bim recognized in her flash of insight in Desai's *Clear Light of Day*, several of Deshpande's characters recognize that their own love has been incomplete. Like Nanda Kaul in Desai's *Fire on the Mountain*, Urmi, the protagonist of *The Binding Vine*, finally rejects nonattachment as an escape. Love necessarily implies attachment, and there can be no escape from its bonds.

Githa Hariharan's Protagonists: Telling Stories to Save Their Lives

The Thousand Faces of Night *(1992)*

Githa Hariharan's first novel, *The Thousand Faces of Night* (1992),[22] would appear to be retreading the same ground as Anita Desai's first novel, *Cry, the Peacock*, published almost thirty years before. The young heroine raised with "modern" expectations is betrayed, flung into an arranged marriage with a coldly rationalist, unimaginative husband who doesn't understand her. She cannot cope with the running of the household or the obligatory entertainment of his colleagues from work. Childless, cloistered at home all day, excluded from her husband's male world, she withdraws into herself and a hypersensitive state bordering on insanity. Interestingly, the two novels even share the motif of the peacock, that flightless bird whose brilliantly plumed male is a national symbol of India. At first reading there would seem to have been no advances at all in middle-class women's fictional self-representation. Hariharan's protagonist, Devi, appears to be as isolated and socially marginalized as her early post-independence predecessors. Even read again and more closely, Githa Hariharan's claustrophobic novel does not easily open up new spaces of action for its protagonist, until it is examined through the lens of a recuperative project of return.

The first point to note is that the main plot traces a double return. In the first chapter the young protagonist, Devi (goddess), is making preparations for her return home to Madras after two years of graduate study in the United States. She has neither been ordered to come home nor has she had a particularly strong desire to do so; a sense of inevitability attends her return. In fact, she has an American boyfriend who has asked her to marry him, but she cannot even conceive of the possibility, feeling that her whole experience in the United States is unreal, merely an interlude before real life begins. Her mother's regular aerogrammes lead her gently but inexorably back "to walk along the shores of an Indian rebirth" (6). As she steps into the plane, the American years fall away as if they had never been. She returns to Madras defenseless and unsuspecting, though filled with uncertainty and "a nameless dread," to a mother who has carefully, methodically, laid plans for her homecoming. The second return, performed in the final chapter of the novel, follows a flight from her husband's house and a miserable marriage. Significantly, both returns are to her waiting mother, both are performed in the wake of the death of a father (Devi's father dies while she is away in America and her father-in-law dies on a visit to America), and both coincide with Diwali, the festival of lights and Hindu New Year.

There are also returns enacted by other female characters in the novel—most importantly, that of Devi's mother Sita, who, after a married life of disciplined self-denial and the death of her husband, returns to an empty house and eventually, to the veena, the musical instrument she loved in her youth. The plot circles back repeatedly from Devi's life and the life stories of the three generations of women in the novel to Devi's grandmother's stories of the goddesses and idealized women of Indian mythology, recounted as role models to Devi as a girl. One of them, that of Gandhari (interestingly, also drawn upon by Jaya in Shashi Deshpande's *That Long Silence*), can be taken as emblematic of the predicaments of both Devi and her mother Sita.

As noted earlier, Gandhari was the wife of the blind King Dhritarashtra and the mother of the one hundred Kauravas in the *Mahabharata*. Not much is said about her in the Critical Edition of the *Mahabharata*, except that she bound her own eyes with cloth when she heard that her husband-to-be was blind, that all her sons died in battle at the hands of their cousins the Pandavas, and that after the war was over, she and her husband, along with her sister-in-law Kunti (the mother of the Pandavas) died in a forest fire.[23] The binding of her eyes has traditionally been taken as a demonstration of Gandhari's wifely devotion and her desire not to upstage her husband in anything or to experience anything that she could not share with him.[24]

The anthropologist Irawati Karve departed sharply from that interpretation in her book, *Yuganta* (End of an Epoch, 1967), where she discussed different individuals in the *Mahabharata* in terms of the kind of warrior society whose values, ethos, and kinship structures she reconstructed from reading the then-newly published Critical Edition. Karve's view of Gandhari, one that is much closer to the spirit of both Deshpande's and Hariharan's, arises from a very different perspective on the seemingly perfect wife, in which Gandhari is not simply an appendage of her husband, but an agent who makes choices. Karve sees her action as altogether destructive, and literally, binding. In her fictionalized retelling, Gandhari binds her eyes out of anger, to spite Dhritarashtra, and then gets trapped in the role of a devoted wife, "chained to the results of [her] own actions." Karve changes Gandhari's end as well: in the final, ascetic phase of his life, Dhritarashtra begs Gandhari to take off her blindfold, "give up [her] fight against life" and "learn to look at the world... objectively." At her husband's request, Gandhari yields at last, agreeing to open her eyes for both of them, and after a few days of adjustment is able to see again. But it is at this point that the forest fire approaches. Dhritarasthra asks her to save herself, but she will not hear of it, and the two walk hand in hand toward the blaze, "a sati... holding her living husband's hand and walking to the pyre."[25]

In Karve's version, although she was wronged in having been married to a blind man without being told, Gandhari was wrong to blindfold herself out of pride and anger. Once she had done so, she could not bring herself to forgive, and thereby kept both herself and her husband in the dark. In the end, Gandhari was able to let go of a lifetime of anger and resentment, and thereby freed herself at last. Walking into the fire with her husband thus became the first really positive act of her married life. Karve's vision is stoic and unyielding, very much like Shashi Deshpande's in *That Long Silence*, where Jaya came to realize that she could not blame her husband or anyone else for their predicament or for her own failings. She herself had chosen to turn a blind eye to his misdemeanors at work and to be a smaller person than she could be. Rather than facing the challenges of life, she had chosen to blindfold herself. In the end she removed the blindfold and faced the fire with her husband.

In *The Thousand Faces of Night*, when Devi asks questions about the ordinary lives around her, Devi's grandmother tells the young girl stories of mythical heroines in explanation. Devi comes across an old black-and-white photograph of her mother, young, dreamy, and holding a veena in her hands. When she takes the photo to her grandmother and asks her if Amma had played the veena as a girl, grandmother tells her the story of Gandhari by way of reply.

"Why didn't they tell her" that Dhritarashtra was blind, Devi wants to know. "Because, my child, a woman meets her fate alone." Grandmother presents Gandhari as proud and angry, yes, but "not just another willful, proud woman ... [s]he embraced her destiny—a blind husband—with a self-sacrifice worthy of her royal blood" (28–29). Gandhari's anger, "the fury that was to become her life-force, the central motive of years of blind suffering," and Devi comes to realize that her own mother Sita is also driven by that proud, blinding anger, that her parents were also "afflicted by a kind of blindness." When Sita had been a young wife, new to the home of her husband's family, her father-in-law had reprimanded her for neglecting her duties in favor of her veena practice, and after that day Sita had plucked the strings right out of the instrument and refused to play again. All her frustrated energy was thenceforth channeled into achieving wifely and motherly perfection, and to the control, advancement, and correction of her mild, unambitious husband and dreamy daughter. As Devi learns through her grandmother's stories and her own experience, her mother's anger has been sustaining, even heroic, but also destructive of herself and those around her.

By valorizing epic heroines like Gandhari, and, by extension, her daughter-in-law Sita, Grandmother teaches Devi that "no heroine died without this powerful and destructive protest that left its mark, a memorial to a fighter, behind her" (40). Citing this passage, Chanda, Ho and Mathai have asserted that *The Thousand Faces of Night* offers an "unambiguous ... message of resistance," with Grandmother teaching Devi not a "a passive acceptance of fate," but rather that "victimization can be transformed into agency." They argue that Grandmother's stories and the real-life stories of Devi's mother Sita and her husband's old housekeeper, Mayamma, open a space for Devi "to take her place among 'her people'—people both as the wider cultural community and, within that, a specific community of women."[26] I agree that the novel seeks to open up space for both refuge and resistance, but suggest that it makes the argument that women's resistance can never be unambiguous within the Indian patriarchal framework, and that the transformation of victim into agent takes place at great personal cost.

In a 1993 essay, Kumkum Sangari problematized the notion of women's "agency" or "empowerment" as a good in itself. She argued that in the contemporary social context, agency for "powerless" women could involve inciting men to violent action, or even being themselves empowered to engage in violent direct action against other women.[27] Sita does indeed perform her socially assigned role to perfection, but she performs it with a vengeance, arguably driving her husband into an early death and her daughter into a bad marriage as well as denying herself the creative fulfilment of her music. In her essay, "Is the Hindu Goddess a Feminist?," Rajeswari Sunder Rajan points out that "agency is never to be found in some pure state of volition or action, but is complexly imbricated in the contradictory structures of patriarchy."[28] Hariharan herself is fully aware of this complexity, and she recognizes that Devi must "de-code" the traditional stories before she can understand how to gain strength from them, recognizing that like all cultural texts, they can be read in more than one way.

Chanda et al. have pointed out that the ending of the novel signals a shift, "from a self-sacrificing to a self-preserving femininity," that allows Devi to challenge dominant national stories by returning to her *mother's* home, to a rebirth and a "reversal of roles," whereby the mother—pointedly *not* the submissive Sita of the epic—will no longer act to shape her daughter into a model of the ideal wife, but has let go of that controlling power and turned to her veena again.[29] Both Chanda et al. and Nilufer Bharucha point to the imagery of Geeta's return to her mother as a return to the womb, but suggest that the second return is not a claustrophobic reenclosure, but a process of development in which she will discover her inner resources.[30] Unlike the womb of grimly blindfolded Gandhari that, after a prolonged period of gestation, gave birth to a hard stone, which in turn became her one hundred sons whose greed precipitated the end of their era, Devi's return to the womb promises an opening-up of possibilities, not a locking-down. The open ending suggests that both mother and daughter will embark together on a journey of self-discovery, whereby Devi will gain the strength necessary to take her place among a "community of women" and "leave a mark of protest worthy of the heroines I grew up with."[31] Although the novel does not specify whether or not Devi will return to her husband, indications are that the one quality she must cultivate is staying power. Since Devi ran away, Old Mayamma has had to hold the fort in her absence as she has so many times before—when her own husband left her, when her mistress (Devi's mother-in-law) left, prematurely taking a vow of renunciation. One person's abdication of responsibility means another person's greater burden. Furthermore, all the stories Devi has been told are stories of women who rose to meet adversity, not women who ran away from it. Devi's father and father-in-law are both dead, Brahmin intellectuals both, both of whom she has been very close to, and the spaces they have left similarly challenge her to find an alternative to their Brahmanical texts that seemed to offer women no access to liberation. *The Thousand Faces of Night* leaves its heroine with this formidable challenge.

While it is indeed true, as Deshpande insists, that women can and do continue to gain sustenance and insights from the two great Indian epics, the failure to find an alternative that is outside of a high-caste, patriarchal frame, even when returning to the mother, points to some of the limits of the worldview that informs Deshpande's and Hariharan's work in the 1980s and early 1990s—*The Dark Holds No Terrors*, *That Long Silence*, and *The Thousand Faces of Night*. In all the above novels, the protagonists returned to stories of women in the *Mahabharata*, which, as Shashi Deshpande notes, offers three-dimensional characters whose actions and choices can be questioned from a number of different perspectives.[32] (They pointedly avoid the *Ramayana's* heroine Sita, except as a negative stereotype of female submissiveness. In *That Long Silence*, it will be recalled, Jaya's pen-name was Seeta, and in *The Thousand Faces of Night*, Sita is Devi's own mother.) In her third novel, Githa Hariharan attempts both to step out of the high-Hindu patriarchal story and to shift perspectives from elite to subaltern.

The Dangers of "Women's Returns" in the 1990s
Feminist projects of return and recovery may risk essentializing the category of Woman, returning to worldviews that most women today would find coercive, and

reinforcing, even if unintentionally, the agenda of political organizations that would strip women of hard-won rights. For instance, Ashis Nandy has suggested that in ancient times, becoming sati may have been a particular prerogative of women, since annihilation of the Self is the highest spiritual ideal of Hinduism, and women were considered to be innately spiritually powerful and self-sacrificing.[33] Rajeswari Sunder Rajan has warned of attempting to recuperate Hindu cultural forms for feminist projects for the very reason that it risks exalting women in such terms: "the problem with women's embrace of alterity is that it is based on an essentialised concept of femaleness, which is also an idealised one" (36–37). She notes that "some Indian feminists would be cautious about buying into the constituency of 'women' by extending the scope and politics of contemporary Hinduism," a Hinduism that is patently *not* the religion of the *Mahabharata*, something more monolithic, less open to interpretation. Besides feminists, Sunder Rajan argues, non-Hindus should be wary of the contemporary attempt to embrace "Hindu religious symbols and practices," especially when they are normalized and incorporated into the "secular" sphere.

In the past decade Indian feminists have had good reason to feel a sense of urgency about the need to envision a different future. In the early 1990s, problems of power, agency, and constituency came to a head for the Indian women's movement with a series of national events whose far-reaching results have come to be referred, in shorthand, as "Mandal-Masjid" and "Fund-Bank." First, there was the upper-caste backlash in 1990 against the Mandal Commission's proposals to expand the long-standing policy of employment and education reservations for low-caste and outcaste Indians, which was greeted with protests and even self-immolations by Brahmin youth. Upper-caste women took an active role in these protests. Then there was the Hindu nationalist Bharatiya Janata Party's (BJP) 1990 campaign to build a Hindu temple on the site of a Muslim mosque (masjid) in Ayodhya (Rama's putative birthplace). This campaign climaxed in December 1992 with the destruction of the mosque by hordes of Hindu "*kar sevaks*" (lit., "those who do service through work"), and which was followed by riots all over the country in which many people were killed, injured, or driven from their homes. Here again, Hindu women played a prominent, even a militant role, and the *sangh parivar* ("family or clan") was seen to have achieved spectacular results in mobilizing women in defense of their religious community. Finally, there was the economic "liberalization" in the late 1980s and 1990s that opened up the Indian market to global capitalism as never before, after years of post-independence protectionist policies intended to promote Indian economic self-sufficiency. This new liberalization was accompanied by privatization and a tremendous consumer boom, leading to a pattern of growth that dramatically increased the spending power of an expanded middle class but simultaneously widened the income gap between rich and poor. Here "the new Indian woman," the idealized middle-class consumer, was the target of an onslaught of advertising campaigns that reconstructed her as open to the world yet always securely and essentially Indian.[34]

In 1993, in the aftermath of the post-Ayodhya riots, the president of the BJP's women's wing, Mridula Sinha, gave an interview that was received with consternation by feminists throughout the country. The BJP defends the giving and receiving of dowry, and opposes divorce, equal property rights for women, and women working outside the home. Sinha enjoined women facing hardship in marriage to "be more adjusting, because they will have nowhere to go if they leave their husbands"; on domestic violence, she asserted that it is very often the woman's fault if she is beaten—that she has probably provoked the man into beating her, and that the best response to beating is "to keep quiet"; and on women's liberation, she insists that "the Indian woman needs strength not freedom... Freedom is fine but duties come first." Asked about her concept of a liberated Indian woman, she replied, "She is a combination of Sita [who left the luxuries of her father's home to accompany her husband in the jungle] and Savitri [who won back her husband from Yama, the God of death]... We need to fight against the atrocities committed on women, but fight without rebelling or upsetting the family goal."[35]

In 1997 the BJP came to power in Delhi for the first time. It pledged to build a Hindu temple in Ayodhya, to develop and test nuclear weapons, and to make India a proud Hindu nation "once again." In the climate of crusading neo-Hinduism throughout the 1990s, feminists became increasingly anxious about the implications for democracy, their hard-won rights, and the century-long legacy of struggle for themselves and the nation. These events precipitated a crisis in the Indian women's movement, forcing women's groups around the country to undertake a rethinking of the very category of "Woman" as an organizing rubric.[36] It was clear that women were fully capable of oppressing other women, and men as well. Furthermore, the danger of essentializing the category, of insisting that there is something inherent about being a woman, was that it could be wielded as a weapon against women themselves. Even middle-class women were forced to recognize that despite their newfound freedom as consumers, they could not take their democratic rights and freedoms for granted. And in this period of globalization and economic "liberalization," even the domestic arena was being policed more powerfully than ever, so that the middle-class home was increasingly subject to the same kinds of forces as is the marketplace; there was no dark place left to hide.

Given the changed social climate, how does Githa Hariharan's third novel, *When Dreams Travel*, published in the late 1990s, differ from *The Thousand Faces of Night*, written at the beginning of the decade? Both are women's attempts to recover something for themselves from old stories, and both involve female protagonists who live sequestered lives and who attempt to sustain themselves through fantasies and dreams—through stories and storytelling, in fact—rather than through direct action in the world.

When Dreams Travel *(1997)*

In this novel, Githa Hariharan has abandoned the Hindu epic for a reimagining of that age-old frame story, *The Thousand and One Nights*, from women's and subaltern perspectives. The narrator of *When Dreams Travel*[37] suggests two reasons why Hariharan's two female protagonists—one a member of the royalty, the other a slave, both powerless—travel imaginatively, through storytelling, "across time, across myth and legend." Caught in the patriarchal frame story, they are seeking Shahrzad (Scheherazade in the Richard Burton translation), the life-saving storyteller who has been marginalized and silenced within her own story, in order to "give voice to (her) route to salvation", and thereby, perhaps, to their own. But there is another motive: "to gain for themselves a view, however obscure, of a different future" (117).

The story of Shahrzad is a secular, worldly tale of sex and power, in which the characters are kings, queens, ministers, and slaves, flawed mortals rather than idealized gods and goddesses. Finding that he has been cuckolded by his wife, who has been consorting with her slaves while he is away, the Sultan Shahryar decrees that he will henceforth marry a fresh virgin every night and execute her the next morning. After three years, with the supply of virgins is dwindling, Shahrazad, the daughter of the Sultan's own wazir (minister) rises to the challenge. Accompanied by her younger sister Dunyazad, she keeps the Sultan spellbound with her cliff-hanging tales for a thousand and one nights, as he repeatedly postpones her execution for just one more night. After that one thousand and first night, the Sultan commutes Shahrazad's death sentence for good. Like so many stories of goddesses, however, *The Thousand and One Nights* is ostensibly about a woman but turns out to be unremittingly patriarchal, depicting a world in which women exist for and are controlled by men. While the newly-wed Shahrzad is in the act of storytelling, she is celebrated as a martyr, and when she wins her life (thereby saving the lives of untold other women as well), she is briefly fêted as a savior. But *The Thousand and One Nights* of high-stakes storytelling—literally telling stories to save her life—ends like any conventional domestic plot: in marriage, with the heroine disappearing into anonymity and royal seclusion. Early in the novel, Shahrzad the woman is about to be effaced forever, encased in a white marble monument that proclaims only her chastity and the wealth and power of her husband. But even the Sultan feels that Shahrzad has somehow escaped him, and her loving sister Dunyazad and her storytelling accomplice Dilshad are determined to get to the heart of the matter.

The novel's plot, which moves between a time shortly after Shahrzad's death/disappearance and flashbacks to her youth during the time she was engaged in the storytelling, is structured as a quest by Dunyazad and Dilshad, a slavegirl who had once served Shahrzad, to find out what happened to Shahrzad, and in so doing, to vindicate her and free themselves and others—including the sultan himself—from the tyranny of the old story. The quest is not so much a physical journey but itself an act of storytelling, in which the younger sister and the slave girl sequester themselves in a room for seven days and nights and each tells a story every night, until finally, "the night is gone...and we can leave it behind" (267). Hariharan's novel locates hope in the dawn that follows that long night.

The Thousand and One Nights, the bare bones of whose frame story can be dated back to the ninth century A.D., is one of the most traveled story collections of the colonial era. With Galland's 1704–08 French translation of an Arabic manuscript, it became "an early landmark of the Oriental Renaissance."[38] Interestingly, the editions that circulated most widely in nineteenth-century India were retranslated into Indian languages from English translations, although *The Thousand and One Nights* was available in Arabic and in Urdu translation from the Persian.[39] Thus, as with so many Indian literary and religious texts, educated Indians encountered it through European Orientalist translations. The oft-told story has traveled from East to West and back again, but Hariharan asks whether it can hold any liberatory potential for women, at least in the versions that are currently circulating. The novel's time-traveling plot, full of stories-within-stories, is located loosely within the familiar frame story of *The Thousand and One Nights*, modified with the Indian Taj Mahal story, in which the emperor is said to have loved his wife Mumtaz Mahal so much that upon her death he vowed to build her the most beautiful tomb in the world as a monument to their love. The monument remains, of course, as a national monument to a glorious past, but where is Mumtaz herself, and can her voice ever be recovered?

When Dreams Travel explores the means by which women can use stories to sustain and even to liberate themselves. It asks when inhabiting old, received stories becomes merely a coping mechanism for women, condemning them and their daughters to endless repetition. Discussing how women have internalized male representations of Woman, Shashi Deshpande cites an article by Gauri Deshpande on translating into Marathi all sixteen volumes of Sir Richard Burton's translation, *The Arabian Nights*, in which she describes its women as entirely male fantasies, "forc[ing] women into distorted views of themselves."[40] It is not through narratives of romantic love that women can find their way out of the labyrinth. No matter how unromantic their lived realities are, women have been particularly susceptible to love stories, but in Hariharan's bleak vision, those love stories end when married life begins. Indian women continue to encounter the old patriarchal master narratives. These colonized narratives perpetuate the imperialist project, as well as a gendered, hierarchical domination of bodies and minds. While fully acknowledging the seductive power of these master narratives, *When Dreams Travel* questions their ability to allow women space to act and to grow.

There are the ancient, endlessly repeated stories that secure the patriarchal *status quo*, claustrophobic stories that imprison women both physically and imaginatively. Then there are the stories that subvert and sustain, stories that women must conceive and nurture in secret, that circulate like fresh air, that enable them to survive. The act of storytelling itself plays a vital, literally life-saving role. And yet the task for the central characters is to free themselves, their sisters, and those who follow after them, from stories both socially imposed and self-perpetuated, that encase them in a kind of living death. Githa Hariharan's narrator warns that all dreams end "before desire is fulfilled," and indeed, in both novels, unfulfilled and unspoken desires fester, numbing the dreamer and poisoning her daughters and granddaughters, serving only to perpetuate the old master narratives. Yet dreams can also be enabling, in that they provide a space in which the powerless can act. When asked about the source of her stories, Shahrazad says that they arise from her very powerlessness:" I don't have a sword, so it seems I cannot rule; I cannot travel, I don't care to weep. But I can dream" (19–20).

Physically confined as the female protagonists are, their narratives are unrestricted in time and space: women have learned to travel in other ways, and are only as limited as their dreams. These limits do not coincide with national borders or geographic barriers: they are both larger and smaller, in that they range as far as the human spirit is capable of reaching and they are confined as closely as the narrowness of social convention or the walls of a house. However, their dreams are themselves limited by the narratives that compose them, and the challenge posed by

Hariharan is the need to dream up new stories that break the confines of the well-traveled patriarchal narrative frameworks. In material terms, it is important to acknowledge that while writing and storytelling may give the powerless a measure of discursive freedom, the realities of women's confinement and social disempowerment still remain. Beneath the taut surface of this novel lies a violent interior, seething with conflict and political intrigue and crisscrossed with structures of power in which even women and servants are both agents and instruments, policing themselves and each other at every level. Neither strategies of engagement nor of escape offer any promises of freedom, agency, or even survival for women; whether they are queens or slaves, their necks remain vulnerable to the executioner's sword. But the very precariousness of the women's positions is what gives the novel its urgency, rendering the domestic sphere of a palace every bit as embattled as the outside world, and thereby deconstructing the notion of an inside and an outside altogether.

The domestic settings of Githa Hariharan's novels are unyieldingly unromantic, even sadistic, and the domestic arena is a battleground. Mothers are never portrayed with the sentimentality of the nationalist plot; hardened with suppressed anger, they give up their daughters without a murmur to the same system that has crushed them, and the married daughters struggle simply to stay alive. Sons and fathers are weak, unable or unwilling to offer protection. The relationship between husband and wife, man and woman, is never one of romantic love. The sustaining thread is sisterhood between and among women. Can women step out of traditional patriarchal frameworks, and is it even advisable for them to do so, given that these structures support as well as suppress, console as well as constrict?

Though women cannot always act, they continue to tell life-saving stories to themselves, each other, and their children. The female characters in both novels draw upon multiple sources of support, both clandestine and socially sanctioned, and offer each other a range of perspectives on life, giving a rich, multilayered texture to lives that might from the outside appear confined. Stories, like silence, are potentially subversive weapons of the weak in that they can allow women a space for resistance; nevertheless they can also be corrosive, poisoning from within. Stories, like people, must not be suppressed, but must be allowed to change and grow over time; otherwise they lose their authenticity and freedom-giving force. At the end of the novel, the aged Shahrazad, "the old warrior" herself, who for so long risked her neck for herself and others in her nightly act of creation, thinks back on the generations of stories that have "colonized her body . . . to paint in their sticky colors and words, their own moral themes" (275). She looks at the complacent young women of the day who owe their very existence to her and wonders if they would have the sharpness to respond with her boldness and presence of mind if they were faced in their turn with her predicament: "I, Shahrazad, saved your grandmothers from being beheaded . . . And you—what will you do when your time comes?" (275). Dunyazad and Dilshad remain connected and indebted to the generations of women who created and sustained them with their lives and their stories, just as they remain indebted to Shahrzad even though they must now find ways to step out of her story.

Trapped in a male narrative that keeps reproducing itself, the two women spend seven days and nights traveling back and forth together in time and space, "through the ultimate wilderness of stories," haunted by the played-out, "shop-worn soul" of

Shahrazad's story, attempting to give it fresh meaning, and "themselves a view … of a different future." Dunyazad, the younger sister, who has been perpetually held in her elder sister's shadow, attempts to retell the Shahrazad story from new, female perspectives. Dunyazad's more sheltered life as the Wazir's daughter has made her vulnerable to romance. Dilshad has no stake in the *status quo*, so she finds it easier to leave it behind. Necessity has taught her the ways of the world and given her no illusions about the corruption of powerful men. Hariharan draws the relationship between Dilshad and Dunyazad as one in which Dilshad leads and Dunyazad follows.

In a novel that is nearly unremitting in its grimness, no doubt in deliberate contrast to the "exotic" splendor of *The Thousand and One Nights*, one of the lightest passages is a story Dilshad tells about how women are manipulated by patriarchal narratives. It includes three versions of "Rupavati's Breasts," one of the Buddhist Jataka tales (stories of the Buddha's former births), with each version taking a different standpoint *vis-à-vis* the dominant Brahmanical ideology. Dilshad's protagonist, Satyasama, leaves home without a qualm and goes out seeking fame and wisdom, confident as only a young woman can be. An old couple, she is told, have some wisdom to impart to her. They live in a dilapidated old house that seems to have been built without a plan, surrounded by overgrown gardens and the strong smell of something that is beginning to decay.

The wife's story, the closest of the three to the standard version of the original Jataka tale,[41] begins with the Bodhisattva as a woman Rupavati, sacrificing her breasts to a starving woman about to devour her child. In the Buddhist fable, Rupavati's self-sacrifice leads to her embodiment as a man; as a man, his merit causes his rebirth as a brahmin; and finally, as a brahmin, his self-sacrifice leads to liberation. The second version is the husband's angry and misogynist counter to his wife's story, which coexists with the wife's, just as the gods of Vedic Brahmanism's Great Tradition and the popular goddess cults of the Little Tradition coexist all over India.[42] His version, which is the closest Hariharan comes to humor in the novel, involves a great deal of tearing-off of breasts, and comments on how women's stories are appropriated by patriarchal power, and also on how Buddhist stories have been drawn into the pantheon of Vedic Brahmanism. When Satyasama herself tries her hand "at this game of remoulding Rupavati's breasts" (185)—a humorous reference to the way Woman is "recast" to serve the interests of those in power—the Brahmin gets his comeuppance, and the old couple eject her angrily from their house. She steps cheerfully out of the misogynist Brahmanical plot, although she is aware that in abandoning rather than accommodating herself to it, she has left the *status quo* intact and herself homeless: "nothing had been settled, except that the old ones stayed put in that stagnant house and she wandered where her bare feet took her" (188).

Hariharan suggests that the danger of abandoning the old stories altogether is that one is unhoused. The greater danger, however, may be that of telling and retelling stories that merely coexist with the dominant power. Nevertheless, the point of telling these three versions is to demonstrate the presence of resistance in cultural texts.[43] Ideological hegemony is never total; dominant narratives are forced to coexist or contend with numerous counternarratives, that may either uphold, challenge, or step right out of the dominant ideology of power. Significantly it is Dilshad, the subaltern woman who has no stake in the *status quo*, whose stories eventually allow them all—herself, Dunyazad, and even the old Sultan—to break out of the hierarchical, patriarchal framework altogether, leaving the long night of the old story behind. But they still pay homage to the original storyteller, who has sustained them all for so long.

In *The Thousand Faces of Night*, Devi had attempted to find sustenance in Goddess stories but had found that they could not free her from the patriarchal tradition of Vedic Brahmanism. She found more strength in the examples of "real" women's lives. *When Dreams Travel* does not vest the same hope in women's stories that do not explicitly challenge or at least seek to subvert the Great Tradition. Hariharan moves from the attempt to subvert the dominant narrative from within to a recognition of the ultimate need to step out of it altogether, with the concomitant recognition that this is not always possible.

Returns and Re-Returns

In Shashi Deshpande's and Githa Hariharan's novels, to what end do the female protagonists return to tread old ground and to retell old stories? Do their returns somehow enable them to act in the present? In a nation in crisis with economic, political, and social reversals being enacted in the public sphere, these characters' lonely preoccupations with return and retelling could be seen as acts of withdrawal or retreat, mirroring the new economic and social privatization and the mood of cultural nativism in the nation at large. They could also be seen as returns to the "site of the Ancestor," where the protagonists pay homage, reconnect with fundamental (not fundamentalist) cultural values, and rethink their strategies for survival.[44] But they also recognize that "women" as a category may not necessarily have any greater investment in social transformation than their male counterparts, and that gaining more power or agency does not in itself constitute a social good.

Within India, women's novels of the past two decades have repeatedly staged "action" as return. For Githa Hariharan and Shashi Deshpande's protagonists, as for Anita Desai's in *Clear Light of Day*, we have seen how a return to the father's home, however problematic for the female protagonists, is often seen as a necessary precondition for their reengagement with their embattled lives, as they "re-return" to break an impasse in their lives, and perhaps to begin to tread new ground. However, it remains an open question to what extent they will be able to reengage on new terms. As Rosalind O'Hanlon has noted in her discussion of the limited possibilities for resistance among nineteenth-century Indian women, "there could be no neutral spaces from which women could defy and hold themselves apart from Indian forms of patriarchy."[45] For both Deshpande and Hariharan, most of the old stories they attempt to retell remain unyieldingly patriarchal. Nevertheless, their heroines must seek their "literary foremothers" within these stories.[46] And as with their literary foremothers, so with their "actual" mothers and foremothers: they must seek their decidedly unmotherly mothers *in* the ancestral houses of their fathers, mothers whom, in sharp contrast to the saccharine representations of mothers in nationalist novels, they refuse to idealize. They may not always be able to tell new stories, but they can offer a range of perspectives on the old ones, and tell them in other ways.

Finally, the material act of cultural production itself can be an act of resistance that challenges the dominant discourse of power. In *When Dreams Travel*, even where Dunyazad and Dilshad envision the possibility of stepping out of the patriarchal frame story altogether, that liberating act is an *imaginative* one that takes place in a closed room. Shahrzad's stories saved her life and the lives of countless other young women who followed after, but the space into which she was liberated was itself another space of confinement. As we have seen in the construction of nationalism, the act of imagining an alternative reality is often a necessary precursor to creating the social space for its future realization. In the present, it also creates imaginative and discursive breathing space that makes life possible; a survival mechanism and source of sustenance whose importance cannot be denied. But out of the mouth of a child, a small, utopian voice from the future persists in asking an innocent question of its mother, reminding us of the limits of discursive action within the social *status quo*: "If you're happy in a dream, Ammu, does that count?"[47]

In my conclusion I consider new trends and tendencies in contemporary Indian English writing, locating them in the now-familiar tradition of the Indian English novel, and pointing to new departures. I comment on Arundhati Roy's Booker Prize–winning novel, *The God of Small Things*, as an Indian English novel, rather than a global phenomenon. Like those of Hariharan and Deshpande, Roy's characters, too, seek to "re-return" with a difference. But like Estha, the child quoted above, Roy's characters point ever more insistently to the limits of discursive maneuvering and dare them to cross the forbidden threshold into action that "counts."

C O N C L U S I O N

R E C A S T (E) I N G G E N R E I N T H E T W E N T Y - F I R S T C E N T U R Y

While literary/cultural forces within India have been paying new attention to the "small"—to the issues of caste, linguistic region, and religious community—and thereby contributing to a decentering of the normative English-educated subject of action, global forces have been conversely functioning to recenter that subject on the world stage. Arundhati Roy's 1997 novel, *The God of Small Things*, performs both acts on both stages, large and small. In this open-ended conclusion, I gesture toward that book's continuities with the by-now-familiar tradition of the Indian English novel, and also to some of its departures from that tradition. Briefly, I consider the nature and subject(s) of action in Roy's novel and in other Indian English novels recently published in and out of India. Looking back to the beginning of our story and then looking ahead, I contemplate the end of action and its binding karma. And finally, I attempt to step out of the framework of colonial karma and consider action from a new perspective.

The God of Small Things as an Indian Novel of the 1990s

For the past century, the Indian English novel has been dominated by the big idea of the Nation. In Arundhati Roy's 1997 Booker Prize–winning novel of the same name, *The God of Small Things* presides over the realm of the personal, the self that is silenced by the national imperative. In an early passage, the withdrawal of the twin protagonist, Rahel, is incomprehensible to her American husband except as a condition "between indifference and despair." The narrator explains Rahel's listless state in terms of the tension between the personal and the national:

> . . . in some places, like the country that Rahel came from, various kinds of despair competed for primacy. And . . . personal despair could never be desperate enough . . . [S]omething happened when personal turmoil dropped by at the wayside shrine of the vast, violent, circling, driving, ridiculous, insane, unfeasible, public turmoil of a nation. The Big God howled like a hot wind, and demanded obeisance. Then Small God (cozy and contained, private and limited) came away cauterized, laughing numbly at his own temerity. Inured by the confirmation of his own inconsequence, he became resilient and truly indifferent. Nothing mattered much. Nothing much mattered. And the less

it mattered, the less it mattered. It was never important enough. Because Worse Things had happened. (20)

Faced with the enormity of suffering on a national scale, private suffering shrivels into insignificance, as the self feels compelled to sacrifice itself at the shrine of the nation. For fifty years, protagonists of Indian English novels have been subject to the same frustrations, but Roy is able to articulate Rahel's alienation—and subsequently, her struggle for reengagement—in these explicit terms only after the crisis in the national idea in the 1970s, after the national narratives of the 1980s, and after the upsurge of women's and Dalits' writing in the 1990s. However, if one were to read *The God of Small Things* (henceforth *GST*) without placing it in an Indian literary tradition, one might easily miss the centrality of the idea expressed in its very title, and see the novel as just an exotic story of illicit love.

Twin Protagonists

Like so many Indian novels that came before it, from *Gora* and *Murugan, the Tiller* to *Midnight's Children*, *GST* is a tale of twin protagonists, but in this case, quite literally. Moreover, while *Gora* and *Murugan, the Tiller* hinged on healing the rift between male friends and *Midnight's Children* played on the duality between polar opposites who are each other's repressed (male) Others, *GST* abandons gender essentialism. It is like *Voices in the City* in that its dual protagonists are siblings, male *and* female, but *GST*'s dual protagonists are actually twins, and unlike *Voices*, in which one sibling must die in order for the other to overcome his alienation, the fraternal twins Rahel and Estha can ultimately overcome their alienation only in each other. In *Gora* and *Murugan, the Tiller*, the differences between the friends were warring elements in the nationalist discourse that had to be reconciled for the national idea to be consolidated and naturalized. *Midnight's Children* self-consciously thematized the ambivalence of nationalism, but one protagonist was clearly favored over his Other, who was conceived as his archrival and his polar opposite. Recognition rather than repression of their polarization yielded an electric charge, but compromise between the warring ideas was ultimately given up as impossible. In *GST*, neither twin is complete without the other, the survival of one hinges on the survival of the other, and the alienation and emptiness of each can be overcome only through an ultimate act of union, which is at once entirely selfish and utterly selfless. *GST* abandons reconciliation at the national level in favor of unashamed sexual healing, yet the novel suggests that attention to this very personal, private self-love is required before healing can be possible at the national level; and conversely, that it is only attention to caste and gender justice at the national level that can prevent further wanton destruction of "small" lives.

Self-Alienation

Before their estrangement, Rahel and her brother Estha were not each other's *alter egos* in metaphorical or even magical terms, but were literally undifferentiated, One, without an Other: "In those early, amorphous years...Estha and Rahel thought of themselves together as Me, and separately, individually as We or Us. As though they were a rare breed of Siamese" (4–5). There is no conflict for the twins between personal identity and group identity because unity enables individual identity just as individuality makes true togetherness possible. Togetherness is not predicated upon self-effacement or denial, and the exercise of individuality does not necessitate a self-ish rejection of the Other. The world's distinctions, however, in separating them from each other, alienate each from her or himself as well. One thinks of the trauma of Partition and the estrangement of Bim and Raja in *Clear Light of Day*. After the traumatic break, Rahel

> thinks of Estha and Rahel as *Them*, because, separately, the two of them are no longer what *They* were or ever thought *They'd* be… Edges, Borders, Boundaries, Brinks and Limits have appeared like a team of trolls on their separate horizons. (5)

Cut apart from Estha and from her mother, who dies soon after the traumatic event of the novel, Rahel drifts into waywardness and seeming indifference, while Estha, cut off from mother and sister and "Returned" to his father, retreats deep into silence (like Saleem the buddha in *Midnight's Children*), slowly withdrawing from the world. Twenty-three years later, Estha is "re-Returned," rejected a second time, when his father, emigrating to Australia, sends him back to his maternal home of Ayemenem, scene of the childhood trauma. Rahel, divorced from her husband and from herself, is summoned back from the United States to help deal with him.

Betrayal and Guilt

The traumatic event, or series of events in the twins' childhood, is an intercaste love affair, a travesty of justice, and a double tragedy. Like so many other protagonists of post-independence Indian English fiction, the twins and their mother, even while powerless victims themselves, feel responsible for the deaths, or at least complicit in them.[1] As we have seen, this exaggerated sense of responsibility is endemic through-out the Indian English novel, bespeaking the authors' ambivalent feelings about their own role as mediators, feelings that have been both projected onto them and inter-nalized by them. In a subplot apparently drawn from L.P. Hartley's *The Go-Between*, the child Saleem in *Midnight's Children* was convinced that he was guilty of the murder of his Aunt Pia's lover Commander Sabarmati by his Uncle Hanif and of Hanif's subsequent suicide.[2] Like Leo in *The Go-Between*, the ten-year-old Saleem was used as an intermediary between his aunt and her secret lover and then blamed himself for the tragic events that followed. While Leo never marries, Saleem did eventually marry but remained impotent. In the public arena, he felt himself respon-sible for no less than the betrayal of his fellow midnight's children that led to their forced sterilization, the destruction of their unfulfilled potentialities. Of course, this exaggerated sense of guilt stemmed from a child's self-confidence as being the center of his small universe, and Saleem's exaggerated sense of responsibility as the media-tor and meaning-maker of the Midnight Children's Conference ("We must think what we are for").

In *GST*, Ammu, the twins' mother, feels responsible for the killing of Velutha, her Untouchable lover, and Rahel and Estha feel responsible for the accidental death-by-drowning of their England-returned cousin Sophie Mol, for their inadvertent betrayal of the lovers, and finally, for their betrayal of Velutha to save their mother. Their childish feelings of guilt are further reinforced by their subsequent rejection by their family and community, with Ammu ostracized, Rahel ignored, and Estha returned to his father. Similarly in *Midnight's Children*, Saleem's innocent message-carrying coincides with his parents' shocking discovery that he is not, in fact, their biological son, and he perceives their sending him to stay with Hanif and Pia as banishment. When this is swiftly followed by the family's relocation to Pakistan, Saleem feels the wrenching loss of both mother love and motherland. Rahel and Estha feel a lack of acceptance from the beginning of the novel, because their mother not only married outside her Syrian Christian community but has also divorced and returned in disgrace to her family home, bringing the twins with them. After the double tragedy, however, they are complete outcasts, and both like Saleem become alienated from their family, their motherland, each other, and themselves.

In *Midnight's Children*, Saleem triumphantly claims to have transformed himself from a victim into a protagonist, but the narrative's ironic recognition is that he has remained a victim. Arundhati Roy's young protagonists deny themselves the comfort of victim status. They could not allow someone to let them off the hook, by saying, "You're not the Sinners. You're the Sinned Against. You were only children. You had no control. You are the *victims*, not the perpetrators." There is no such easy way out for Rahel and Estha—they acknowledge their complicity in what happened to Velutha. They "both knew that there were several perpetrators (besides themselves) that day. But only one victim" (182). We have seen that the low-caste Murugan was not the protagonist of Venkataramani's *Murugan, The Tiller*, but a symbol of the noble peasant who knew his place in the social hierarchy; and that, however sincerely the socialist-humanist Anand tried to make Bakha the subject of *Untouchable*, the pressures of his time prevented his conferring on his hero an identity in conflict with the dominant Congress image of the Harijan. Even though *GST*'s title valorizes Velutha and the novel arguably romanticizes him as well, it does not presume to confer the status of protagonist or subject-agent upon him, since to do so would be patently false. Velutha remained resistant to cooptation by the status quo, which is why he had to be destroyed.

"Re-Return"

In *Midnight's Children*, Saleem never really returns to his family. They betray his trust and wrench him from the midnight's children when they move to Pakistan, where he loses his sister to the State, his parents to each other (as they belatedly fall in love with each other in their old age), and his entire family to the Indo-Pakistan war of 1965, after which he withdraws into alienated silence as the buddha. For the rest of the novel he must find surrogate parent-figures, most of whom also betray him. What seems to be essential to Saleem's reengagement both with himself and the world is his return to India. In *GST*, both Rahel and Estha, who had taken refuge with Ammu in their maternal home of Ayemenem after their parents' divorce, are cast out again as a result of their mother's affair and its aftermath. As the novel begins, they have both been "re-Returned" to Ayemenem, but this double return has been an act of choice for neither of them. For the twins, the physical return to Ayemenem is a prerequisite for reengagement; however, it is not expressed as a return to the motherland or to the bosom of nation or the family but as a return to a geographical place of their childhood which they must now remap as adults. It is the twins' return to each other and to themselves that is crucial, something that must take place in Ayemenem, but does not ultimately rely on their reconciliation with nation, family, or religious community. Like so many novels with domestic plots, *GST* also figures a return to the ancestral home. However, the protagonists do not stay within its confines, or those of the patriarchal social order, but take that step across the line to embrace the Other, breaking the Law of the Threshold, and being fully prepared to face the terrible consequences.[3]

Karma at the Millennium

A cursory glance at three very different Indian English novels published at the time of the millennium is enough to see that, whatever the perspective of the writer, karma and the Gita still remain key referents of the action.

Anuradha Marwah Roy's novel, *Idol Love* (1999), addresses the rise of the Hindu Right. The "Ramins," as she calls them, in a clever conflation of "Brahmins" and a newly reincarnated deity, "Poornaramin," rule over the new-old Raminland in an Indian dystopia reminiscent of Margaret Atwood's *The Handmaid's Tale*. Significantly, it is a strategic use of the *Bhagavad-Gita* that is decisive in converting a "no-win situation" into a landslide victory for the Ramins in the general election. The novel's female protagonist, an English-educated writer who has been working with a secularist coalition, finds herself co-opted and used by the very forces she has been opposing. By the end of the novel, her voice has been completely silenced and her "karma" defined for her by the state as the "action of dedicating her womb to her race," her social status based upon her caste and her power to give birth to sons.[4]

In *The Glass Palace* by Amitav Ghosh (2000), the significantly named Arjun, an Anglicized, hitherto-loyal, officer in the colonial British Indian army, faces a personal crisis like his epic namesake, and takes decisive and courageous action by crossing over to fight in the Indian National Army, where he eventually faces death alone in the forests of Burma.[5] But in Ghosh's novel Arjun is a tragic figure in spite of his heroism; the conflicting codes of the British Army and his belatedly awakened national conscience torment him to the point that he welcomes his end when it comes.

Manil Suri's novel, *The Death of Vishnu*, which climbed the best-seller charts in the United States and the United Kingdom in 2001, begins with a now near-obligatory nod to the Gita in its epigraph: "I am Vishnu . . . sustaining the entire world with a fragment of my being."[6] Despite the title, it is not the dying, impoverished stairwell-dweller, Vishnu, but the middle-class residents of the apartment building who are in fact the novel's main characters. In terms of the novel's action, Vishnu's death serves only to restore the *status quo* of the social order: the young Hindu–Muslim lovers break up in the end, so that a suitable marriage can be arranged for the Hindu girl, and the Muslim resident who dares to have a vision from the "Indian" Gita is besieged and nearly killed by a Hindu mob. In his vision, he had seen the dying, impoverished Vishnu as the Lord Vishnu, sustainer of the universe, but the mob was enraged by his presumption in assuming that as an Indian he has a "right" to a vision inspired by the Gita: "How dare you throw our Gita in our faces like that!"[7] As for Vishnu himself, despite his dreams of ascent, he remains on the same landing throughout the novel, and when he dies at last, it is only to be reincarnated all over again.

In India of the 1990s, fiction once again stepped out of the pages of a novel, as it did a century ago, as the fighting ascetics from *Anandamath* reemerged wielding shiny new tridents. This time, though, they were fighting not colonial oppressors but fellow citizens in a democratic pluralist state. Karma today would seem to be far from the Gandhian strategy of confounding the colonizers by turning weakness into a strength. Instead, India seeks to compete with the world powers on their own terms by laying claim to the hypermasculine power of the nuclear bomb, which promises to its people not food, not agency, but potentially, the end of all human action.

In "The End of Imagination," an essay written in response to the May 1998 nuclear tests conducted by the government of India, Arundhati Roy commented on the schizophrenic nature of the pro-nuclear argument. She noted that acquiring nuclear capacity was the Indian government's bid for power on a global stage. And yet it labeled those who opposed the bomb "inauthentic" Indians. Wrote Roy, "We storm the heart of whiteness, we embrace the most diabolical creation of western science and call it our own. But we protest against their music, their food, their clothes, their cinema and their literature...We're back on the old ship. The SS Authenticity & Indianness."[8] Just over a century ago, Indian nationalists began to use a dual strategy to cope with British colonial supremacy: they capitulated to it in the material realm, seeking to learn from their rulers the secrets of their power, and resisted it in the realm of culture, seeking to keep their own pride and identity as Indians intact.[9] On the eve of the twenty-first century, Indian aspirants to power were trying the same strategy again to compete with global power, but this time the stakes were higher. And yet again they invoked the *Bhagavad-Gita.*

July 1945: as Robert Oppenheimer watched the fireball of the first nuclear bomb test in the New Mexico desert, he struggled to justify his action in terms of the Gita's dilemma and solution. Did the Gita sanction killing in war as long as one did not spare one's own family and friends? He knew that the blinding light signified death, but was it also Krishna? And was to see Krishna to know that one *was* Krishna, "both the slayer and the slain" as the Gita puts it? As he told it later, Oppenheimer came out of his reverie with the solution to the dilemma: "There floated through my mind a line from the *Bhagavad-Gita* in which Krishna is trying to persuade the Prince that he should do his duty: 'I am become death, the shatterer of worlds.' I think we all had this feeling more or less."[10]

May 1998: Half a century later, in the Rajasthan desert, Indian nuclear scientists watched their own fireballs—five of them—and also identified them, and themselves as well, with the power of Lord Krishna.[11] Ironically, the maker of India's bomb, and India's president, A.P.J. Abdul Kalam, is "an observant Muslim...immers[ed] in the broader culture of India...and...an avid reader of Hindu scriptures...[who] knows by heart sections of...the *Bhagavad-Gita.*" Ironically, too, an Indian echoes an American quoting an Indian text. Dr. Kalam insists on the bomb's authentic Indianness and his own; that it was "developed...substantially unaided" and that he himself is "completely indigenous."[12]

We have seen the importance of return to the site of a trauma in order to begin a process of recovery. Thus the renewed literary preoccupation with Partition in the last two decades, and the efforts to reunite family members who have been cut off from each other for half a century. In such cases, as in *The God of Small Things*, forward action cannot take place until there has been a doubling back. National unity cannot be imposed from above by smoothing over differences and inequities; it is only after the past has been faced, and complicity with its betrayals acknowledged, that healing and union become possible. A nuclear weapons program takes the opposite approach to action. In attempting to compete with India's estranged twin, its divided self, and to prove India's potency to the "West," it threatens to perform, instead of union, the ultimate act of splitting, colonial karma in the extreme.

Postcolonial Karma

In a 1998 talk, Meenakshi Mukherjee predicted that caste would be a central theme in Indian English fiction of the twenty-first century.[13] In a body of work that had largely ignored caste or denied its importance for so long, whether due to the blindness of its privileged caste position, or to idealism in a newly postcolonial nation whose constitution had been drafted by a member of the lower castes, or to the difficulty of capturing the language and nuances of caste interactions in English, this new sensitivity to caste issues and acknowledgment of the persistence of caste and casteism is certainly evident in *The God of Small Things* and *Idol Love*.[14] But if we look not merely for literary depictions of Dalits, but for depictions of caste-related issues by Dalits, we reach the limit of the Indian English novel, at least at this time. As mentioned earlier, there are very few Dalit writers who write in English, and even those few do not use the novel form, preferring autobiography, poetry, the essay, and the short story. One of the trademarks of Dalit literature has been its refusal to speak in the standard form of a given language, and its insistence on using its own spoken idiom and dialect. This kind of language is difficult to translate without loss, but more importantly, if Dalits stopped writing in their mother tongues they would largely cease to reach other Dalits. As for the novel form, its middle-class origins hardly need to be stated. As a uniquely middle-class form of expression, it is not the genre of choice for Dalits. In fact, it is arguable that if a Dalit were to write a novel in English, he or she would no longer have a Dalit perspective.

Subaltern historian Ranajit Guha once wrote that the only real critique of a ruling culture comes from a position outside of the structure of power the critique seeks to change. It is therefore fitting to close with Dalit perspectives on karma and the problem of action. I do not suggest that all Dalits share any single standpoint, or indeed that they are positioned entirely outside Indian society's structures of power. Nevertheless, after an entire book in which I have presented a series of high-caste Hindu perspectives, it will be salutory to offer another view, from below.

"Justice"

The narrator of Urmila Pawar's short story, "Justice" [translated from the Marathi *Nyay*], is a Bombay-based attorney who returns to his native village after fifteen years to dispose of some ancestral land.[15] Unfortunately the sale will displace old Kushaba, a hardworking old tiller who has cultivated the land all these years and "turned it into a gold mine," but that can't be helped. He learns from the Village Elder (to whom he is to sell the land) that Kushaba's beautiful young widowed daughter Paru (Parvati) is pregnant, and it is rumored that the well-off, highly educated young Shantanu is the father.[16] The whole village is agog with the scandal, and the general tendency is to blame Paru and pity Shantanu. Paru's layabout brother from Bombay has arrived in the village, threatening to kill people if his sister does not get justice. The matter is to be settled by the village council rather than in a formal court of law, and while the Elder had been hoping simply to fine Shantanu, he is afraid that if Paru openly accuses Shantanu of the act, he will have to force him to marry her. Shantanu's mother is terrified for her son, and approaches the Bombay attorney for help, but he has no desire to get involved. He finds himself vacillating, at first grudgingly admiring Paru's spirit in "exploiting" the situation to her advantage, then pitying Shantanu, who has so much promise and so much to lose, and then feeling a fatherly desire to support Paru. After a time he decides to wash his hands of the whole affair.

The day of the council comes and the whole village turns up expectantly, with the men ranged on one side, women on the other; "all arrows were ready to shoot. Shantanu and his mother are there, looking like death, so is Nagya the goonda [hooligan] brother, his eyes glowing red with country liquor." When the time comes, Paru steps forward and answers the questions put to her by the oldest man in the village. She speaks clearly, "with no trace of fear" and answers the questions "directly and promptly" (109)—her name, marital status, what she does for a living. Then the moment of truth arrives. Paru is asked to name the father, and it is here that she confounds everyone: she will not do so. Old Subhanrao asks her again and again, but she stands firm; she does not know, she says, because she was attacked and raped from behind on her way to sell fruit at the market. She tells her story in an unashamed, straightforward manner and demands justice. When asked why she has not told this story before, she asks the unanswerable question: what would they have done in her place? "Everyone [is] nonplussed." Then attention turns to the child: "What about that sin...growing inside of you?" It is illegitimate and cannot be allowed to be born. But Paru stands her ground and insists on keeping the child. She declares herself a woman with a heart and feelings, a mother with the need to love a child, and a widow who will need support in her old age. She challenges anyone in the crowd to stand forward and offer her his support in a child's stead. Again, nobody has an answer. The narrator "st[eals] a glance" at Shantanu. His eyes are full of pride in Paru's strength and gratitude to her for not having exposed him.

The next day the narrator tells the Village Elder that he has decided not to sell his land after all. "Quite proud of myself and what I was doing, I said, 'Would you have me make my daughter homeless?'"(111).

With its simple call for justice, this story reverses the social and moral norms both of patriarchal society and the postcolonial state. The social norms of the village construct and condemn Paru as a manipulative seductress who has engineered Shantanu's ruin, and construct Shantanu as her victim who should not have to pay too dearly for a momentary lapse. The social expectations of the narrator, villagers, and readers alike are that Paru will collude with her vengeful, gold-digging brother in exposing Shantanu and demanding that he save their honor by marrying her. On the other hand, the postcolonial state constructs Paru as a poor victim of high-caste privilege who is owed some sort of restitution. Both the social and the legal codes expect Paru and her family to be ashamed of her condition, and for her to come to the council or the state as a cowed supplicant. Her widowed status confers an even greater social stigma upon her illegitimate pregnancy, despite widow remarriage having been legal for 150 years. Both the social and legal *status quo* is challenged by her brother's posture of defiance and the threat that public exposure poses to the respectability of Shantanu and his family. The postcolonial state prefers that such domestic matters be settled at the family and community level and kept out of the courts. But Paru's simple, direct self-representation confounds them all. She comes forward dressed in a traditional nine-yard sari, challenging their image of her as a seductress and a slut. She refuses to blame or even implicate the high-born Shantanu, confounding the village's expectations that she will manipulate the situation for her financial benefit, and side-stepping her brother's male code of honor and desire for vengeance. Despite the rape, she refuses to present herself as a victim, an ingratiating supplicant asking for a handout, or a dishonored woman bowed down with shame. Instead, she enacts a reversal by which Shantanu comes to be grateful to her. She is neither ashamed of her condition nor afraid to work hard to support herself and her child. She has no desire to force Shantanu unilaterally into marriage merely for the sake of "honor" or "respectability." Instead, she simply invokes as her natural right the justice due to any woman in her situation.

Further reversals are enacted at the level of the narrative. The story's Dalit author has created a middle-class, presumably upper-caste male narrator, thereby reversing the narrative norms by which a middle-class, upper-caste male writer created a narrator like himself or an upper-caste female narrator through and for whom he spoke. Furthermore, Urmila Pawar has created a widowed peasant protagonist who speaks for herself, rather than the normative upper-caste widow constructed as abject victim and object of pity. Rather than an omniscient figure, she makes her narrator an unreliable figure, vacillating between condemnation, compassion, and indifference. Even when he finally does the right thing, he expresses pride in himself and his action— clearly it has not been entirely a selfless act, and is a result of his half-guilty paternalism. However, it is clear that to Paru his motives are immaterial. She did what she had to do, and asserted her desire and her right to keep her child, astounding the narrator and everyone else around her, who were unable to conceive a way out of her dilemma.

In a 1998 interview, Pawar discussed the real-life model for "Justice," revealing a final act of reversal in her story. When she was a teenager, a widow in her village had also become pregnant, but "could not say anything" when she was asked to name the father at the village meeting, since he was one of her interrogators. The other women "took justice into their own hands" by holding her down and kicking her until she bled, causing her fetus to abort. Pawar remembers that these women had later boasted of their atrocity "as if they had performed some act of bravery." The incident had remained with her and eventually "came out as a story; as 'Nyay.'"[17] The widow in the fictional story does not name the father either, but because she will not, not because she cannot. Instead, she demands justice for herself, preempting both the villagers and her own brother, who were ready to dispense it according to their own lights. In real life, the widow fell victim to society's construction of her situation; in real life, other women shamelessly became the agents of patriarchal "justice." Urmila Pawar has refused to reproduce "reality."

Contributing to *Wages of Freedom*, a collection of essays that look back on fifty years of the Indian nation-state, Dalit scholar Kancha Ilaiah sees the *Bhagavad-Gita* as a text used by "all brahminical nationalists to construct an ideology of Hindu nationalism."[18] Of the Gita's famous prescription of action without desire for the fruit, he writes:

> The Bhagavadgita propagated the notion that those engaged in *karma* (work) should not expect a *phala* (wage) for it. The karmacharis (*workers*) must fulfil their *karma*, but the *phala* must be left for the lord, i.e. the Brahmin, the Baniya or the Kshatriya...Any revolt against *phalarahitakarma* (work without wages) was defined as adharma (*against dharma*) and was suppressed by killing the rebellious Sudras and Chandalas concerned. (267)

From Ilaiah's perspective, karma is labor, and work without concern for the reward is wageless labor. He charges that the idea that the notion of inaction as the highest ideal can only be the creation of a Brahmin who looks down on physical work. Ilaiah puts forward an entirely different proposition from that of Vivekananda a century before him, who spoke of raising the population to the Brahmin's level: "Dalitization is a reversal of that process. It begins to construct human relations based on the labour process (as against the ritual process) and assigns the highest dignity to the most difficult and creative labour." In Ilaiah's view,

> A nation is not merely a notion, but a living reality of people. Brahminism is to this day attempting to construct the Indian nation in the image of a fantasy..."a nation is not made with imagination, but by putting your hands in its soil." Even after fifty years of independence, we have been endeavouring to make the Indian nation by chanting mantras, but now it is time to soil our hands. (289–290)

∗   ∗   ∗

Calling this book *Colonial Karma* was intended not to suggest a kind of closed historical determinism in my readings of Indian English novels, but to call attention to some of the colonialist and nationalist assumptions and paradigms that continue to condition Indian cultural discourse. Identifying them and beginning to disentangle their overlapping histories could be a preliminary to freeing us from their determining influence, even if there is no prospect of their disappearing from the cultural mix in the near future. The late Edward Said used to like to quote Antonio Gramsci's observation that history has deposited in us an infinity of traces without leaving an inventory, and felt that it was the great human task to try to produce that inventory. This is what I set out to do in some small measure in approaching a critical understanding of the Indian English novel. In *Midnight's Children*, speaking of the failure of the once-dominant model of Indian nationalism, Salman Rushdie wrote, "New myths are needed." I end by questioning that need. At the present time, on the dangerous threshold of a new age of Belief, I would vote for demystification rather than new myths. A sober reckoning of the continuing power of the colonial past is required before the cultural imagination can create anew, not myths or mantras, but models for a society in which there is room for all its people to live.

There are other forms of collectivity besides the nation, and other forms of literary expression besides the novel. In the past century the Indian English novel has necessarily been preoccupied with problems of nation and the struggle to construct a national subject. These problems persist, but in the preceding chapters we have suggested some of the limits of the novel's reach. Indian English, that "bastard child of history," has a legitimate place in modern India, and will surely retain a position of privilege in India because of its status as the most powerful global language and a passport to jobs and higher education abroad. Nevertheless, it is incapable of speaking for everyone as it has long attempted to do. Noting the persistent, even growing imbalance of power and global prominence between Indian English literary texts and the literatures in the Indian languages, S. Shankar writes of the latter as "Midnight's Orphans."[19] After more than a century of shouldering the "burden of English," it may be time for the writers and critics of Indian English literary texts to lay it down, or at least to share it. In 1987 Gayatri Chakravorty Spivak suggested a critical practice that yokes "in [their] persistently asymmetric intimacy" the teaching of English literature in India "to the teaching of the literary or cultural production in the mother tongues."[20] It is this persistent asymmetry that produces the "sanctioned ignorance" that prevents teachers of Indian literature outside India from doing the same. Rather than merely "diagnos[ing] the hegemonic reading into place," Spivak calls for teachers of "Other" texts "to do enough homework in language and history" to produce active, critical readings.[21] If they are to attempt this, they cannot continue to read the master texts of Indian literature such as the Gita without attention to the colonialist and nationalist historiography which has produced them in modern times, or to read the Indian English novels that increasingly make the crossing to Britain and America in complete isolation from the contemporary Indian literary scene, which is at once regional, national, global, and multilingual.

The Indian English novel must now take its place in the linguistic multiplicity and vitality of the larger Indian literary scene, where the past decade or so has seen a dramatic increase in intra-national literary translation. More regional literary works are becoming available in English and other Indian language translations across the country. This new literary cross-fertilization is producing a more dynamic picture, not only of different regional literatures, but also of the national literary consciousness. There is less of a time lag between the publication of a work in a regional language and its becoming part of the national scene. Thus there is a growing awareness of differences and parallels among the concerns and trends in the literatures of the different regions, and Indian literary trends can thus begin to be compared with each other and to particularities of their own settings, instead of solely to trends and traditions in Britain or America. Several publishers have launched translation series, and a publisher like Katha not only works exclusively with translation and holds translation training seminars at universities all over India, but also publishes magazines and books for neoliterates and teenage readers, so that its reach is vertical as well as horizontal.[22]

It is the challenge of postcolonial studies to develop a new kind of scholarship that draws upon the many intellectual traditions that it is our "privilege and curse" to have inherited, a scholarship that strives—despite inevitable ambivalence—to be free from both colonialist paternalism and nationalist apologetics. The multiple layers and versions of history—Orientalist, colonial, nationalist, postcolonial, global—do not supersede each other, but exist simultaneously, overlapping and contending in ever-changing combinations. In the opening paragraph of *Midnight's Children*, the postcolonial baby-boomer Saleem Sinai is born "handcuffed to history"; in the closing sequences of *Clear Light of Day*, the resistant Bim is forced to look open-eyed upon her past and acknowledge that "nothing's over, ever." We cannot expect to transcend history, or wish away the pernicious effects of the past, but—in the words of Chinua Achebe—we can look back to find "where the rain began to beat us," and thereby loosen the bonds of colonial karma.

Notes

Preface

1. The sixth edition of *The Oxford Companion to English Literature*, edited by Margaret Drabble (Oxford: Oxford University Press, 2000), 29, inexplicably uses the term "Anglo-Indian literature" to refer to Indian literature in English, with no mention of its usage to refer to English writers about British India (such as E.M. Forster and Rudyard Kipling). The entry on "Anglo-Indian literature" is ascribed to Salman Rushdie, but it should be entitled "Indo-Anglian literature," and Rushdie surely knows this. I am tempted to suggest that it is a Freudian slip on the part of the editors, as they continue to reappropriate Indian writing under the banner of English literature, even in the postcolonial period. I am reminded of an exultant article in the British press soon after Arundhati Roy won the Booker Prize in 1997, claiming her as an example of the New Britain.
2. See K.R. Srinivasa Iyengar's *Indo-Anglian Literature*, first published in 1962, 5th ed. (New Delhi: Sterling, 1985).
3. See, for instance, Fawzia Afzal-Khan's 1993 *Cultural Imperialism and the Indo-English Novel*, which discusses R.K. Narayan, Anita Desai, Kamala Markandaya, and Salman Rushdie, all of whom write exclusively in English.
4. Salman Rushdie, e.g., uses "Indo-Anglian" in his now-notorious introduction to *Mirrorwork: 50 Years of Indian Writing, 1947–1997* (New York: Henry Holt and Company, 1997), where he refers to it self-mockingly as that "bastard child of Empire, sired on India by the departing British" (like Rushdie's own narrator, Saleem Sinai, in *Midnight's Children*). In the same introduction Rushdie also makes the exaggerated claim for the centrality of Indian writing in English that infuriated those who had a firsthand familiarity with any other Indian literary tradition.

Introduction

1. Amit Chaudhuri, "A Bottle of Ink, a Pen and a Blotter," *London Review of Books* (August 9, 2001): 21–22.
2. Meenakshi Mukherjee makes this point in her essay, "Nation, Novel, Language," in *The Perishable Empire: Essays on Indian Writing in English* (Delhi: Oxford University Press, 2000), 1–29: "the 'tradition' of Indian writing in English is discontinuous; there is no genealogy that can be traced satisfactorily, however much scholars might attempt to create one."
3. I use "figuring" here to refer to the act of giving imaginative form to an idea that then repeats itself in text after text as an allegorical trope. By figuring the national subject and the national arena of action, early cultural nationalists sought to summon them into being, to make the Word flesh. Hayden White elaborates on such allegorical "figuring" in *Tropics of Discourse* (Baltimore: Johns Hopkins University Press, 1978). Gayatri Chakravorty Spivak discusses the literary sleight-of-hand of "figuring the impossible." See *A Critique of Postcolonial Reason* (Cambridge: Harvard University Press, 1999), as also Jenny Sharpe's *Allegories of Empire: The Figure of Woman in the Colonial Text* (Minneapolis: University of Minnesota Press, 1993).

4. Edward Said's *Orientalism* (New York: Random House, 1978) establishes most firmly the self-justifying purpose of such Orientalist stereotypes.

5. See Mrinalini Sinha, *Colonial Masculinity: The "Manly" Englishman and the Effeminate Bengali in the Late Nineteenth Century* (New York: Manchester University Press, 1995); and Revathy Krishnaswamy, *Effeminism: The Economy of Colonial Desire* (Ann Arbor: University of Michigan Press, 1998).

6. James Mill, *A History of India*, quoted in Tharu and Lalita, eds., Introduction, *Women Writing in India, Vol. I* (New York: Feminist Press, 1991), 46.

7. The quote is Gayatri Chakravorty Spivak's, from "Can the Subaltern Speak? Speculations on Widow Sacrifice," in Nelson and Grossberg, eds., *Marxism and the Interpretation of Culture* (Urbana-Champaign: University of Illinois Press, 1988), 271–313.

8. See Said's *Orientalism* and David Kopf's *British Orientalism and the Bengal Renaissance* (Berkeley: University of California Press, 1969).

9. F. Max Müller, *India—What Can It Teach Us?* (New Delhi: Munshiram Manoharlal Publishers, 1991), 76.

10. "The definitions of women and literature which emerge at this time in India are initially produced in the *entangled* space of colonizers, indigenous literati and middle-class intelligentsia…in England in an embattled space (of worker's and women's protest)… Together these definitions and ideologies enter a single, albeit complex and shifting ideological configuration." Kumkum Sangari, "Relating Histories: Definitions of Literacy, Literature, Gender in Early Nineteenth Century Calcutta and England," in Svati Joshi, ed., *Rethinking English: Essays in Literature, Language, History* (New Delhi: Trianka, 1991), 40.

11. In Lord Macaulay's 1835 *Minute on Indian Education* that established English as the language of colonial education in India: "We must…do our best to form a class who can be interpreters between us and the millions whom we govern, a class of persons, Indian in blood and colour, but English in taste, in opinions, in morals, and in intellect." They were eventually to become "the vehicles for conveying knowledge to the great mass of the population." Rita Raley's *History of English Studies Page*, UCSB. Accessed August 13, 2003. <http://www.english.ucsb.edu/faculty/rraley/research/english/macaulay.html>.

12. See Rajeswari Sunder Rajan, ed., *The Lie of the Land* (New Delhi: Oxford, 1992), and Joshi, ed., *Rethinking English*.

13. From Salil Tripathi, *Postcolonial Listserv*, November 2, 2002: "According to the Indian census, in 1991, India's population was 838 million, of which some 180,000 called English their first language, 64 million called it their second language, and another 25 million called it their third language. That figure, of about 89 million, is about 11% of the population…those who call it their second language are more than reasonably fluent; and those who call it their third language would certainly have sufficient fluency to read simple documents. The 2001 census has been completed and limited data is on the web;…the rest is still being compiled. The population has risen to 1.02 billion, and if other things are equal, the number of Indians 'familiar' with English would then rise to about 108 million." Indian Census: <http://www.censusindia.net/cendat/language/table4_E.PDF>.

14. Khushwant Singh, "English Zindabad Versus Angrezi Hatao," in *We Indians* (New Delhi: Orient Paperbacks, 1982), 115–117.

15. K.R. Srinivasa Iyengar, *Indian Writing in English*, 5th ed. This was originally written in 1972, for the 2nd ed. Dr. Srinivasa Iyengar is one of the pioneering scholars of Indian English (in his terms, Indo-Anglian) literature.

16. Rushdie himself thematizes the disjunction between English and other Indian languages in post-independence India, in the scene in *Midnight's Children* where the English-educated Saleem, ignorant of the languages and language-politics of Gujarati and Marathi in 1950s Bombay, stumbles into a language march and unwittingly sets off a riot by repeating a Gujarati chant whose significance in the charged political setting he does not fully understand.

17. Salman Rushdie, "Damme, This is the Oriental Scene for You," in *The New Yorker*, June 23 and 30, 1997.

18. In arguing for this historical confluence between the Indian nation, the novel, and the English-educated middle class, I am aware of the controversy generated by Fredric Jameson's "The Third World Literature in the Era of Multinational Capital" (*Social Text,* vol. 15, Fall 1986, 65–88) and Aijaz Ahmad's trenchant reply, "Jameson's Rhetoric of Otherness and the 'National Allegory'" *Social Text* Vol. 17, Fall (1987, 3–25). However, mine is not an essentialist or exclusive argument.

19. Shivarama Padikkal, "Inventing Modernity: The Emergence of the Novel in India," in Niranjana Tejaswini et al., eds., *Interrogating Modernity* (Calcutta: Seagull, 1993); Sumit Sarkar, *Modern India 1885–1947* (Madras: Macmillan India, 1983); Veena Naregal, "Colonial Bilingualism and Hierarchies of Language and Power: Making of a Vernacular Sphere in Western India," *Economic and Political Weekly* (December 4, 1999): 3446–3456.

20. Mukherjee, "Nation, Novel, Language," 1–29.

21. Naregal, "Colonial Bilingualism and Hierarchies of Language and Power," 3448.

22. See Sunil Khilnani's *The Idea of India* for an articulation of the Nehruvian ideal.

23. Salman Rushdie, Introduction to *The Vintage Book of Indian Writing 1947–1997* (Vintage Books, London: Random House, 1997), xii. Published in the United States as *Mirrorwork: 50 Years of Indian Writing, 1947–1997*. Much earlier, in *The Twice-Born Fiction: Themes and Techniques of Indian Novel in English* (New Delhi: Heinemann, 1971) Meenakshi Mukherjee had used the term "twice-born" in the same sense, to refer to the dual heritage of the Indian novel in English. Fittingly, the same term is also used in India to refer to members of the upper castes.

24. A favorite expression of Rushdie's.

25. Meenakshi Mukherjee, "The Anxiety of Indianness," in *The Perishable Empire*, 181.

26. Malashri Lal, *The Law of the Threshold: Women Writers in Indian English* (Simla: Indian Institute of Advanced Study, 1995), 4.

27. "The Hindu Reformation . . . was indeed a significant fact, but it would have remained basically a religious movement but for the rediscovery of the *Bhagavad Gita* as the political and social gospel of Hindu India." K.M. Panikkar, *Foundations of New India* (London: Allen & Unwin, 1963), 36.

28. Literally, Lokamanya means, "Revered by the People," an honorary title popularly conferred upon him after his 1897 sentencing to imprisonment by the British. Stanley Wolpert, *Tilak and Gokhale* (Delhi: Oxford University Press, 1989), 102.

29. Mahatma means "Great Soul," and was conferred upon Gandhi by Rabindranath Tagore.

30. Nationalist leaders who translated or wrote on the Gita while serving terms in British jails included B.G. Tilak, M.K. Gandhi, Jawaharlal Nehru, Vinoba Bhave, and C. Rajagopalachari. Other prominent nationalists who either translated or wrote on the Gita during the colonial period included Aurobindo Ghose (later Sri Aurobindo), Annie Besant, Lala Lajpat Rai, and S. Radhakrishnan.

31. B.G. Tilak, *Shrimad Bhagavad-Gita Rahasya* translated into English by B.S. Sukthankar, 7th ed. (Poona: Tilak Brothers, 1986).

32. In a speech in 1896, Tilak drew upon the Gita to justify the use of violence: "No blame attaches to any person if he is doing deeds without being actuated by a desire to reap the fruit of his deeds . . . If thieves enter our house and we have not strength enough in our fists to drive them out, we should without hesitation lock them up and burn them alive . . . Do not circumscribe your vision like a frog in a well; get out of the Penal Code, enter into the lofty atmosphere of the Shrimat Bhagavad-Gita and then consider the actions of great men." Wolpert, *Tilak and Gokhale*, 87.

33. Gayatri Chakravorty Spivak discusses Krishna's Time in *A Critique of Postcolonial Reason* (Cambridge: Harvard University Press, 1999), 37–67.

34. Ibid., 95.

35. M.K. Gandhi. "Anasaktiyoga," in *The Collected Works of Mahatma Gandhi, Vol. XLI June–October 1929* (New Delhi: The Publications Division, Ministry of Information and Broadcasting, 1970), 93.

36. Jawaharlal Nehru, *The Discovery of India* (Delhi: Oxford University Press, 1989), 108–110.
37. C.F. Andrews, 1912, cited in Eric Sharpe, *The Universal Gita* (La Salle (IL): Open Court, 1985), 69.
38. Surendranath Dasgupta, *A History of Indian Philosophy Vol. I* (Delhi: Motilal Banarsidass, 1991. First published 1922), 406–494; J.L.Mehta, lecture notes, *Vedanta Philosophy* (Havard Divinity School, Fall 1974).
39. It is perhaps no coincidence that the only Congress leader who was neither a Brahmin nor a Kshatriya was able to capture both the imagination of the peasants and the confidence of the industrialists.
40. For a critical Marxist perspective on the function of the Gita in Hindu thought, see D.D. Kosambi's essay, "Social and Economic Aspects of the Bhagavad-Gita," in *Myth and Reality: Studies in the Formation of Indian Culture*, 12–41.
41. Gita 9:32: "For those who take refuge in Me, O Partha (Arjuna), though they are lowly born, women, Vaisyas, as well as Sudras, they also attain to the highest goal," S. Radhakrishnan's translation. Sudras are the lowest caste in the fourfold caste hierarchy, apart from the outcastes, who are outside it altogether.
42. While it may be overstating the case to assert, as Pankaj Mishra has done in characteristically trenchant fashion, that the British "invented" Hinduism, there are many scholars who are in substantial agreement. Pankaj Mishra, "How the British Invented Hinduism," *New Statesman* (August 26, 2002): 19–21.
43. Panikkar, *Foundations of New India*, 36.
44. M.K. Gandhi, "My Meaning of the Gita," in *Prefaces* (Ahmedabad: Navajivan Trust, 1969), 65.
45. Vivekananda was addressing a gathering in Madras in 1897. In R.N. Minor, ed., *Modern Indian Interpreters of the Bhagavadgita*, 142.
46. Ashis Nandy comments critically on this notion that Hindus could rise only by becoming more Western, less like themselves: "In a moment of terrible defeatism Vivekananda had said that the salvation of the Hindus lay in three Bs: beef, biceps and Bhagvad-Gita (*sic*)" (in *The Intimate Enemy: Loss and Recovery of Self Under Colonialism* [Delhi: Oxford University Press, 1983], 47). However, the Gita's idea of harmonizing the three *gunas* and of accepting the the different paths to *moksha* must have been tremendously attractive to early Indian nationalists, who were seeking ways of reconciling different and often-conflicting goals, both within themselves and in the larger public sphere. Indira V. Peterson, "Rethinking History: Swami Vivekananda's East and West," paper presented at The Association of Asian Studies National Meeting, Chicago, 1990.
47. Translation is from *Srimad Bhagavadgita* (with Sanskrit text and English translation) (Gorakhpur: Gita Press, 1969), 82.
48. Hayden White, *Tropics of Discourse* (Baltimore: Johns Hopkins University Press, 1978), 3.
49. Partha Chatterjee, *Nationalist Thought and the Colonial World: A Derivative Discourse*, 30.
50. "Dominance Without Hegemony and Its Historiography," in Ranajit Guha, ed., *Subaltern Studies VI*, 210–309.
51. Ibid., 257.
52. Veena Naregal's term, in "Colonial Bilingualism and Hierarchies of Language and Power."
53. The term is Partha Chatterjee's, discussed in ch. 3, *Nationalist Thought and the Colonial World*, 54–84.
54. Ibid., ch. 4, 85–130.
55. Ibid., ch. 5, 131–166.

Chapter One

1. See Sumit Sarkar's discussion of the social roots of the intelligentsia between 1885 and 1905, in *Modern India:1885–1947* (Madras: Macmillan India, 1983), 65–70.

2. Gauri Viswanathan's *Masks of Conquest: Literary Study in British-Ruled India* (New York: Columbia University Press, 1989) remains the definitive work here.

3. See Meenakshi Mukherjee's *Realism and Reality: The Novel and Society in India*, for a discussion of the tensions between the realism of the imported novel genre and the colonial realities for its practitioners in nineteenth-century India.

4. Earlier scholarship tended to characterize the two in polar terms, as "reform" and "revivalism." However, as we shall see in the writers we discuss in this chapter it is more accurate to say that both tendencies were likely to be present to varying degrees in any one person or position.

5. The word vernacular, which refers to the native language, mother tongue, or the everyday speech of the people, derives from the Latin *verna*, a slave born in his master's house (Webster's Dictionary). Under Anglicist educational policy in colonial India, English was to replace Sanskrit as the language of high culture, and to serve as a model for modernizing the vernacular, or Indian languages.

6. Sisir Kumar Das, *A History of Indian Literature, Vol. VIII: 1800–1910* (Delhi: Sahitya Akademi, 1991).

7. A handful of earlier works may be able to lay claim to the genre of "novel," but it is generally agreed that, flawed as it is, *Rajmohan's Wife* (hereafter *RW*) was one of the first Indian novels written in English. See Das, *A History of Indian Literature, Vol. VIII*, and Mukherjee, *Realism and Reality*.

8. Tapan Raychaudhuri, "Bankimchandra Chattopadhyay," in *Europe Reconsidered: Perceptions of the West in Nineteenth Century Bengal* (Delhi: Oxford University Press, 1988), 126.

9. Bankimchandra died leaving an unfinished commentary on the *Bhagavad-Gita*. Ajit Ray, "Bankim Chandra Chatterji's New Hinduism and the Bhagavadgita," in R.N. Minor, *Modern Indian Interpreters of the Bhagavadgita* (Albany: SUNY Press, 1986), 34–43.

10. Mukherjee, *Realism and Reality*, 49.

11. Raychaudhuri, "Bankimchandra Chattopadhyay," 104, 124. Not surprisingly, sitting for English examinations is a recurrent theme in Indian English fiction, as well as in Anglophone colonial/postcolonial literatures more generally.

12. 1858 was the same year that, in the wake of the Revolt of 1857, Queen Victoria assumed the title of Empress of India, officially incorporating India into the British Empire.

13. Raychaudhuri, "Bankimchandra Chattopadhyay," 117.

14. Ibid., 125–126.

15. Ibid., 104.

16. Sudipta Kaviraj, *The Unhappy Consciousness: Bankimchandra Chattopadhyay and the Formation of Nationalist Discourse in India* (Delhi: Oxford University Press, 1995), 168.

17. Serialized in the weekly *Indian Field* in 1864, *RW* was not issued in book form until 1935, long after Bankim's death. The existence of an English novel by Bankim was forgotten until all but the first three issues of the journal, *Indian Field*, in which the novel had been published were discovered. The reconstructed whole was published in Calcutta in 1935, and again in the collected works in 1969. It was not until 1996 that a new edition brought it back into print again, with a Foreword, Notes, and an Afterword by Meenakshi Mukherjee.

18. Clearly imitative of the English novel in both language and style, it is only in flashes that Bankimchandra's distinctive voice emerges out of the purple prose. However, while Salman Rushdie calls it "a poor melodramatic thing" (*The Vintage Book of Indian Writing*, xvii), Meenakshi Mukherjee asserts that, on the contrary, it is "very nearly realistic in its representation of East Bengal middle-class life" (vi). For all its flaws, *RW* has important continuities with Bankim's mature work as well as illuminating differences from it. The continuities lie in its strong female protagonist, its recognition of the need for social reform, and its frustration at the powerlessness of the educated Bengali (man), while the major difference can be located in its lack of a clearly formulated response to that lack of power to act.

19. Matangini takes this bold action at a time when married, upper-caste Bengali women generally lived in seclusion in women's quarters, appearing unveiled only before their husbands. In fact, even Matangini's sister Hemangini, who is married to Madhav, is too timid to give him the news of the robbery plot in person.

20. Bankimchandra uses the legal term "relict" rather than "widow."

21. This detail is an example of the author's ambivalence toward social reform. Even though he sympathizes with Matangini's powerlessness in her unfortunate marriage, he clearly feels threatened by the colonial reforms of laws pertaining to widow remarriage and inheritance of their husband's property.

22. Chatterjee, *Rajmohan's Wife*, 104. See Mrinalini Sinha's *Colonial Masculinity: The "Manly Englishman" and the "Effeminate Bengali" in the Late Nineteenth Century* (Manchester (UK): Manchester University Press, 1995), for an examination of British attitudes to English-educated Bengalis.

23. The feudal lord's suicide by hanging is interestingly reminiscent of Chinua Achebe's novel, *Things Fall Apart*. He is a residual figure who cannot survive in the new order, though he was used to unquestioned power in the old. But here he is not a noble or exemplary figure, and Bankim neither mourns nor celebrates his passing. As an employee of the British and a man of the law himself, Bankim is bound to see the guilty prosecuted and justice done. But one senses his unspoken approval of the robber chief who warns the feudal Mathur of his imminent arrest and then vanishes into the night with a "*Me* they shall not catch" (123).

24. "Bankim . . . formulates and fills out a violent Hindu agenda and immediately proceeds to deconstruct it." Tanika Sarkar, "Imagining Hindurashtra: The Hindu and the Muslim in Bankimchandra's Writings," in David Ludden, ed., *Contesting the Nation*: 184. See also Kaviraj, *The Unhappy Consciousness*.

25. See Uma Chakravarti, "Whatever Happened to the Vedic Dasi? Orientalism, Nationalism, and a Script for the Past," in *Recasting Women: Essays in Indian Colonial History* (New Brunswick, (NJ): Rutgers University Press, 1990), 27–87.

26. See Meenakshi Mukherjee, ch. IV, "Women in a New Genre," in *Realism and Reality* for a documentation of the large number of female protagonists in the nineteenth-century novel.

27. "[L]ong before women had become conscious of their position in society . . . male reformers had taken up the standard for them," wrote Lakshmi Menon in 1942, citing more than a century of male reformers from Rammohan Roy to D.K. Karve. Lakshmi Menon, *The Position of Women*, Oxford Pamphlets on Indian Affairs No. 2 (London: Oxford University Press, 1944), 28.

28. Quoted in Partha Chatterjee, *The Nation and Its Fragments*, 135.

29. See Krupabai Satthianadan, *Saguna* (1887–88) and *Kamala* (1894); Pandita Ramabai, *The High-Caste Hindu Woman* (1888).

30. "Knowledge of English was a gender-specific skill in 19th-century India," Meenakshi Mukherjee, "Nation, Novel, Language," in *The Perishable Empire*, 19.

31. Oyyarattu Chandu Menon. *Indulekha: A Novel of Malabar*, translated by W.F. Dumergue, 1890 (Calicut: Mathrubhumi, 1965). The novel was so popular that in 1892 another Malayalam novel, *Parannotiparinayam* by K. Ramankutty Menon, parodied contemporary imitations of *Indulekha*. Das, *A History of Indian Literature, Vol VIII*. Between 1889 and 1956, it was published in 53 editions (T.C. Sankara Menon, Foreword, 1965 English ed.).

32. Chandu Menon was first appointed as a junior clerk by a judge in the Madras Presidency, and over his long career was promoted to the post of Munsiff, and eventually, Sub-Judge (Foreword, *Indulekha*).

33. The English translation was published in 1890, only a year after the first Malayalam edition.

34. Chandu Menon elaborated on these intentions at length in his Preface to the First Edition, and in his letter to Dumergue, both part of the prefatory material in the English edition.

35. In her discussion of early Indian novels with female protagonists, Mukherjee notes that *Indulekha* was more an exception than the rule in ending with a happy marriage, *Realism and Reality*, 71.

36. Most scholars of the *Mahabharata* agree that while the epic is based on actual historical events, several of its main characters, including Krishna, were deified over time.

37. See Homi Bhabha's essay, "Signs Taken for Wonders: Questions of Ambivalence and Authority under a Tree Outside Delhi, May 1817," in *The Location of Culture* (London: Routledge, 1994), for a consideration of the English book as a sign of colonial dominance.

38. Appendices I and II of *Anandamath* give accounts of the Sannyasi disturbances of the 1770s from various British sources (Nares Chandra Sen-Gupta translation). However, in the novel, Bankim "twisted the Sannyasi rebellion to transform it into a battle organized by a secret society against the British," drawing upon histories of Italian secret societies and the Phadke Rebellion (see note 39). Das, *A History of Indian Literature, Vol. VII*, 213–214.

39. However, in distant Bombay Presidency, where another terrible famine had recently been raging, there had recently been an secretly organized uprising that had been suppressed by the British, and Bankim additionally drew upon that revolt in his depiction of "the Children." Sumit Sarkar discusses the 1879 Phadke Rebellion in *Modern India*, 48–49.

40. Bankim Chandra Chatterjee, *The Abbey of Bliss* (hereafter *AB*), translated by Nares Chandra Sen-Gupta (Calcutta: Padmini Mohan Neogi, 1906).

41. Cf. Meenakshi Mukherjee's discussion of *Anandamath* in *Realism and Reality*, 47–56.

42. In Vedic Brahmanism, *moksha* is the highest of the four ends of human life (the other three being *dharma* (sacred duty), *artha* (wealth), and *kama* (pleasure).

43. Gita 12:6–9: "On the other hand, those who depending exclusively on Me, and surrendering all actions to Me, worship me, constantly meditating on Me with single-minded devotion. These, Arjuna, I speedily deliver from the ocean of birth and death, their mind being fixed on Me. Therefore fix your mind on Me and establish your intellect in Me alone; thereafter you will abide solely in Me. There is no doubt about it. If you cannot steadily fix the mind on Me, Arjuna, then seek to attain me through the Yoga of repeated practice," *Srimad Bhagavadgita* (Gorakhpur: Gita Press), 561–564.

44. As we shall see in our discussion of Rabindranath Tagore's novel, *Gora*, there were different tendencies among the Brahmos, some of them identifying themselves as Hindus and others very emphatically rejecting Hinduism and considering themselves closer to Christianity.

45. I have included the revolutionary Aurobindo Ghose's English translation of the the first stanza of *Bande Mataram* in the text, because it better captures the rapturous lyricism of the original. Below is Nares Chandra Sen-Gupta's translation:

> Hail thee mother! [*Bande Mataram*] To her I bow
> Who with sweetest water o'erflows
> With dainty fruits is rich endowed
> And cooling whom the south wind blows
> Who's green with crops as on her grow
> To such a mother down I bow. (31)

46. Arguing in *The Wretched of the Earth* for the necessity of violence in the decolonizing struggle, Frantz Fanon asserts that the native must "vomit out" the colonizer.

47. Mukherjee, *Realism and Reality*, 49.

48. *AB*, 36.

49. A chapter excised in Basanta Koomar Roy's abridged English translation of *Anandamath*, first published in 1941, on the eve of the Quit India Movement (New Delhi: Vision Books, 1992).

50. This is from the 1906 edition, *AB*, translated by Nares Chandra Sengupta, 197.
51. *Mleccha* is a derogatory term for a foreigner, referring to a barbarian, a low character who does not speak Sanskrit, or one who speaks indistinctly or confusedly, *V.S. Apte, The Practical Sanskrit-English Dictionary* (Delhi: Motilal Banarsidass, 1965).
52. *AB*, 166–167. Priya Joshi discusses Bankimchandra's clever splitting of the narrative voice into two, so that he is able to give voice to seditious impulses through the character of Satyananda, while maintaining a loyalist omniscient narration that presents British rule as providential, *In Another Country: Colonialism, Culture, and the English Novel in India.*
53. *AB*, 200–201. In another translation, by Sri Aurobindo and his brother Barindra K. Ghosh, this same closing passage reads: "He takes Satyananda by the hand. How sublime! In that magnificent Vishnu temple...stood the two great personalities...one holding the hand of the other. Who has gripped whom? Knowledge stands wedded to devotion—religion has embraced karma or action—renunciation is coupled with success—Kalyani has grasped the hand of Santi. This Satyananda was Santi; this Sage is Kalyani. Satyananda is success, and this Saint stands for renunciation. Renunciation came and took success away" (132). Quoted in Sunil Kumar Banerjee, *Bankimchandra: A Study of His Craft* (Calcutta: Firma K.L. Mukhopadhyay, 1968), 127.
54. Sarkar, "Imagining Hindurashtra," 184.
55. *AB*. The Preface continues, "Revolutions are very generally processes of self-torture and rebels are suicides. The English have saved Bengal from anarchy. These truths are elucidated in this work."
56. Jasodhara Bagchi, "Positivism and Nationalism—Womanhood and Crisis in Nationalist Fiction: Bankimchandra's *Anandamath*," *Economic and Political Weekly*, vol. 20, no. 43, *Review of Women's Studies* (October 26, 1985): WS-59.
57. Sangeeta Ray, *Engendering India: Woman and Nation in Colonial and Postcolonial Narratives* (Durham: Duke University Press, 2000), 23, 166.
58. Basanta Koomar Roy's English version also downplays the anti-Muslim character of the Bengali original, substituting "British" everywhere that Bankim had originally used phrases that translate as "low Muslims" or "dissolute swine."
59. Sarkar, "Imagining Hindurashtra," 180–181, Mukherjee, *Realism and Reality*, 52–53.
60. Sudipta Kaviraj, e.g., in *The Unhappy Consciousness*, focuses on his complex relationship to modernity and his inner conflicts.
61. Translated as culture by Partha Chatterjee, praxis by Sudipta Kaviraj.
62. Ajit Ray, "Bankim Chandra Chatterji's New Hinduism and the *Bhagavadgita*," in R.N. Minor, *Modern Indian Interpreters of the Bhagavad-Gita*, 34–43.
63. Meditating on the Gita in prison, Aurobindo had a religious experience that led him to move away from politics after his release. He founded a new journal called *The Karmayogin*, and rather than advocating violent anticolonial action, began to use the Gita to advance a balanced cultivation of its three paths to liberation, followed by a transcendence of them to a higher plane of consciousness. In 1910 he abandoned political activism altogether and founded the Ashram of the Mother in Pondicherry, where he was to remain until the end of his life as Sri Aurobindo. According to Sumit Sarkar, "...the much-quoted Gita doctrine of *nishkama karma* stimulated a rather quixotic heroism, a martyrdom for its own sake in place of effective programmes: 'The Mother asks us for no schemes, no plans, no methods. She herself will provide the schemes, the plans, the methods...'" (Aurobindo in *Paril* 1908). Sarkar, *Modern India*, 124–125.
64. Ibid., 125. In 1918, out of 186 killed or convicted revolutionaries, 165 came from the three upper castes.
65. East Bengal was to become East Pakistan at the Partition of India, and later still, Bangladesh, after East Pakistan's secession from West Pakistan.
66. In Bengal alone, these included Bepin Pal's *New India*, Brahmobandhab Upadhyay's *Sandhya*, Barindrakumar Ghose's *Yugantar*, and Aurobindo Ghosh's *Bande Mataram*. Sarkar, *Modern India*, 113.

67. He edited *Bangardarshan* for five years starting in 1901. Krishna Dutta and Andrew Robinson, *Rabindranath Tagore: The Myriad-Minded Man* (New York: St. Martin's Press, 1996), 82–83, 142.

68. The term "transcreation" was coined by Brazilian poet Harold de Campos to refer to a translation that has a strong creative element, seeking to capture the spirit rather than the letter of the original. I use the term transcreation here because critics such as Mahasweta Sengupta have shown that Tagore's English *Gitanjali* was very different from his Bengali one. See her "Colonial Poetics: Rabindranath Tagore in Two Worlds," in Susan Bassnett and Andre Lefevre, eds., *Translation, History, Culture* (London: Pinter Publishers, 1990).

69. Sarkar, *Modern India*, 115.

70. Dutta and Robinson emphasize Tagore's many-sidedness. His responses were unpredictable, and he was different things to different people and constituencies. Nevertheless, he can be broadly located in the Brahmo Samaj tradition, although his views shifted a great deal over the course of his life. As late as March 1917, he believed that British rule in India was providential (209).

71. Rabindranath Tagore, *Gora*, translated by Sujit Mukherjee. (New Delhi: Sahitya Akademi, 1997). Serialized in the Bengali monthly *Probasi* between 1907 and 1909, *Gora* was first published as a book in 1909.

72. Noted by Lalita Pandit in "Caste, Race and Nation: History and Dialectic in Rabindranath Tagore's *Gora*," in Hogan and Pandit, eds., *Literary India: Studies in Aesthetics, Colonialism, and Culture* (Albany: SUNY Press, 1995).

73. *Gora*, xii–xiii. Since Gora's biological father was Irish, another model who has been suggested is Margaret Noble, the Irishwoman who became a disciple of Vivekananda and took the name Sister Nivedita.

74. The nationalist organization Rashtriya Swayamsevak Sangh [RSS], founded in 1926, still runs youth training camps in the same paramilitary mode.

75. Mukherjee thinks not, and suggests that Tagore's vision is more complex.

76. The term "nation-in-the-making" was used by early nationalists and Congress leaders such as B.G. Tilak and Surendranath Banerjea to acknowledge that India was not yet a nation, but was still a wide diversity of peoples being brought together by historical forces. It was felt to be necessary to promote a sense of unity and national identity in order to aid in that historical process. Bipan Chandra et al., *India's Struggle for Independence*, 74.

77. Binoy agrees that there will be no idol at the ceremony.

78. Gayatri Spivak asserts that Anandamoyi's final words about sending for Binoy are "a request to [Gora] to acknowledge the love of the emancipated Brahmo heroine [Sucharita], expressed obliquely as a request to summon a male friend." In "The Burden of English," in Rajeswari Sunder Rajan, ed., *The Lie of the Land* (New Delhi: Oxford University Press), 285–286.

79. Mukherjee, Introduction, *Gora*, xvii. In his own life, Tagore and his family were considered outside the pale of Hindu orthodoxy and the Tagore family elegantly and eclectically mixed Hindu, Muslim, and European cultures, but when it came to marrying off his children, Tagore, like Binoy, observed caste, although he did not adhere strictly to Hindu marriage rituals.

80. "…*Ghare-Baire*['s] …noble but quite ineffective and isolated hero Nikhilesh stands in significant contrast to the optimistic ending of his earlier novel *Gora*." Sarkar, *Modern India*, 122–123.

81. Rabindranath Tagore, *Nationalism* (New York: Macmillan, 1917), 42.

82. Tagore, *The Home and the World*, translated by Surendranath Tagore, introduced by Anita Desai (Harmondsworth: Penguin, 1985), 120.

83. Martha Nussbaum, "Patriotism and Cosmopolitanism," vol. 19, no. 5, *Boston Review* (October–November 1994).

84. Tagore was soon to become engaged in an argument with Gandhi about English education. Gandhi wrote in 1921 that it was an essential of Swaraj to "get rid of the

infatuation for English," which was "doing violence to the manhood and especially the womanhood of India" and leading to the neglect of the mother-tongue. He also stated that the "contagion" of their English education had made "pigmies" of modern leaders like Rammohan Roy and Tilak compared to great Indians of old like Chaitanya and Shankara. Mahatma Gandhi, *Young India: 1921–1922* (New York: B.W. Huebsch, 1923), 454–464. Tagore took offence at Gandhi's characterization of his hero, Rammohan Roy and the suggestion that women not study English. In *The Home and the World*, however, Bimala's husband's (unilateral) decision to give her an English education marks the beginning of her downfall, Dutta and Robinson, *Rabindranath Tagore: The Myriad-Minded Man*, 264.

85. Anita Desai's Introduction to the Penguin edition discusses Bimala as the personification of Bengal.
86. Sarkar, *Modern India*, 122–123.

Chapter Two

1. M.K. Naik, *A History of Indian English Literature* (New Delhi: Sahitya Akademi, 1982), 116, 152–176. Established by the Government of India in 1954, the Sahitya Akademi, India's national academy of letters, was intended "to foster and coordinate literary activities in all the Indian languages and to promote through them the cultural unity of India." <http://www.sahitya-akademi.org/sahitya-akademi/org1.htm> 19 July 2003.
2. Stanley Wolpert, "Reunification without Reconciliation," in *Tilak and Gokhale* (Delhi: Oxford University Press, 1989), 273–295.
3. In this "basic Gandhian strategy of struggle … phases of a vigorous extra-legal mass movement and confrontation with colonial authority alternate with phases during which direct confrontation is withdrawn, political concessions or reforms, if any, [are] wrested from the colonial regime … and silent political work [is] carried on among the masses within the existing legal framework, which, in turn, provides scope for such work." Bipan Chandra et al., *India's Struggle for Independence*, 313. This strategy of "Struggle-Truce-Struggle" culminated "with a call for 'Quit India' and the achievement of independence" (509).
4. In Tamilnadu, "Periyar" E.V. Ramaswani Naicker founded the Self-Respect Movement in the mid-1920s. The year 1927 was the year of the Mahad Satyagraha, at which Dr. B. R. Ambedkar, leader of the "depressed classes" in Maharashtra, publicly burned the *Manusmriti* after a struggle to drink water from the town tank. Sarkar, *Modern India*, 239–244. The *Manusmriti* is the scripture that contains the edicts passed down by the patriarch Manu, including a justification of the fourfold caste hierarchy represented by a human body in which the Brahmins are the head, the Kshatriyas the arms, the Vaishyas the legs, and the shudras the feet. The "untouchables" do not even figure in this scheme.
5. Gail Omvedt, *Dalit Visions* (Hyderabad: Orient Longman, 1995), 42.
6. Meenakshi Mukherjee, "The Anxiety of Indianness," in *The Perishable Empire*, 174.
7. Ibid., 174. Mukherjee further asserts that "there is no getting away from the burden of India" for the Indian writer in English, especially for the contemporary migrant writer who feels compelled to represent "India" to the world, no matter how slight his/her acquaintance may be with Indian literary traditions (175–176).
8. Ibid., 174.
9. K.S. Venkataramani, *Murugan, the Tiller* (Mylapore (Madras): Svetaranya Ashrama, 2nd ed., 1929).
10. K.R. Srinivasa Iyengar, *Indian Writing in English*, first published in 1962, 5th ed. (New Delhi: Sterling Publishers, 1985), 279.
11. See Ashis Nandy's analysis of Gandhi's use of the feminine in *The Intimate Enemy: Loss and Recovery of Self under Colonialism* (Oxford: Oxford University Press, 1983).
12. Tagore, however, also draws attention to the Hindu exclusivity of the nationalist movement, which Venkataramani virtually ignores.

13. It is interesting to compare Ramu's position at the end of the novel with that of Madhav, the protagonist of *Rajmohan's Wife*. In *Rajmohan*, Madhav was kidnapped by the robbers and had to be rescued by a woman; it was only the British who could eventually despatch the miscreants; and Madhav had to live without the woman he loved while paying for her upkeep. In *Murugan*, Ramu gets himself captured deliberately, converts the robbers into law-abiding subjects, and gets to live with both women in the end.

14. Chatterjee, *Nationalist Thought and the Colonial World*, 113.

15. *Murugan, the Tiller*: excerpts of reviews in the twelve-page advertising section at the back.

16. Chatterjee, *Nationalist Thought and the Colonial World*, 114.

17. Ranajit Guha, "Discipline and Mobilize," in *Subaltern Studies VII* (Delhi: Oxford University Press, 1992), 99.

18. "Land to the Tiller" was proposed by Nehru but never taken up effectively by the Congress Party in its post-independence land reform. It was a slogan of the Socialist All-India Kisan Sabha (Farmer's Assembly) in the 1930s.

19. Chatterjee, *Nationalist Thought and the Colonial World*, 125.

20. Ranajit Guha, "Discipline and Mobilize," in Partha Chatterjee and Gyanendra Pandey, eds., *Subaltern Studies VII: Writings on South Asian History and Society* (Delhi: Oxford University Press, 1992), 69–120.

21. Sita, or Janaki (Janaka's daughter) was the wife of King Rama, epic hero of the *Ramayana*, ideal man, and to many, an incarnation of the God Vishnu.

22. Ibid., 335.

23. Mulk Raj Anand, *Untouchable* (London: Penguin Books), 1986. *Untouchable* was first published in 1935 after four years, during which time it was turned down by nineteen British publishers. It had an introduction by E.M. Forster who, as Gauri Viswanathan has noted, denied the possibility of agency through self-representation to untouchables in his praise of Anand's fitness as an Indian insider-outsider to represent Bakha with "just the right mixture of insight and detachment" and his assertion that an untouchable could not have written such a story, because "he would have been involved in indignation and self-pity." By 1986, *Untouchable* had been translated into thirty-eight languages. Many of Anand's other novels have enjoyed considerable worldwide popularity, *Across the Black Water*, e.g., having been translated into eleven different languages.

24. *Untouchable*, 129. Bhangis are a hereditary scavenger and sweeper caste, "untouchables" in pre-Independence India.

25. Other early novels with untouchables as major characters are Unnava Lakshminarayana's *Malapalli* (The Village of the Untouchable, Telugu, 1922), *Comana Dudi* (The Drum of Choma, Kannada, 1933), Premchand's *Karmabhumi* (Hindi, 1932) and *Godan* (The Gift of a Cow, Hindi, 1936), V.S. Khandekar's *Don Mane* (Two Minds, Marathi, 1938), and Thakazhi Sivasankara Pillai's *Thottiyude Makan* (Scavenger's Son, Malayalam, 1947), Tarashankar Bandhopadhyay's *Kabi* (The Poet, Bengali, 1942). In addition there were a number of novels that focused on untouchability although the protagonists were not untouchables. Premchand's short stories are also important for their early treatment of untouchability (Das, *A History of Indian Literature: 1910–1956*).

26. It was not until 1947, though, that the first poem by an untouchable was published and not until the 1960s that a "Dalit" ("broken," oppressed) writers' movement emerged, rejecting the paternalistic label conferred on them by Gandhi.

27. Sarkar, *Modern India 1885–1947*.

28. Gauri Viswanathan, *Outside the Fold: Conversion, Modernity, and Belief* (Princeton: Princeton University Press, 1998); Teresa Hubel, *Whose India? The Independence Struggle in British and Indian Fiction and History* (Durham (NC): Duke University Press, 1996).

29. The socialist Anand may have felt a similar tension in adjusting himself to the Gandhi-led Congress, as he certainly did in submitting to the restrictions of the Sabarmati Ashram.

30. I thank the publisher's anonymous reader of my manuscript for this insight.

31. Viswanathan, *Outside the Fold*.

32. It was not until the early 1930s, the time *Untouchable* was written, that Dalits were officially classified as Hindus. They had not been considered part of the Hindu fold in the past, but the British included them as Hindus for census purposes and for the electoral changes brought about by the 1932 communal award. See James Massey, "Dalits-Tribals at the Crossroads: Faced with a New Form of Violence," *Dalit International Newsletter*, vol. 5, no. 3 (October 2000): 1, 4.

33. Viswanathan, *Outside the Fold*, 145.

34. For the first time he admires Indian dress and feels no desire to look like an Englishman.

35. It should be noted that Bakha was by no means Anand's only low-caste character. The Dalit protagonist of the title story of his 1946 collection *The Barber's Trade Union and Other Stories* is a much stronger character who cleverly acts to subvert the prejudices of caste Hindus to his benefit.

36. Gail Omvedt, *Dalit Visions*, 47.

37. Mukherjee, *The Twice-Born Fiction*, 77–78.

38. Mulk Raj Anand, *Seven Summers: The Story of an Indian Childhood* (Bombay: Kutub-Popular, 1959), 262.

39. Ibid., 75. See also Chronology, in M.K. Naik, *Mulk Raj Anand* (New York: Humanities Press, 1973), ix–xii.

40. Mulk Raj Anand, *Pilpali Sahab* (New Delhi: Arnold-Heinemann, 1985), 242–243.

41. Naik, *Mulk Raj Anand*. A comment on his father's hybrid style of dress in Anand's autobiographical *Seven Summers* (London: Penguin Books, 1986), 67, may sum up how Anand sees the influences that contributed to the early formation of his own patchwork philosophy: "a queer motley of English and Indian habiliments such as has been the dominant note in the fashionable dress of India, neither purely Indian nor even adequately imitative, but just anyhow, sadly lacking in form for all its studied effort at a respectable compromise, assimilating as it does some items of the superior, foreign English dress into the scheme work of Indian styles, and yet somehow symbolic of modern India, which is nothing if not a patched-up compromise of, mechanistic Europe and feudalist Asia."

42. Meenakshi Mukherjee also notes this curious inaction in Anand's protagonists, in *The Twice-Born Fiction*, 75.

43. E.M. Forster in the case of *Untouchable* and Graham Greene in the case of *Swami and Friends*.

44. John Lowe, "A Conversation with R.K. Narayan," in Geoffrey Kain, ed., *R.K. Narayan: Contemporary Critical Perspectives* (E. Lansing: Michigan State University Press, 1993), 181.

45. K.R. Srinivasa Iyengar, *Indian Writing in English*.

46. Ved Mehta, *John is Easy to Please: Encounters with the Written and the Spoken Word* (New York: Farrar, Straus and Giroux, 1971).

47. Eleventh- and Seventeenth-Century Muslim rulers who are said to have destroyed Hindu temples. These two figures have been demonized in the Hindu collective memory. The notion that there are "good" and "bad" Muslims is embedded in the mainstream (Hindu) nationalism discourse. Even Indians who declare themselves committed to secularism tend to make this distinction. Good Muslims are quiet, unobtrusive, and fall in with the Hindu mainstream; bad Muslims are demonstrative about their religion and hold out for their political interests. This student is clearly a "good Muslim," and Swami would seem to be using him to demonstrate the progressiveness of his school.

48. M.C.C. shares its initials with England's Marylebone Cricket Club.

49. Meenakshi Mukherjee, *The Twice-Born Fiction*, 155.

50. Fawzia Afzal-Khan, *Cultural Imperialism and the Indo-English Novel* (University Park (PA): Penn State University Press, 1993), 57.

51. *The Bachelor of Arts* (London: Thomas Nelson, 1937), *The Dark Room* (London: MacMillan, 1938), and *The English Teacher* (London: Eyre & Spottiswoode, 1946), first published in the United States as *Grateful to Life and Death*, 1953.

52. See Sumathi Ramaswamy's *Passions of the Tongue: Language Devotion in Tamil India, 1891–1970* (Berkeley: University College Press, 1997), for a fascinating account of Tamil linguistic nationalism. See especially "Language and the Nation: Indianizing Tamil" for a discussion of *tamillparru* or the "Indianist" imaginary within Tamil nationalism, 46–62.

53. Meenakshi Mukherjee, "The Anxiety of Indianness," in *The Perishable Empire*, 171.

54. Raja Rao, *Kanthapura*, 1938 (New York: New Directions, 1963).

55. Incidentally, Tagore was the first to call Gandhi Mahatma, or Great Soul, and Gandhi was the first to call Tagore Gurudev, or Great Teacher.

56. "There is no village in India, however mean, that has not a rich *sthala-purana*, or legendary history, of its own. So god or godlike hero has passed by the village—Rama might have rested under this pipal tree, Sita might have dried her clothes, after her bath on this yellow stone, or the Mahatma himself, on one of his many pilgrimages through the country, might have slept in this hut, the low one, by the village gate…One such story from the contemporary annals of a village I have tried to tell," author's Foreword, *Kanthapura*, vii.

57. See *Kanthapura*, pp. 180–181. In *Myths of the Nation: National Identity and Literary Representation* (Oxford: Clarendon Press, 1999), Rumina Sethi discusses the beginnings of a socialist party in early 1930s jails by a younger generation of Congress volunteers disillusioned with Gandhi's politics, particularly after he dropped several key Congress demands in his solo negotiations with Lord Irwin. (According to Sumit Sarkar, one of those concessions was the demand to return confiscated lands already sold to third parties, and another was the effort to prevent the hanging of the revolutionary Bhagat Singh, who stayed in jail while the civil disobedience prisoners were released (310).) Like Nehru, these left-leaning Congress members were also critical of Gandhi's opposition to industrialization, and what they saw as his paternalistic notion of trusteeship, which rendered workers passive.

58. Sethi, *Myths of the Nation*, 98–101.

59. Tabish Khair, *Babu Fictions: Alienation in Contemporary Indian English Novels* (New Delhi: Oxford University Press, 2001), 204, 206–207, 216–217, 221.

60. Ibid., 122. See Ketu H. Katrak's "Indian Nationalism, Gandhian Satyagraha, and Representations of Female Sexuality," in Andrew Parker et al., eds., *Nationalisms and Sexualities*, 395–406.

61. The eulogy continues: "And Rama will come back from exile, and Sita will be with him, for Ravana will be slain and Sita freed, and he will come back with Sita on his right in a chariot of the air, and brother Bharatha will go to meet him with the worshipped sandal of the Master on his head. And as they enter Ayodhya there will be a rain of flowers," *Kanthapura*, 181.

62. K.R. Srinivasa Iyengar, *Indian Literature in English*, 394.

63. B.G. Tilak, *Gita Rahasya*. Pub. Mandalay Jail, 1910–11; Pub. in Marathi 1915; English translation B.S. Sukthankar; M.K. Gandhi, Gujarati Gita translation and commentary 1929, Yeravda Prison; English translation Mahadev Desai, *The Gita According to Gandhi*; Vinoba Bhave, *Talks on the Gita*. First delivered in Dhulia jail, 1932.

64. Bipan Chandra et al., *India's Struggle For Independence* (New Delhi: Penguin India, 1989), 323 ff.

65. N.S. Phadke, *The Whirlwind*, translated from Marathi by the author (Bombay: Jaico, 1956), 147, 149–150, 185, 187.

Chapter Three

1. Mulk Raj Anand and Krishna Hutteesing, *The Bride's Book of Beauty: Sringar* (Bombay: Kutub, August 1947).

2. Sisir Kumar Das, "Triumph and Tragedy," in *A History of Indian Literature, 1911–1956*, 370–395.

3. See Ritu Menon and Kamla Bhasin, *Borders and Boundaries: Women in India's Partition*; Urvashi Butalia, *The Other Side of Silence: Voices from the Partition of India* (New Delhi: Viking Penguin, 1998); Jill Didur, "At a Loss for Words: Reading the Silence in South Asian Women's Partition Narratives," in *Topia: A Journal for Canadian Cultural Studies*, Number 4 (Fall 2000): 53–71.

4. William L. Shirer, *Gandhi: A Memoir* (New York: Simon and Schuster, 1980), 228.

5. Dhananjay Keer, *Veer Savarkar* (Bombay: Popular Prakashan, 1988): 416.

6. See Malashri Lal's *The Law of the Threshold: Women Writers in Indian English*, ch. 6 on *Inside the Haveli*.

7. Bhabani Bhattacharya, *Music for Mohini*, 93.

8. Radha Kumar, *The History of Doing: An Illustrated Account of Movements for Women's Rights and Feminism in India 1800–1990*. (London: Verso, 1993), 97.

9. Partha Chatterjee, "The Nationalist Resolution of the Women's Question" in Sangari and Vaid, eds., *Recasting Women: Essays in Indian Colonial History*, 233–253.

10. R. Radhakrishnan, "Nationalism, Gender, and the Narrative of Identity," in Parker et al., eds., *Nationalisms and Sexualities* (New York: Routledge, 1992), 84.

11. Inspired by Homi Bhabha's evocative neologisms in *Nation and Narration* (New York: Routledge, 1990).

12. Cited in Desai, "Women Well Set Free," *New York Review of Books,* vol. 39, no. 1 and 2 (January 16, 1992), 45.

13. See Meenakshi Mukherjee, *The Twice-Born Fiction: Themes and Techniques of the Indian Novel in English* (New Delhi: Heinemann, 1971), 79.

14. Adil Jussawalla, ed. *New Writing in India* (Harmondsworth: Penguin, 1974), 35.

15. Gordon Roadarmel, Introduction, *Modern Hindi Short Stories* (Berkeley: University of California Press, 1974), 2–3.

16. Agehananda Bharati quoted in Khushwant Singh, *We Indians,* 1982 (New Delhi: Orient Paperbacks, 1987), 57.

17. Partha Chatterjee, "The Moment of Arrival: Nehru and the Passive Revolution," in *Nationalist Thought and the Colonial World: A Derivative Discourse?* 131–166.

18. In *The Twice-Born Fiction*, 78–91 and 208–209, Meenakshi Mukherjee cites several novels published in the late 1950s and early 1960s as examples of the kind in which "traditional" values inevitably triumph: *Remember the House* (1956), *A Time to Be Happy* (1957), *Some Inner Fury* (1957), *The Dark Dancer* (1959), and *Sunlight on a Broken Column* (1961). In contrast, she singles out Anita Desai's *Voices in the City* (1965) and Arun Joshi's *The Foreigner* (1968) as examples of the more complex kind of novel, influenced, but not entirely shaped, by French Existentialism, and characterized by three-dimensional characters and the "refusal of simple solutions."

19. "The political and social gospel of Hindu India" is K.M. Panikkar's term, from *Foundations of New India*, 36.

20. For some of the ideas in this paragraph I am indebted to a 1993 conversation with Shiv Visvanathan of the Center for the Study of Developing Societies in Delhi.

21. For a detailed overview of the relationship between literature—particularly by women—and the post-independence Indian nation-state, see "The Twentieth Century: Women Writing the Nation," in Susie Tharu and K. Lalita, eds., *Women Writing in India. Vol. II: The Twentieth Century* (New York: The Feminist Press, 1993), 43–116.

22. Tharu and Lalita, *Woman Writing in India*, 93.

23. P. Lal, "Indian Writing in English: A Reply to Mr. Jyotirmoy Datta," in Abu Sayeed Ayyub and Amlan Datta, eds. *Ten Years of Quest*, (Bombay: Manaktalas, 1966), 297–303.

24. Jyotirmoy Datta, "On Caged Chaffinches and Polyglot Parrots," in *Ten Years of Quest*, 291.

25. Meenakshi Mukherjee, "The Anxiety of Indianness," in *The Perishable Empire*.

26. In *Nationalism in Indo-Anglian Fiction*, G.P. Sharma sees the *karma* theory running through the entire narrative of *Cry, the Peacock* and "the depiction of woman's plight in

modern Indian society" as a mirror of the Indian nationalist spirit in an era of awakening. Cited in Usha Bande, *The Novels of Anita Desai: A Study in Character and Conflict* (New Delhi: Prestige Books, 1988), 13. As we shall see, the fact that Desai feels compelled to engage with the Gita ideals is certainly evidence of the continued pervasiveness and force of the nationalist discourse, but her critical examination of these ideals in action problematizes nationalism rather than upholding it. Still, books such as Sharma's amply demonstrate the anxiety to "prove" that Indian English novels are as patriotic as those written in the Indian languages.

27. In an interview, Desai said, "There was a time in my life when I was enormously influenced by Camus. *The Outsider* influenced a great deal of my early writing. Some of it was posturing of course." In Feroza Jussawalla and Reed Way Dasenbrock, eds., *Interviews with Writers from the Post-Colonial World* (Jackson (MI): University Press of Mississippi, 1992), 170.

28. As Gordon Roadarmel reminds readers: "the modern Indian writer is living very much in the twentieth century, dealing with a relatively universal range of problems, though these problems are of course seen primarily in the distinctive context of life in his own country." Introduction, *Modern Hindi Short Stories* (Berkeley: University of California Press, 1972), 1.

29. Discussing Partha Chatterjee's analysis of the internal contradictions of Indian nationalism, R. Radhakrishnan writes, "In a real sense . . . the nationalist subject does not exist. Conceived within this chronic duality, the nationalist subject is doomed to demonstrate the impossibility of his own claim to subjecthood. The inner and outer in mutual disarray, the nationalist subject marks the space of a constitutive debacle." In *Nationalisms and Sexualities*, 91.

30. Eunice de Souza, " 'Indianness' and the Critic in a Post-Colonial Culture," *The Bombay Review,* 1 (1989): 28–41.

31. An earlier and shorter version of Part I was published as "Codes in Conflict: Post-Independence Alienation in Anita Desai's Early Novels," in *Journal of Gender Studies*, vol. 5, no. 3 (1996): 317–328.

32. Desai herself has stipulated that her four earliest novels not be re-issued in new editions: *Cry, The Peacock, Bye Bye Blackbird, Voices in the City,* and *Where Shall We Go This Summer?* (Anita Desai, personal correspondence, 1995).

33. Even in its fifth edition, K.R. Srinavasa Iyengar's *Indian Writing in English* still discusses all "The Women Novelists" together in one chapter, and M.K. Naik discusses Jhabvala, Markandaya, Sahgal, Desai together in quick succession as "the major Indian English women novelists" in *A History of Indian English Literature*, 241.

34. For example, see Raji Narasimhan, *Sensibility Under Stress: Aspects of Indo-English Fiction* (New Delhi: Ashajanak Publications, 1976). Referring to Desai's narrative voice in *Cry, the Peacock*, she writes, "her cries suggest the orphan, from the overall cultural thinning and dereliction, which gives them a metallic poignance" (20); to her description of a sitar concert in *Voices in the City*: "The visual response to Indian music . . . is the hallmark par excellence of remoteness from the culture" (33).

35. For an example of the latter critical tendency, see Aijaz Ahmad's throwaway mention of Desai as an Indian English writer with "currency . . . in the global category of Third World Literature," by virtue of her "claim to represent . . . the Indian national experience." *In Theory* (Delhi: Oxford University Press, 1994), 75.

36. R.S. Sharma writes, "Hers is a small world . . . her characters have a near-neurotic quality about them." In *Anita Desai* (New Delhi: Arnold-Heinemann, 1981), 12–13. E.V. Ramakrishnan takes Desai to task for the "limitations of her political vision" in her 1984 novel *In Custody* in "The Politics, of Language and the Language of Politics," in Bharucha and Sarang, eds., *Indian-English Fiction 1980–90: An Assessment* (Delhi: B.R. Publishing Corporation, 1994), 19–32.

37. Anita Desai, "The Indian Writer's Problems," in R.S. Srivastava, ed., *Perspectives on Anita Desai,* 1–4.

38. Anita Desai, "The Use of English by Indian Writers," lecture, April 24, 1989, University of Massachusetts, Amherst. Raja Rao's foreword to *Kanthapura* (1938) is a classic statement on Indian writing in English. For responses to critical attacks on English in the 1960s and 1970s, see P. Lal, *The Alien Insiders: Essays on Indian Writing in English* (Calcutta: Writers Workshop, 1987).

39. Anita Desai, *Voices in the City*, 139–140.

40. This is reminiscent of an essay by Virginia Woolf in which she responds to an essentializing characterization of women as excelling in "close analytic miniature work"and being "more happy when they reproduce than when they produce." Woolf argued that women were forced into limited forms by their confined lives. In Andrew MacNeillie, ed., *The Essays of Virginia Woolf Vol. 1: 1904–1912* (San Diego: Harcourt Brace Jovanovich, 1986), 16.

41. Anita Desai. "Women Writers," *Quest* 52 (April–June 1970), 39–43.

42. Anita Desai, "Women Well Set Free," 45.

43. Anita Desai, *Games at Twilight and Other Stories* (Harmondsworth: Penguin, 1982), 1–10. Also anthologized in Rushdie and West, eds., *The Vintage Book of Indian Writing 1947–1997* (published in the United States as *Mirrorwork*), 121–130.

44. In *The Law of the Threshold*, Malashri Lal describes Indian women's multiple, cross-cutting realities as a "twilight zone of indeterminacies," 165.

45. *Gita* 2:58 "When like a tortoise, which draws in its limbs from all directions, he withdraws his senses from the sense-objects, his mind is stable," Jayadayal Goyandka, *Srimad Bhagavadgita* (Gorakhpur: Gita Press, 1969).

46. In the last chapter of the novel, Gautama's mother and sister have taken Maya back to her father's home in Lucknow, and are awaiting his return from abroad. She is to be sent to a mental asylum, where word of what happened will not get out. In the final paragraph, Maya is up on the roof and starts to scream in terror—presumably she has suddenly realized the enormity of what she has done. Her mother-in-law hurries up to her, and all is suddenly quiet. "There was silence, and then both disappeared into the dark quiet. All around the dark was quiet then" (218). Some critics have suggested that Maya commits suicide, but the novel ends ambiguously.

47. Jasbir Jain, *Stairs to the Attic: The Novels of Anita Desai* (Jaipur: Printwell, 1987), 16.

48. Ibid., 19–20.

49. Anita Desai, *Voices in the City*, 199.

50. M.K. Gandhi, *Anasaktiyoga*, 100.

51. It is a common practice in Advaita (nondualistic) Vedanta to remind oneself, "I am not my body," in order to move toward realization of the eternal Self within and without, which alone is ultimately real.

52. In their Introduction to *Recasting Women: Essays in Indian Colonial History* (11), Kumkum Sangari and Sudesh Vaid note that during the nineteenth-century reconstruction of the "respectable" Bengali middle-class woman, "women who have hitherto had greater access to a 'public' sphere of street, marketplace, fair and festival" were consciously "excluded from the private space of the *bhadralok* (lit. respectable people) home" and what is seen to constitute acceptable cultural activity is narrowed. It is the ravaged street singer's entry into her cloistered space that precipitates Monisha's realization that she has never really lived.

53. Lata Mani, "Contentious Traditions: The Debate on Sati in Colonial India," in Sangari and Vaid, eds., *Recasting Women: Essays in Indian Colonial History,* 88–126. Mani demonstrates how the sati debate was more about hammering out the terms of a colonial discourse rather than "about" women; more about what constituted tradition than whether or not women should be burned to death.

54. Like Rajeswari Sunder Rajan in her approach toward the subjectivity and agency of the *sati* by "shifting the emphasis from sati-as-death to sati-as-burning," Desai demystifies the act by engaging with "the subject of/in pain," refusing to pull back from its horror and

thereby allow her to become unreachable. "The Subject of Sati: Pain and Death in the Contemporary Discourse on Sati," in *Real and Imagined Women*, 15–35.

55. In *The Twice-Born Fiction*, Meenakshi Mukherjee comments that Desai's protagonist Nirode in *Voices in the City* is: "a complex character whose predicament cannot be explained away by any glib discussion of the conflict of cultures. It is tempting to relate this hero to the heroes of Camus … but a more relevant observation—an observation that once again establishes the close connection between Indo-Anglian fiction and contemporary fiction in other Indian languages—is that Nirode is a counterpart of the new protagonists of Bengali fiction (who in their turn are also influenced by French existentialism) as seen in the controversial novels of Samaresh Basu and Sunil Gangopadhyay."

56. Meanings of their names: Nirode is from Sanskrit *nirodh*: Confinement, hindrance, annihilation, disappointment; Monisha: wish, desire; Arun: sun; Jiban: life.

57. In their discussion of the model of liberal, nationalist feminism in the period of the 1920s through the 1940s, Susie Tharu and K. Lalita discuss the phenomenon of the superwoman, who takes everything upon herself, scorns to exhibit weakness or to depend on men, and who blames only women themselves for their problems or failures. Gautama's mother in *Cry, The Peacock* is one of the women of this generation, bewildered by Maya's incompetence and passivity; so is Aunt Lila, in *Voices in the City*. "Women's Organizations and Liberal Nationalist Feminism," in *Women Writing in India*, 84–90.

58. P. Lal. *The Alien Insiders : Essays on Indian Writing in English*, 126.

59. "From a disintegrated consciousness, all seek wholeness in themselves and a reconnection with the voltage of social dynamism." Nadine Gordimer (another writer upon whom race, nationality, and gender confer a complex and sometimes painful positioning) in her 1979 essay, "Relevance and Commitment" in Stephen Clingman, ed., *The Essential Gesture: Writing, Politics and Places* (New York: Knopf, 1988), 135–136. Gordimer also makes a useful distinction between the Marxist concept of alienation caused by one's "relation to the means of production" and alienation in the broader sense as "a condition of rejecting and/or being rejected."

60. Rajeswari Sunder Rajan, *Real and Imagined Women*, 2–3, 12.

61. Anita Desai, *Where Shall We Go This Summer?* 1975 (New Delhi: Orient Paperbacks, 1982), 35.

62. Sita and Raman are named ironically, in contrast to the epic ideal of the *Ramayana*. Here Desai's female characters differ from the droves of women in modern Indian English novels who are nothing but Sita, Savitri, or Shakuntala figures, whether by name or by nature. See Meenakshi Mukherjee's *Twice-Born Fiction*, 163–166.

63. Bhabani Bhattacharya, *Music for Mohini*.

64. *Where Shall We Go This Summer?* 37.

65. In *The Law of the Threshold*, Malashri Lal describes the typical Indian English woman writer balancing on a line, but not crossing it, maintaining a "strenuous poise—between the outer world of patriarchy and colonial influences and an inner world of energy let loose by selected visions of the 'Other,'" 5. This aptly describes both Monisha's crisis in *Voices in the City* and Nanda Kaul's crisis in *Fire on the Mountain*, except that the strenuous poise is not entirely maintained: Monisha kills herself after a vision of the "Other" in the courtyard, and while Nanda sits at the phone, after the news of Ila's death, Raka sets everything on fire.

66. Anita Desai, *Fire On the Mountain*, 144.

67. Anita Desai, "The Seed of Destruction," *The New York Review of Books*, vol 38, no. 12 (June 27, 1991): 4.

68. *Clear Light of Day*, 182. It is notable that Bim and Raja learned this from T.S. Eliot, who himself learned it from India.

69. Loved by Hindus and Muslims alike, Muhammad Iqbal (1873–1938), a contemporary of Tagore's, struggled against quietism very much as the nationalist Hindus had. He taught that "action is life and inaction is death," and struggled against injustice and

tyranny whether it was colonialist, nationalist, capitalist, or feudal. He believed both in reason and in faith, and was a devout Muslim. Like Tagore, he moved away from nationalism because he found it too exclusive. Toward the end of his life, he gave his support to Jinnah because he feared for the survival of the Muslims in India. He is now canonized as the national poet of Pakistan. From Stephen Hay, ed. *Sources of India Tradition, Vol. Two* (New Delhi: Penguin India 1991), 2nd ed., 205–207. Living in Old Delhi in a neighborhood with as many Muslims as Hindus and ten years old at Partition, Desai herself lost half her schoolfriends and neighbors overnight and forever. The novel is thus a personal act of recovery as well as a literary and a cultural one (Anita Desai, Personal interview. S. Hadley, Massachusetts, November 1992).

70. Vidyut Bhagwat, "Marathi Literature as a Source for Contemporary Feminism," *Economic and Political Weekly*, (April 29, 1995): WS24–WS29.

71. Anita Desai, *Clear Light of Day*, 174.

Chapter Four

1. *Indian Literature*, vol. XXV, no.1 (1982): 128.

2. Susie Tharu. "Tracing Savitri's Pedigree," in Kumkum Sangari and Sudesh Vaid, eds., *Recasting Women: Essays in Indian Colonial History* (originally delivered as a paper in November 1981).

3. Salman Rushdie, *Midnight's Children* (London: Picador, 1982). Further references to this work will be abbreviated *MC* and all citations are from this edition.

4. An earlier version of this chapter was published in *Studies in the Novel*, vol. 97, no. 3 (Fall 1997): 342–375.

5. *MC*, 9.

6. Quoted from Shyamala Narayan, in the 1983 Bibliography, *Journal of Commonwealth Literature*, vol. XIX, no. 2 (1984): 79–82. Rushdie had lived in England since 1962, when his father sent him to Rugby at the age of fourteen. He went on to read history at King's College, Cambridge, during which time his family moved from Bombay to Karachi, Pakistan. Since his childhood, he had been back to India only once, in the late 1970s, when *MC* was conceived.

7. From Una Chaudhuri, "Imaginative Maps," New York: Turnstile Press. A 1983 interview with Rushdie, conducted by Una Chaudhuri, Subir Grewal's Rushdie page, <hostmaster@ trill-home.com> downloaded March 8, 1997.

8. Mukund Padmanabhan et al. "The Empire Writes Back," in *Sunday*, December 4–10, 1988.

9. 1983 Bibliography, *Journal of Commonwealth Literature*.

10. See Debashish Mukerji's article, "An Area of Brightness," on the increased acceptance of Indian writers in English both in the West and in India itself. Downloaded from SAWNET: <www.umiacs.umd.edu/users/sawweb/sawnet/SAW.books.html> November 28, 1996.

11. Two examples of Indian critiques of Rushdie's literary influence are Aijaz Ahmed's *In Theory*, and Harish Trivedi's essay, "The St. Stephen's Factor," *Indian Literature*, vol. XXXIV, no. 5 (September/October 1991): 183–187. Trivedi also uses the term "post-Rushdie" critically in his *Colonial Transactions: English Literature and India*. (Manchester: Manchester University Press, 1995). Two studies of Rushdie as diasporic writer are Vijay Mishra's "Postcolonial Differend: Diasporic Narratives of Salman Rushdie," *Ariel*, vol. 26, no. 3 (1995): 7–45, and Jean Kane's "The Migrant Intellectual and the Body of History: Salman Rushdie's *Midnight's Children*," *Contemporary Literature*, vol. 37, no.1 (Spring 1996): 94–118.

12. Although Rushdie accidentally (-on-purpose?) calls him the scribe of the *Ramayana*.

13. These critics are too numerous to list, but some of the scholars who have discussed the relationship of history, politics, and the individual in *MC* are: Uma Parameswaran, R.S.

Pathak, Dieter Riemenschneider, Aruna Srivastava, Neil ten Kortenaar, and Jonathan White. Thanks to Michael Reder for his useful review of the critical literature in "Narration and Identity in Salman Rushdie's *Midnight's Children*," unpublished Master's thesis, 1994.

14. Mukund Padmanabhan et al. "The Empire Writes Back," *Sunday*, December 4–10, 1988.

15. "Damme, This is the Oriental Scene for You!" Special Fiction Issue, *The New Yorker* (June 23 and 30, 1997): 50–61.

16. Hence Saleem's desperate anxiety to set down his story before it is too late and his recognition that his son-who-is-not-his-son's generation will not live by his generation's ideals. "Out of Time" was a popular Rolling Stones' song of Rushdie's teenage years, whose lyrics express a lover's contemptuous rejection of a former love who has "been away for much too long."

17. Jerome Segal, *Agency and Alienation: A Theory of Human Presence* (Savage (MD): Rowman & Littlefield, 1991), 129.

18. Ibid., 102, 116.

19. Carlos Moya, *The Philosophy of Action: An Introduction* (Oxford: Polity Press, 1990).

20. Una Chaudhuri interview, 1983.

21. Kumkum Sangari, "The Politics of the Possible," *Cultural Critique* 7 (Fall 1987): 157–186.

22. Salman Rushdie, "Imaginary Homelands," in *Imaginary Homelands: Essays and Criticism 1981–1991* (New York: Granta/Viking, 1991), 21.

23. These passive-aggressive forms of resistance are reminiscent of suffragettes' tactics, and more relevant here, of Gandhi's use of mass nonviolent civil disobedience. See Ashis Nandy's discussion of Gandhi's "feminine" modes of anticolonial resistance in *The Intimate Enemy: Loss and Recovery of Self Under Colonialism*, 47–57. For a feminist critique of these tactics, see Ketu H. Katrak's essay, "Indian Nationalism, Gandhian 'Satyagraha' and Representations of Female Sexuality," in Andrew Parker et al., eds., *Nationalisms and Sexualities*, 395–406.

24. See Ambreen Hai, "'Marching In from the Peripheries': Rushdie's Feminized Artistry and Ambivalent Feminism," in M. Keith Booker, ed., *Critical Essays on Salman Rushdie* (New York: G.K. Hall & Co, 1999), 16–50, for a useful discussion of Rushdie's ambivalent shifting use of women and gender in his novels, as he appropriates feminine forms and feminist resistance in the service of his postcolonial project, while his narratives at the same time "undermine their own (proto) feminist strains." She examines the contradictory uses of women and gender in his work by examining plot and narrative structure, tone, representations of women, rhetorical tropes, and tropes of women's art. Although her essay covers several of his novels, her discussion of *MC* examines Rushdie's stereotyped and somewhat crude representations of women like the Widow, Reverend Mother, and Aunt Alia, Saleem's simultaneous desire for and competition with his sister, the effeminized or impotent male figures like Nadir Shah and Saleem himself, and the narrative uses of figures like Durga and Padma as enablers of the male-authored narrative.

25. Pathak, R.S. "History and the Individual in the Novels of Salman Rushdie," in G.R. Taneja and R.K. Dhawan, eds., *The Novels of Salman Rushdie* (New Delhi: Indian Society for Commonwealth Studies, in association with Prestige Books, 1992), 123.

26. Guruprasad, Thakur. "The Secret of Rushdie's Charm," in Taneja and Dhawan, eds., *The Novels of Salman Rushdie*, 169.

27. Anita Desai, "Where Cultures Clash By Night," *The Washington Post*, March 15, 1981.

28. *MC*, 194. Also see Ambreen Hai's discussion of Rushdie's use of the Padma figure in "Women Marching In from the Peripheries," 26.

29. Bipan Chandra et al., *India's Struggle for Independence* (New Delhi: Penguin Books, 1989), 71.

30. Nayantara Sahgal, *Prison and Chocolate Cake* (New York: Alfred A. Knopf, 1954), 220–221.

31. Una Chaudhuri interview, 1983.

32. The depth of Rushdie's current disillusionment with sociopolitical trends in India is reflected in his *The Moor's Last Sigh* in which Saleem's son Aadam, his last repository of hope in *MC*, has grown up to be a power-hungry, amoral, 1990s-style yuppie capitalist.

33. In his essay, "The Riddle of Midnight: India, August 1987," Rushdie returns for the fortieth anniversary of Independence and the fortieth birthday of the "Class of 47." In view of the increasing exclusiveness of the nationalist idea in India, he muses over the "paradox: that, in a country created by the Congress's nationalist campaign, the well-being of the people might now require that all nationalist rhetoric be abandoned." Given the continuing nationalist history India has been rehearsing, that does not look very likely anytime soon, *Imaginary Homelands*, 32–33.

34. Homi K. Bhabha. Introduction, *Nation and Narration* (London: Routledge, 1990), 1–2. Here, Bhabha draws from Benedict Anderson's *Imagined Communities*, Tom Nairn's *The Breakup of Britain*, and Hannah Arendt's *The Human Condition*.

35. K.R. Srinivasa Iyengar uses the term in its purely descriptive sense. However, he quotes another critic, Shyam Ratna Gupta, who uses it in the more critical sense as a sign of schizophrenic tendencies or alienation, *Indian Writing in English*, 5th edition, 774.

36. William Safire, "On Language: Janus Lives," *New York Times Magazine* (May 4, 1997): 22.

37. Homi K. Bhabha, *Nation and Narration*, 3.

38. M. Keith Booker, "Beauty and the Beast: Dualism as Despotism in the Fiction of Salman Rushdie," *ELH*, vol. 57, no.4 (1990): 977–997.

39. M.C.C. also stands for the British Marylebone Cricket Club. Thanks to Stephen Clingman for pointing this out to me. It also intertextually evokes the Malgudi Cricket Club in R.K. Narayan's *Swami and Friends*.

40. "The gander is the animal mask of the creative principle, which is anthropomorphically embodied in Brahma...a symbol of sovereign freedom through stainless spirituality... The Hindu ascetic...freed from the bondage of rebirth, is said to have attained to the rank of 'gander' (hamsa), or 'highest gander' (paramahamsa)...The wild gander... exhibits in its mode of life the twofold nature of all beings. It swims on the surface of the water, but is not bound to it. Withdrawing from the watery realm, it wings into the pure and stainless air, where it is as much at home as in the world below...Thus it is the homeless free wanderer, between the upper celestial and the lower earthly spheres, at ease in both, not bound to either...it symbolizes the divine essence, which, though embodied in, and abiding with, the individual, yet remains forever free from, and unconcerned with, the events of individual life...On the one hand earth-bound, limited in life-strength, in virtues and in consciousness, but on the other hand a manifestation of the divine essence ...we, like the wild goose, are citizens of the two spheres." Heinrich Zimmer, *Myths and Symbols in Indian Art and Civilization*, (New York: Harper & Row, 1962): 48–9.

41. Kathleen Flanagan, "The Fragmented Self in Salman Rushdie's *Midnight's Children*," *Commonwealth Novel in English*, vol. 5, no. 1 (Spring 1992): 38–45.

42. This is typical Rushdiesque deflationary humor, but with a serious point—the English democratic institutions inherited by independent India may have held promise at Independence, but it is increasingly being asked whether they hold the seeds of their own destruction.

43. To Rushdie, the fragment implies a whole, even if the whole is itself composite; it loses meaning in isolation. While he defends the fragment's right to a voice and an independent existence and condemns the coerciveness of the centralized State, he is clearly ambivalent about the loss of a controlling Center. For a 1990s perspective, see Partha Chatterjee's *The Nation and Its Fragments*.

44. Two of the protagonists in I. Allan Sealy's epic family chronicle-national-narrative, *The Trotter-Nama* (New York: Knopf, 1988), are also ballooning miniaturists, literally and figuratively. As the Seventh Trotter's body balloons grotesquely, his paintings (ironically, copies of Mughal miniatures) get smaller and smaller. He claims that they do not simply

imitate the original, but progressively improve upon it, eventually "dispensing with the world" altogether. His illustrious ancestor, also a portly figure, was killed while hot-air ballooning.

45. Richard Cronin, "The Indian English Novel: *Kim* and *Midnight's Children*," *Modern Fiction Studies*, vol. 33, no. 2 (1987): 201–202.

46. In Maharashtra, the Shiv Sena organization built its power base in Bombay by organizing local, lower-level workers against "outsiders."

47. "Washing dirty linen" invitably calls to mind the novel's episode of the washing-chest. If you hide in dirty laundry, you are bound to get exposed. You can only retreat "from the demands of parents and history" for so long before they catch up with you. And as with Saleem, both exposing and exposed, so also with Rushdie himself.

48. Anita Desai, Personal interview, S. Hadley, Massachusetts, November 1992.

49. Two Indian collections of essays on new Indian English writers of the 1980s are Viney Kirpal, ed., *The New Indian Novel in English: A Study of the 1980s* (New Delhi: Allied Publishers Ltd., 1990) and Nilufer E. Bharucha and Vilas Sarang, eds., *Indian-English Fiction 1980–1990: An Assessment* (Delhi: B.R. Publishing Corporation, 1994).

50. The Parsis came to India in the eighth century A.D. and Anglo-Indians have been a presence since the early seventeenth century.

51. "The mind is restless, Krishna, impetuous, self-willed, hard to train: to master the mind seems as difficult as to master the mighty winds. The mind is indeed restless, Arjuna: it is indeed hard to train. But by constant practice and by freedom from passions the mind in truth can be trained." Upamanyu Chatterjee, *English, August: An Indian Story* (Calcutta: Rupa, 1989), 83–84. In his *Colonial Transactions*, Harish Trivedi notes with some contempt that the English-educated protagonist (and author) uses a Gita in English translation. The novel, however, thematizes this very point, Agastya himself thinking that his orthodox uncle (the one who had never forgiven his Bengali father for having married a Christian) "would have been displeased ('It is not written by Racine, you know, that you have to read it in English')" (83). It is also worth remembering that Gandhi himself first read his Gita in English translation.

52. Sanjay Iyer, "East, West: No Home is Best," *Indian Review of Books*, vol. 4, no. 3 (January–February 1995): 2.

53. Here I must acknowledge my colleague Pennie Ticen, who first used "on the hyphen" years ago in a conversation with me, long before it was in common use.

54. Antonio Gramsci via Nadine Gordimer, from the epigraph to her novel *July's People*: "The old is dying and the new cannot be born, in this interregnum there arises a great diversity of morbid symptoms." Gramsci's position here is that, while the precise direction is unknown, it is clear that the mass of the people have become "detached from their traditional ideologies…through the 'crisis of authority.'" There can be no easy resolution through a "restoration of the old," he asserts; it is necessary to create a new culture. "State and Civil Society," in Quintin Hoare and Geoffrey Nowell Smith, eds., *Selections from the Prison Notebooks* (New York: International Publishers, 1971), 276.

55. Neil ten Kortenaar's term to describe Rushdie's allegorical method in *MC*. "*Midnight's Children* and the Allegory of History," *Ariel*, vol.26, no. 2 (1995): 41–62.

56. Mukul Kesavan, *Looking Through Glass* (New York: Farrar, Straus and Giroux, 1995).

57. Rajeswari Sunder Rajan, "The Feminist Plot and the National Allegory: Home and World in Two Indian Women's Novels in English," *Modern Fiction Studies*, vol. 39, no. 1 (Spring 1993): 71–92.

58. In her reading of *MC*, in *Cultural Imperialism and the Indo-English Novel* (University Park (PA): Penn State University Press, 1993), Fawzia Afzal-Khan says that Saleem is trying to "debunk myth" when he declares that he will not see his son's miracles, that he will not see them "because, in fact, they will not happen" (159). While it is true that Saleem does suggest that his son's generation will be more "pragmatic" than his own, I do not believe

that he rules out "new myths" altogether. Saleem cannot partake of a new collective myth because he has been formed by the old one, and with its demise will come his own.

59. Amitav Ghosh, *The Circle of Reason* (New York: Viking Penguin, 1986), 416–417.

Chapter Five

1. Jill Ker Conway, "The Politics of Women's Education," in *A Woman's Education* (New York: Knopf, 2001), 120.

2. Kumkum Sangari and Sudesh Vaid's *Recasting Women: Essays in Indian Colonial History* (New Brunswick, NJ): Rutgers University Press, 1990), was an influential early collection of feminist "returns" to rethink colonial history. Ranajit Guha and other historians of the Subaltern Studies Group have similarly returned to colonialist and nationalist history in *Subaltern Studies*.

3. Madhu Kishwar, "In Defence of Our Dharma," *Manushi* (1990), 60. Madhu Kishwar is a cofounder of the women's magazine *Manushi* (Womankind).

4. Shashi Deshpande, "The Indian Woman—Myths, Stereotypes and the Reality," Swiss-India Society and Völkerkundermuseum der Universität Zürich, October 30, 1997. <http://ch.8m.com/shashi.htm> last accessed November 6, 2003.

5. Deshpande's writing career and publishing history can be compared to Desai's in that she had a large body of work published in India before she received a wider recognition or readership either inside or outside the country.

6. This chapter abounds with Sitas: Desai's protagonist in *Where Shall We Go This Summer*, Devi's mother in *The Thousand Faces of Night*, and Jaya's penname *in That Long Silence*. Each text makes a different, critical use of the name, which, of course, evokes the ideal of Rama's loyal, long-suffering wife in the *Ramayana*. Pre-independence Indian English novels tended to employ the idealized image of Sita uncritically.

7. My source for this story is a four-part set of Indian comic books for children, *Shri Krishna Leela* (Delhi: Dreamland Publications, retold and edited by T.R. Bhanot), published in English, Hindi, Bengali, Gujarati, and Marathi. The original source is Book 10 (of 12) of the *Bhagavata Purana*. Gaurinath Sastri, *A Concise History of Classical Sanskrit Literature* (Delhi: Motilal Banarsidass, 1974), 45.

8. Toni Morrison's characterization of *Beloved*: "Unspeakable Things Unspoken: The Afro-American Presence in American Literature," *Michigan Quarterly Review*, vol. 28, no. 1 (Winter 1989).

9. The same realization brings a sense of calm and relief to Bim in Desai's *Clear Light of Day* (also published in 1980). Perhaps what is liberating to both is that ultimately they alone are responsible for their actions, no matter how much they may feel bound to other people by need, duty, and social custom. Perhaps, too, the reminder of one's aloneness at the point of death makes them resolve to set things to rights in their family relationships while they still have the opportunity. Significantly, Desai's character gains her insight from a history text, and that, too, about the Mughal Emperor Aurangzeb, while Deshpande's draws her inspiration from a Hindu epic.

10. The contemporary movement against dowry murders and domestic violence began only in 1977–78, and gathered force over the next five years. See Radha Kumar, ch. 7: "The Campaign Against Dowry," in *The History of Doing: An Illustrated Account of Movement for Women's Rights and Feminism in India 1800–1990* (London: Verso, 1993), 115–126.

11. Flavia Agnes, "My Experiences of Being Single and Why I Returned" (1982), cited in N. Gandhi and N. Shah, eds., *The Issues at Stake: Theory and Practice in the Contemporary Women's Movement in India* (New Delhi: Kali for Women, 1991), 316.

12. Shashi Deshpande, *That Long Silence* (London: Virago, 1988).

13. It was a corruption scandal at the very top that precipitated the State of Emergency called by Indira Gandhi. Her son Rajiv was also dogged by corruption charges. The

Maharashtra-based women's Anti-Price Rise Movement in the early 1970s was an important part of the popular reaction against high-level government corruption that led to the crisis at the Center.

14. *Vimrsya etat asesena yathecchasi tatha kuru, Gita* 18:63. "Reflect on it fully and then act as you wish." Translation in *Srimad Bhagavad Geeta* (Delhi: Shree Geeta Ashram, 1985).

15. Rosemary Marangoly George, *The Politics of Home* (Berkeley: University of California Press, 1999), 147, 149.

16. Shashi Deshpande, *A Matter of Time* (Delhi: Penguin India 1996; New York: The Feminist Press, 1999). The Feminist Press has also reissued Deshpande's previous novel, *The Binding Vine.*

17. Shashi Deshpande, "The Indian Woman—Myths, Stereotypes and the Reality."

18. Anita Desai, "Women and Fiction in India," in *The Toronto South Asian Review*, vol. 10, no.2 (1992): 27. Based on a talk delivered at the University of Toronto, November 1990.

19. In *The Issues at Stake: Theory and Practice in the Contemporary Women's Movement in India* (New Delhi: Kali for Women, 1992), Nandita Gandhi and Nandita Shah point out the limitations of Mahatma Gandhi's model of self realization and self-reliance, which "puts too much emphasis on personal life and individual judgement, and fails to integrate that realization to other spheres." They assert that "individual freedom is part of society's freedom, personal responsibility merges with the social, the private with the public, the family links to the state . . . Self assertion can no longer be applied to only personal lives" (322).

20. See my review of Deshpande's novels in *South Asian Novelists in English: An A-to-Z Guide*, Jaina Sanga, ed. (Westport (CT): Greenwood Press, 2003), 54–60.

21. See Arvind Rajagopal, "Thinking about the new Indian Middle Class: Gender, Advertising and Politics in an Age of Globalization," in *Signposts: Gender Issues in Post-Independence India*, Rajeswari Sunder Rajan, ed. (New Delhi: Kali for Women, 1999), 57–100. Also, Rajeswari Sunder Rajan, *Real and Imagined Women: Gender, Culture, Postcolonialism* (New York: Routledge, 1993), 130–138.

22. Githa Hariharan, *The Thousand Faces of Night* (New Delhi: Penguin Books India, 1992).

23. From Irawati Karve, *Yuganta*. Although *Yuganta* was first published in Marathi in 1967, it was not until after 1974 when the English translation was first published that Githa Hariharan and Shashi Deshpande would have had the opportunity to read it.

24. C.V. Narasimhan, *The Mahabharata: An English Version Based on Selected Verses* (Delhi: Oxford University Press, 1996), 17. Shanta Rameshwar Rao, *The Mahabharata* (Hyderabad: Orient Longman, Disha Books, 1992), 21–22.

25. *Yuganta*, 38–40.

26. Geetanjali Singh Chanda, Elaine Yee Lin Ho, and Kavita Mathai, "Women in 'India': Four Recent Novels," in *Wasafiri* 26 (Autumn 1997): 59.

27. Kumkum Sangari, "Consent, Agency and Rhetorics of Incitement," in *Economic and Political Weekly*, May 1, 1993, 867–882. The contemporary context is that of Hindu nationalism and a high-caste backlash against caste-based employment and educational reservations.

28. Rajeswari Sunder Rajan, "Is the Hindu Goddess a Feminist?" *Economic and Political Weekly* (October 31, 1998): WS-34–38.

29. Chanda et al., "Women in 'India.'"

30. Nilufer Bharucha, "Inhabiting Enclosures and Creating Spaces: The Worlds of Women in Indian Literature in English," *Ariel*, vol. 29, no. 1 (January 1998): 102, 104.

31. *The Thousand Faces Of Night*, 95, quoted in Chanda et al.,"Women in 'India' Four Recent Novels," 59–60.

32. Shashi Deshpande, "The Indian Woman—Myths, Stereotypes and the Reality."

33. Ashis Nandy's essay, "Sati in Kali Yuga: The Public Debate on Roop Kanwar's Death," in his collection, *The Savage Freud and Other Essays on Possible and Retrievable Selves* (Princeton: Princeton University Press, 1995), 32–52. Such an argument is particularly

disturbing in the context of a highly glorified and publicized return of a sati in the 1980s after the practice had been illegal for over 150 years. To be fair, Nandy denounces the Roop Kanwar sati in no uncertain terms, but in my view that does not make his argument any less dangerous. He argues that those modern Indian liberals and leftists who censure the contemporary degradation of the rite as a way for the family of the sati to make a fortune cannot distinguish between that degraded practice and the ancient mythological and spiritual legitimacy of the idea of sati. Because they do not have any respect for the spiritual ideal that lies behind the act, they will never be able to understand its colonial and postcolonial resurgence.

34. See Arvind Rajagopal's essay, "Thinking About the New Indian Middle Class: Gender, Advertising and Politics in an Age of Globalisation" in *Signposts: Gender Issues in Post-Independence India*, 57–100.

35. "Leader or Misleader?" *Savvy* (May 1993), 56–59.

36. See Susie Tharu and Tejaswini Niranjana, "Problems for a Contemporary Theory of Gender," in Shahid Amin and Dipesh Chakrabarty, eds., *Subaltern Studies IX* (Delhi: Oxford University Press, 1996), 232–260.

37. Githa Hariharan, *When Dreams Travel* (Picador India, 1999; London: Macmillan, 1999).

38. David Beaumont, "Introduction," *Alf Laylah wa Laylah* or *The One Thousand and One Nights* <http://www.arabiannights.org/intro.html> last accessed August 5, 2003.

39. According to Sisir Kumar Das's *A History of Indian Literature 1800–1910*, there were at least seven translations published from English translations between 1838 and 1893, into Bengali, Marathi, Tamil, Gujarati, and Telugu.

40. Shashi Deshpande, "The Indian Women—Myths, Stereotypes and the Reality," referring to Gauri Deshpande in *Indian Review of Books*, Translation Issue (September–November 1995).

41. Reiko Ohnuma, "The Story of Rupavati: A Female Past Birth of the Buddha," *Journal of the International Association of Buddhist Studies*, vol. 23, no. 1 (2000): 103–145.

42. See the work of Milton Singer on the Great Tradition and the Little Tradition in India. Also, A.K. Ramanujan's Introductions to *Speaking of Siva* (Baltimore: Penguin Books, 1973) and *Folktales from India* (New York: Pantheon, 1994).

43. The *Ramayana* is a case in point: it is thought to be an unremittingly patriarchal master-narrative, but it circulates in a multitude of regional versions from Sita's, the monkeys', and the demons' perspectives. See Paula Richman, ed., *Many Ramayanas: The Diversity of a Narrative Tradition in South Asia* (Berkeley: University of California Press, 1991).

44. The return to the "Site of the Ancestor" is Farah Jasmine Griffin's term for African American narratives that return to the South, which is the site of oppression and trauma, but also the site of their American history and roots. *"Who Set You Flowin'?": The African American Migration Narrative* (New York: Oxford University Press, 1995).

45. Rosalind O'Hanlon, "Issues of Widowhood: Gender and Resistance in Colonial Western India," in Haynes and Prakash, eds., *Contesting Power: Resistance and Everyday Social Relations in South Asia* (Delhi: Oxford University Press, 1991), 103–104.

46. Chanda et al., "Women in 'India': Four Recent Novels," 58–61.

47. Arundhati Roy, *The God of Small Things*, 208.

Conclusion

1. Other examples include Tara in Anita Desai's *Clear Light of Day*, who still feels guilty about having abandoned her sister Bim to shoulder all the family responsibilities; Sita in Shashi Deshpande's *The Dark Holds No Terrors*, who still feels guilty about the accidental drowning death of her brother as a child; and the child Lenny in Pakistani novelist Bapsi Sidhwa's *Cracking India*, who inadvertently betrays her Hindu Ayah to the rampaging mob at Partition, and thus is complicit in her rape and abduction.

2. I have never seen this explicitly asserted either by Rushdie or anyone else, but Rushdie does begin his famous essay, "Imaginary Homelands," with the opening sentence from *The Go-Between*, and once one notices the similarity it is striking.

3. Malashri Lal, *The Law of the Threshold*, 5.

4. Anuradha Marwah Roy, *Idol Love* (New Delhi: Ravi Dayal, 1999), 222, 97.

5. Amitav Ghosh, *The Glass Palace* (New Delhi: Ravi Dayal and Permanent Black, 2000). See Pankaj Mishra's review of *The Glass Palace*, " There Will Always Be an England in India," *The New York Times Book Review* (February 11, 2001): 7.

6. From the *Bhagavad-Gita*, ch. 10. Translated by Barbara Stoler Miller. Epigraph in Manil Suri, *The Death of Vishnu* (London: Bloomsbury, 2001).

7. Ibid., 268.

8. Arundhati Roy, "The End of Imagination," Introduction, Praful Bidwai and Achin Vanaik, eds., *New Nukes: India, Pakistan and Global Disarmament* (New York: Interlink Publishing Group, 2000), xxvi–xxvii.

9. Partha Chatterjee, "The Nationalist Resolution of the Women's Question," in Sangari and Vaid, eds., *Recasting Women*.

10. Nuel Phar Davis, *Lawrence and Oppenheimer* (New York: Simon and Schuster, 1968), 240.

11. One scientist on seeing it said, "I can now believe stories of Lord Krishna Lifting a Hill." *India Today*, cited in Arundhati Roy, "The End of Imagination," xix.

12. John Burns, "Self-Made Bomb Maker," *New York Times*, May 20, 1998, A6.

13. Meenakshi Mukherjee, lecture on the Indian English novel, Mount Holyoke College, Fall 1998.

14. Most English writing about caste has restricted itself to the fourfold order (*varna*—Brahmin, Kshatriya, Vaishya, Shudra), whereas caste is lived in the much more complex and regionally various *jati* system that is made up of many subcastes, whose hierarchical ranking is not always strictly according to *varna*.

15. Urmila Pawar, "Justice," in Geeta Dharmarajan, ed., *Separate Journeys* (New Delhi: Katha, 1998), 99–112. The original Marathi story, *Nyay*, was first published in the 1980s.

16. It is no accident, I think, that Shantanu was the king in the *Mahabharata* who married the fishergirl Satyavati. In that story, it will be recalled, the girl's father insisted not only that the king own up to his paternity, but that Satyavati's son become king, so that her status and security in her old age would be assured. As we shall see, Urmila Pawar's story departs radically from this plot.

17. Urmila Pawar, *Amhihi Itihas Ghadawala: Urmila Pawar and the Making of History*, SPARROW Publication No. 6 (Mumbai: Sound and Picture Archives for Research on Women, 1998), 14.

18. Kancha Ilaiah, "Towards the Dalitization of the Nation," in Partha Chatterjee, ed., *Wages of Freedom: Fifty Years of the Indian Nation-State* (Delhi: Oxford University Press, 1998).

19. S. Shankar, "Midnight's Orphans, or A Postcolonialism Worth Its Name," *Cultural Critique*, vol. 56 (Winter 2004).

20. Gayatri Chakravorty Spivak, "The Burden of English Studies," in Rajeswari Sunder Rajan, ed., *The Lie of the Land* (Delhi: Oxford University Press, 1992), 295.

21. Gayatri Chakravorty Spivak, *A Critique of Postcolonial Reason: Toward a History of the Vanishing Present* (Cambridge: Harvard University Press, 1999), 50.

22. Publishers of translations and translation series include: Katha, Disha Books (Orient Longman), Modern Indian Novels in Translation (Macmillan India), Yatra (Harper Collins), Gender, Culture, Politics (Stree), Manas (East West Books), Seagull Books, Kali for Women, Permanent Black, and of course, the Sahitya Akademi in Delhi.

Bassnett, Susan and Harish Trivedi, eds. *Post-Colonial Translation: Theory and Practice*. London & New York: Routledge, 1999.

Bhabha, Homi K., ed. *Nation and Narration*. London: Routledge, 1990.

Blackburn, Stuart and Vasudha Dalmia. *India's Literary History: Essays in the Nineteenth Century*. Delhi: Permanent Black, 2004.

Das, Sisir Kumar. *A History of Indian Literature. Vol. VIII. 1800–1910. Western Impact: Indian Response*. New Delhi: Sahitya Akademi, 1991.

———. *A History of Indian Literature, 1911–1956. Struggle for Freedom: Triumph and Tragedy*. New Delhi: Sahitya Akademi, 1995.

Embree, Ainslie, ed. *Alberuni's India*. Translated by Edward C. Sachau. New York: W.W. Norton & Co., 1971.

Ghosh, Bishnupriya. *When Borne Across: Literary Cosmopolitics in the Contemporary Indian Novel*. New Brunswick (NJ): Rutgers University Press, 2003.

Hogan, Patrick Colm and Lalita Pandit, eds. *Literary India: Comparative Studies in Aesthetics, Colonialism, and Culture*. Jaipur: Rawat Publications, 1997.

Iyengar, K.R. Srinivasa. *Indian Writing in English*, 5th ed. New Delhi: Sterling Publishers, 1985.

Jain, Jasbir. *Feminizing Political Discourse: Women and the Novel in India*. Jaipur: Rawat Publications, 1997.

John, Mary E. and Janaki Nair, eds. *A Question of Silence? The Sexual Economies of Modern India*. New Delhi: Kali for Women, 1998.

Joshi, Priya. *In Another Country: Colonialism, Culture, and the Indian English Novel in India*. New York: Columbia University Press, 2002.

Joshi, Svati, ed. *Rethinking English: Essays in Literature, Language, History*. New Delhi: Trianka, 1991.

Karve, Iravati. *Yuganta: The End of an Epoch*. First published in Marathi, 1967, 2nd rev. ed. Hyderabad: Disha Books, Orient Longman, 1991.

Khair, Tabish. *Babu Fictions: Alienation in Contemporary Indian English Novels*. New Delhi: Oxford University Press, 2001.

Khilnani, Sunil. *The Idea of India*. New York: Farrar, Straus, Giroux, 1998.

Kumar, Amitava. *Bombay-London-New York*. New York: Routledge, 2002.

Lal, Malashri. *The Law of the Threshold: Women Writers in Indian English*. Simla: Indian Institute of Advanced Study, 1995.

Loomba, Ania and Suvir Kaul, eds. "On India: Writing History, Culture, Postcoloniality." Special Issue, *Oxford Literary Review,* Vol. 16 (1994).

Mankekar, Purnima. *Screening Culture, Viewing Politics: An Ethnography of Television, Womanhood, and Nation in Postcolonial India*. Durham (NC): Duke University Press, 1999.

Mehrotra, Arvind Krishna, ed. *A History of Indian Literature in English*. New York: Columbia University Press, 2003.

Mehta, Rama. *The Western Educated Hindu Woman*. Bombay: Asia Publishing House, 1970.

Menon, Ritu and Kamla Bhasin. *Borders and Boundaries: Women in India's Partition*. New Delhi: Kali for Women, 1998.

Mukherjee, Meenakshi. *Realism and Reality: The Novel and Society in India*. Delhi: Oxford University Press, 1985.

—————.*The Perishable Empire: Essays on Indian Writing in English*. New Delhi: Oxford University Press, 2000.

Naik, M.K. *A History of Indian Writing in English*. Delhi: Sahitya Akademi, 1982.

Nair, Rukmini Bhaya. *Lying on the Postcolonial Couch: The Idea of Indifference*. Minneapolis: University of Minnesota Press, 2002.

Naregal, Veena. *Language Politics, Elites and the Public Sphere: Western India Under Colonialism*. London: Anthem Press, 2002.

Niranjana, Tejaswini. *Siting Translation: History, Post-Structuralism and the Colonial Context*. Berkeley: University of California Press, 1992.

Niranjana, Tejaswini, P. Sudhir, and Vivek Dhareshwar, eds. *Interrogating Modernity: Culture and Colonialism in India*. Calcutta: Seagull, 1993.

Orsini, Francesca. *The Hindi Public Sphere 1920–1940: Language and Literature in the Age of Nationalism*. New Delhi: Oxford University Press, 2002.

Parker, Andrew et al., eds. *Nationalisms and Sexualities*. New York: Routledge, 1992.

Radhakrishnan, R. *Diasporic Mediations: Between Home and Location*. Minneapolis: University of Minnesota Press, 1996.

—————. *Theory in an Uneven World*. Oxford: Blackwell, 2003.

Ramaswamy, Sumathi. *Passions of the Tongue: Language Devotion in Tamil India, 1891–1970*. Berkeley: University of California Press, 1997.

Ray, Sangeeta. *En-Gendering India: Woman and Nation in Colonial and Postcolonial Narratives*. Durham: Duke University Press, 2000.

Raychaudhuri, Tapan. *Europe Reconsidered: Perceptions of the West in Nineteenth Century Bengal*. Delhi: Oxford University Press, 1988.

Roy, Parama. *Indian Traffic: Identities in Question in Colonial and Postcolonial India*. Berkeley: University of California Press, 1998.

Said, Edward W. *Orientalism*. New York: Random House, 1978.

—————. *Culture and Imperialism*. New York: Vintage Books, Random House, 1993.

Sangari, Kumkum and Uma Chakravarti, eds. *From Myths to Markets: Essays on Gender*. Shimla: Indian Institute of Advanced Study, 1999.

Sarkar, Tanika. *Hindu Wife, Hindu Nation: Community, Religion, and Cultural Nationalism*. Bloomington: Indiana University Press, 2001.

Schwab, Raymond. *The Oriental Renaissance*. Translated by G. Patterson-Black and V. Reinking. New York: Columbia University Press, 1984.

Sen, Geeti. *India: A National Culture?* New Delhi, Thousand Oaks (CA): Sage Publications, 2003.

Sethi, Rumina. *Myths of the Nation: National Identity and Literary Representation*. Oxford: Clarendon Press; Oxford University Press, 1999.

Sharpe, Jenny. *Allegories of Empire: The Figure of Woman in the Colonial Text*. Minneapolis: University of Minnesota Press, 1993.

Spivak, Gayatri Chakravorty. *A Critique of Postcolonial Reason: Toward a History of the Vanishing Present*. Cambridge (MA): Harvard University Press, 1999.

Sunder Rajan, Rajeswari. *Real and Imagined Women: Gender, Culture and Postcolonialism*. London and New York: Routledge, 1993.

—————. *Scandal of the State: Women, Law, and Citizenship in Postcolonial India*. Durham (NC): Dule University Press, 2003.

Sunder Rajan, Rajeswari, ed. *The Lie of the Land: English Literary Studies in India*. Delhi: Oxford University Press, 1992.

———. ed. *Signposts: Gender Issues in Post-Independence India*. New Delhi: Kali for Women, 1999.

Thapar, Romila. *Sakuntala: Texts, Readings, Histories*. New Delhi: Kali for Women, 1999.

Trivedi, Harish and Meenakshi Mukherjee. *Interrogating Postcolonialism: Theory, Text and Context*. Shimla: Indian Institute of Advanced Study, 1996.

Williams, Raymond. *Culture and Society: 1780–1950*. Garden City (NY): Doubleday Anchor, 1960.

Viswanathan, Gauri. *Masks of Conquest: Literary Study in British-Ruled India*. New York: Columbia University Press, 1989.

———. *Outside the Fold: Conversion, Modernity, and Belief*. Princeton: Princeton University Press, 1998.

Colonial, Nationalist, and Postcolonial History and Historiography

Anderson, Benedict. *Imagined Communities*. London: Verso, 1983.

Bose, Sugata and Ayesha Jalal. *Modern South Asia: History, Culture & Political Economy*. London and New York: Routledge, 1998.

Brass, Paul R. *The Politics of India Since Independence*. The New Cambridge History of India, IV: 1. 1st Corrected Indian ed. Cambridge: Cambridge University Press, 1992.

Chandra, Bipan et al. *India's Struggle for Independence*. New Delhi: Penguin Books India, 1989.

Chakravarti, Uma. *Rewriting History: The Life and Times of Pandita Ramabai*. New Delhi: Kali for Women, 1998.

Chatterjee, Partha. *Nationalist Thought and the Colonial World: A Derivative Discourse*. 1986. Delhi: Oxford University Press, 1993.

———. *The Nation and Its Fragments: Colonial and Postcolonial Histories*. Princeton (NJ): Princeton University Press, 1993.

———. ed. *Wages of Freedom: Fifty Years of the Indian Nation-State*. Delhi: Oxford University Press, 1998.

Chatterjee, Partha and Pradeep Jeganathan, eds. *Community, Gender, and Violence*. Subaltern Studies XI. New Delhi: Permanent Black, 2000.

Embree, Ainslie. *India's Search for National Identity*. New York: Alfred A. Knopf, 1972.

Gellner, Ernest. *Nations and Nationalism*. Ithaca. Cornell University Press, 1983.

Guha, Ranajit. *Dominance Without Hegemony: History and Power in Colonial India*. Cambridge: Harvard University Press, 1998.

Haynes, Douglas and Gyan Prakash, eds. *Contesting Power: Resistance and Everyday Social Relations in South Asia*. Delhi: Oxford University Press, 1991.

Hobsbawm, E.J. *Nations and Nationalism since 1780: Programme, Myth, Reality*. Cambridge: Cambridge University Press, 1990.

Jayawardena, Kumari. *Feminism and Nationalism in the Third World*. London: Zed Books, 1986.

Kosambi, D.D. *Myth and Reality: Studies in the Formation of Indian Culture*. 1962. Bombay: Popular Prakashan, 1992.

Kumar, Nita, ed. *Women as Subjects: South Asian Histories*. Charlottesville: University Press of Virginia, 1994.

Kumar, Radha. *The History of Doing: An Illustrated Account of Movements for Women's Rights and Feminism in India 1800–1990*. London: Verso, 1993.

Ludden, David, ed. *Contesting the Nation: Religion, Community, and the Politics of Democracy in India*. Philadelphia: University of Pennsylvania Press, 1996.

Majumdar, R.C. *History of the Freedom Movement in India*, Vol. I, Book 2: *The Indian Nation in the Making*. Calcutta: Fimma. K.L. Mukhopadhyay, 1962–1963.

Nandy, Ashis. *The Intimate Enemy: Loss and Recovery of Self Under Colonialism*. Delhi: Oxford University Press, 1983.

Sangari, Kumkum and Sudesh Vaid, eds. *Recasting Women: Essays in Indian Colonial History*. New Brunswick (NJ): Rutgers University Press, 1990.

Sarkar, Sumit. *Modern India, 1885–1947*. Madras: Macmillan India, 1983.

———. *Beyond Nationalist Frames: Relocating Postmodernism, Hindutva and History*. New Delhi: Permanent Black, 2002.

Sinha, Mrinalini. *Colonial Masculinity: The "Manly Englishman" and the "Effeminate Bengali" in the Late Nineteenth Century*. New York: Manchester University Press, 1995.

Tagore, Rabindranath. *Nationalism*. New York: Macmillan, 1917.

Talbot, Ian. *India and Pakistan*. London: Arnold, 2000.

Other Literary Texts

Chatterjee, Bankim Chandra. *Kamalakanta*. Translated by Monish Ranjan Chatterjee. New Delhi: Harper Collins, 1997.

Chaudhuri, Nirad C. *The Autobiography of an Unknown Indian*. 1951. Reading (MA): Addison-Wesley, 1989.

Deshpande, Gauri. *The Lackadaisical Sweeper: Short Stories*. Madras: Manas, 1997.

Deshpande, Shashi. *Small Remedies*. New Delhi: Viking Penguin India, 2000.

Dharmarajan, Geeta, ed. *Separate Journeys*. New Delhi: Katha, 1998.

Hariharan, Githa. *In Times of Siege*. New Delhi: Viking Penguin, 2003.

Karlekar, Malavika. *Voices from Within: Early Personal Narratives of Bengali Women*. Delhi: Oxford University Press, 1991.

Marwah-Roy, Anuradha. *Idol Love*. Delhi: Ravi Dayal, 1999.

Satthianadhan, Krupabai. *Kamala: The Story of a Hindu Life*. 1894. Edited and introduced by Chandani Lokuge. Delhi: Oxford University Press, 1998.

SPARROW (Sound and Picture Archives for Research on Women). *Amhihi Itihas Ghadawala: Urmila Pawar and the Making of History*. Mumbai: SPARROW, 1998.

Tharu, Susie and K. Lalita, eds. *Women Writing in India, Vols I and II*. New York: Feminist Press, 1991, 1993.

Translations, Commentaries, and Nationalist Interpretations of the *Bhagavad-Gita*

Arnold, Sir Edwin, Transl. *The Song Celestial or Bhagavad Gita*. Bombay: Jaico Books, 1957.

Bakker, J.I. (Hans). *Gandhi and the Gita*. Toronto: Canadian Scholars Press, 1993.

Besant, Annie. *The Bhagavad-Gita or Lord's Song.*, 16th ed. Madras: G.A. Natesan & Co., 1946.

Bhave, Vinoba. *Talks on the Gita*. New York: The Macmillan Company, 1960.

Chidbhavananda, Swami. *The Bhagavad Gita*. Tirupparaitturai: Sri Ramakrishna Tapovanam, 1972.

Gandhi, M.K. "*Anasaktiyoga*: The Message of the Gita" in *The Collected Works of Mahatma Gandhi, Vol. XLI* (June–October 1929). New Delhi: The Publications Division, Ministry of Information and Broadcasting, 1970, 90–133.

———. *The Bhagavadgita*. New Delhi: Orient Paperbacks, 1991.

Lal, P., Transcreator. *The Bhagavadgita*. Delhi: Orient Paperbacks, 1965.

Minor, Robert N., ed. *Modern Indian Interpreters of the Bhagavadgita*. Albany: State University of New York Press, 1986.

Prabhavananda, Swami and Christopher Isherwood. *The Song of God: Bhagavad-Gita*. 1944. Introduction by Aldous Huxley. New York: Mentor, New American Library, 1951.

Radhakrishnan, Sarvepalli. *The Bhagavadgita*. New York: Harper & Brothers, 1948.

Rajagopalachari, C. *Bhagavad-Gita: Abridged and Explained, Setting Forth the Hindu Creed, Discipline and Ideals*. New Delhi: The Hindustan Times, 1941.

Sharpe, Eric J. *The Universal Gita: Western Images of the Bhagavad Gita, a Bicentenary Survey*. La Salle (IL): Open Court, 1985.

Tilak, B.G. *Shrimad Bhagavadgita Rahasya*. 1935. B.S. Sukthankar, translator, 7th ed. Pune: Tilak Brothers, 1986.

van Buitenen, J.A.B. *The Bhagavadgita in the Mahabharata*. Chicago (IL): University of Chicago Press, 1981.

Vivekananda, Swami. *Karma Yoga*. Calcutta: Advaita Ashrama, 1991.

Wilkins, Charles. *The Bhagvat-Geeta or Dialogues of Kreeshna and Arjoon*. London: C. Nourse, 1785. Reprinted in New York: Geo. P. Philes, New York University, 1867.

Philosophy and Culture

Dasgupta, Surendranath. *A History of Indian Philosophy, Vols I & II*. 1922. Delhi: Motilal Banarsidass, 1975.

Ilaiah, Kancha. *Why I Am Not a Hindu: A Sudra Critique of Hindutva Philosophy, Culture, and Political Economy*. Calcutta: Samya, 1996.

Madan, T.N. *Non-Renunciation: Themes and Interpretations of Hindu Culture*. Delhi: Oxford University Press, 1987.

Mele, Alfred R., ed. The *Philosophy of Action*. Oxford: Oxford University Press, 1997.

Moya, Carlos J. *The Philosophy of Action: An Introduction*. Cambridge: Polity Press, 1990.

Segal, Jerome M. *Agency and Alienation: A Theory of Human Presence*. Savage (MD): Rowman & Littlefield, 1991.

Wagner, Valeria. *Bound to Act: Models of Action, Dramas of Inaction*. Stanford: Stanford University Press, 1999.

Index

Joshi, Svati, 168n
Jussawalla, Adil, 85, 180n
Jussawalla, Feroza and Reed Way
    Dasenbrock, 181n
"Justice" (Pawar), 161–4, 191n

Kane, Jean, 184n
Kanthapura (Rao), 74–9, 179n
Kanwar, Roop, 189–90n
karma *xi, xii, xiii,* 2, 18, 21, 39, 42, 93,
    130, 138, 155, 159, 160, 161, 180–1n
    colonial/postcolonial, *xi, xii,* 2, 9, 21, 32,
        50, 84, 106, 155, 161, 166
    nationalist concept of, *xi, xii,* 2, 18, 19, 42
    Gandhian notion of, 53; *see also* action,
        Gandhian model of
karma yoga, 39
    as caste duty, 64
    as cause and effect, *xii*
    nishkama (desireless, nonattached), 11,
        16, 37, 66, 174n
    as renunciation, 11, 13, 33, 37, 55,
        59, 174n
    as solution to problem of action, *xi*
    as labor, 164
kar sevaks, 147
Karve, D.K., 29, 172n
Karve, Irawati, 144, 189n
Katrak, Ketu H., 179n, 185n
Kaviraj, Sudipta, 25–6, 171n, 174n
Keer, Dhananjay, 180n
Kesavan, Mukul, 127, 187n
Khair, Tabish, 76, 179n
Khilnani, Sunil, 169n
Kirpal, Viney, 187n
Kishwar, Madhu, 131, 188n
Kortenaar, Neil ten, 185n, 187n
Kosambi, D.D., 170n
Krishnaswamy, Revathy, 168n
Kumar, Radha, 180n, 188n

Lajpat Rai, Lala, 12
Lal, Malashri, 9, 169n, 180n, 182n,
    183n, 191n
Lal, P., 87, 98, 180n, 182n, 183n
The Law of the Threshold (Lal), 9–10, 159,
    169n, 180n, 182n, 183n, 191n
liberalization (economic), 147, 148

Little Tradition, 152, 190n
Lokasamgraha, 15
lok sabha, 119, 122
Looking Through Glass (Kesavan), 127, 187n

Macaulay, Thomas Babington (Lord), 4, 168n
MacNeillie, Andrew, 182n
Mahabharata, 11, 13, 14, 32, 110, 123,
    126, 132, 134, 135, 137, 144, 146,
    147, 173n, 189n, 191n, 197
Mahad Satyagraha, 176n
Malayalam novel, 19, 24, 29–32,
    172n, 177n
Mani, Lata, 182n
Manichean, 85, 114, 120
Mansfield Park, (Austen), 46
Manusmriti, 61, 176n
marriage, 30, 56
    as cultural synthesis, 18, 30, 68
    as nationalist trope, 30, 79–80
    in Indian novels, 27, 30, 31, 44, 56, 57,
        59, 73, 79–80, 84, 92, 94, 99,
        101, 104, 132, 134, 136, 137,
        138, 139, 143, 145, 149, 159,
        163, 172n, 173n
    reforms, 175
    women and, 84, 136, 138, 147–8
Massey, James, 178n
Matter of Time, A (Deshpande), 139–41
mediate(d), *xiii,* 4, 6; mediator(s), 2, 6, 7
Mehrotra, Arvind Krishna, 194
Mehta, J.L., 170n
Mehta, Rama, 84
Mehta, Ved, 68, 178n
Memory of Elephants, The (Desai), 125
Menon, Lakshmi, 172n
Menon, Ritu, 139
Menon, Ritu and Kamla Bhasin, 180n
Midnight's Children (Rushdie), 5, 20, 99,
    106, 107–28, 156, 157, 158, 164, 166,
    168n, 184n
Mill, James, 3, 168n
Minor, R.N., 174n
Mishra, Pankaj, 170n, 191n
Mishra, Vijay, 184n
Moksha, 11, 13, 170n, 173n
Moor's Last Sigh, The (Rushdie), 110
Morrison, Toni, 188n